EXAMINING RELIGIONS

Islam

Rosalyn Kendrick

HEINEMANN
EDUCATIONAL

Heinemann Educational,
a division of Heinemann Educational Books Ltd,
Halley Court, Jordan Hill, Oxford OX2 8EJ

OXFORD LONDON EDINBURGH
MELBOURNE SYDNEY AUCKLAND
IBADAN NAIROBI GABORONE HARARE
KINGSTON PORTSMOUTH N H (USA)
SINGAPORE MADRID

© Rosalyn Kendrick

First published 1989

British Library Cataloguing in Publication Data
Kendrick, Rosalyn
   Islam.
   1. Islam
   I. Title   II. Series
   297

ISBN 0 435 30314 7

Designed and produced by Gecko Ltd, Bicester, Oxon
Printed and bound in Great Britain by Butler & Tanner
Ltd, Frome and London

Acknowledgements

To my agent Carolyn Whitaker, for her staunch faith in
me, which has kept me going through some very hard
times;
to Gulam Sarwar of the Muslim Educational Trust, for his
unwitting help to me, in that I have learned so much from
a study of his writings, and again for his replies to my
urgent letters;
to Abu Hussein and Qasim al-Malawi from the local
mosque in Hull, who were my first real teachers of Islam.
God knows our weaknesses and our strengths; men of
truer humility and devotion to God I have yet to meet.
Qasim went through the entire text of my first draft and
guided me gently away from many errors and false
interpretations;
to Rahmat Aziz Salik, the Imam of Hull Mosque for
allowing me to visit and use the facilities, and to Abdul
Wali for helping me to conduct interviews and for
rephrasing my questionnaire. Many Muslims all over
Britain went through the chore of filling this in and giving
me much valuable information. I thank them all, and
especially my friend Hussein Omar who started me off by
introducing me to so many of his friends;
to my friends Muhammad Rahouma, Abdul Karim al-
Ghamdi, Abdullah Bakhashwain, Ghazi al-Naji, Yahya
al-Khazraj, Abdul Azim, Ali Muthannah and Muhammad
Khamali for answering so many of my questions and
Abdul Al-Heeti for teaching me Arabic;
to Dr Owen Cole, and Dr Ahsan of the Islamic Foundation
(Leicester) for being such detailed and conscientious
critics; and to Dr Ahsan's colleague S. Faiyazuddin
Ahmad for his speedy replies to my letters;
to Bashir Ahmad Orchard of the Ahmadiyya Movement
and to Imam Ebrahim Y. Bawa of Gloucester, for their
letters, pamphlets and encouragement;
to Jane Kandur, Zahrah Nicolle and Samir Elatar of
Dar-al-Taqwa, 7a Melcombe St, London, for prompt help
and support;
to Gwyneth Major, Ann Willey, Denise Hall and Trevor
Norman, my long-suffering librarians;
to Begum Zarina Choudry (and her husband Siddiq) and
Dr Hesham el-Essawy of the Society for the Promotion of
Religious Tolerance, and my brother-in-Islam Rashid
Ahmed Hassan – for supplying so much help and
encouragement in the way of prayers, letters, books and
press cuttings (not to mention Mr Hassan's especial
efforts to get me into purdah, a business pursued with
unstinting generosity and the acquisition of gifts from
both Britain and Pakistan. I could fill another book with
his letters of encouragement!).

*'My success in my task can only
come from Allah.
In him I trust, and
to Him I turn.'*

(surah 11:88)

Thanks are due to Religious Studies Consultant W. Owen
Cole, M. H. Ahsan and F. M. Gosling for commenting on
the manuscript.

The publishers would like to thank the following for
permission to reproduce photographs: Abbas/Magnum
pp.66, 126; J. C. Allen pp.20, 102, 128 (bottom); Art
Directors p.107; Associated Press p.106; Bollinger/Stern
p.104; Camera Press pp.144, 148, 150, 153; Colorific p.113;
Daily Telegraph p.93; Gamma/Frank Spooner Pictures
p.38; Sonia Halliday Photographs pp.139, 142; Hulton-
Deutsch Collection pp.105, 152 (left); Hutchison pp.8, 15
(Christopher Tordai), 16 (Bernard Régent), 35, 42 (Bernard
Gérard), 44, 57, 60, 66, 68, 89 (right), 124 (bottom) (Juliet
Highet), 125 (bottom) (Christine Pemberton); IPA pp.74–
75; Islamic Foundation pp.72, 80 (bottom); NAAS pp.61,
79, 86, 88; NAAS/C. Mould pp.24, 77, 83, 84–85, 122;
Palomar Observatory p.32; Ann and Bury Peerless pp.124
(centre), 147; Popperfoto pp.122 (top), 137; Peter Sanders
pp.36, 40, 64–65, 78, 80 (top), 87, 89 (left), 94, 100, 108,
112, 114, 124 (left and right), 125 (top), 128 (left); Topham
Picture Library pp.26, 152 (right).

All other photographs supplied by the author.
Cover photographs by Peter Sanders.

The publisher would also like to thank the following for
their kind permission to reproduce copyright material:
Accrington Observer and Times Ltd for the article on
p.126; Zahara Barry of the UK Islamic Propagation Centre
for the letter to *The Guardian* on p.105; William Brandon
for the letter to *The Independent* on p.120; Mrs Zarina
Choudry of the Islamic Society for the Promotion of
Religious Tolerance in the UK for the letter to the *Glasgow
Herald* on p.121, *The Economist* for the letter on p.120;
Hesham El Essawy for the letter to *The Independent* on
p.120; *Nelson Leader* and *Colne Times* for the letter on p.120;
Times Newspapers Ltd 1988 for the article on p.79;
Torquay Herald Express for the article on p.109 and the
letter on p.120.

The publishers have made every effort to trace copyright
holders. However, if any material has been incorrectly
acknowledged we would be pleased to correct this at the
earliest opportunity.

CONTENTS

'He is my Lord. There is no God but He,
"who created me and guides me,
who gives me food and drink,
who heals me when I am sick,
who will cause me to die and
will raise me up again, and who,
I hope, will forgive me my sins
in the Day of Reckoning."

(surah 26:78–82)

In Him do I put my trust,
To Him I return.'

(surah 2:156)

(A **surah** is a chapter in the Muslim holy book, the Qur'an. Surahs are divided into **ayats** or verses, as shown in the example above.)

Surrender

Islam is an Arabic word which means 'submission', 'surrender' or 'obedience'. Another meaning of the word is 'peace'. It stands for a person's decision to surrender totally to the will of God. Followers of the religion are known as Muslims, and they believe that submission and obedience to the will of God is the *only* way in which a person can ever achieve real peace in the heart and mind, and in society as a whole.

Their knowledge of the will of God comes through the Qur'an, a series of revelations or messages from God, given over a period of twenty years to the Arab Muhammad, who lived in the sixth century **CE** (Christian Era).

Submission to God is not passive, but a positive act of bringing your likes and dislikes, attitudes and behaviour into harmony with God's will. Both belief (**iman**) and action (**amal**) are absolutely vital. One is worthless without the other.

Muslims believe that God exists. They submit to God's will as revealed in the Qur'an. They believe that all surahs were messages revealed by God to Muhammad, and keep the Five Pillars of the faith – bearing witness, praying five times a day, giving one-fortieth of savings to the poor, fasting the thirty days of Ramadan and making the pilgrimage to Makkah.

'It is not righteousness
to turn your face
towards east or west;
but this is righteousness –
to believe in God
and the Day of Judgement,
and the angels,
and the Book,
and the messengers;
to give from your wealth
out of love for God
to your family
to orphans
to the needy
to the wayfarer
to those who ask,
and for the freeing of slaves;
to be steadfast in prayer,
and practise regular giving;
to fulfil all the promises
which you have made;
to be firm and patient
in pain and suffering
or any other adversity,
and through all periods of panic.
Such are the people of truth,
the God-fearing.'

(surah 2:177)

Islam is often misunderstood in the West, due not only to ignorance but also to bad publicity. People have reacted to newspaper reports concerning the strict penalties given for theft, drunkenness, adultery and treason, and the recent terrorist activity carried out by various extremists throughout the war-torn Middle East.

That Islam is misunderstood is particularly sad, as it is a world religion of over 1000 million followers (of whom perhaps some two million live in Britain).

People often confuse the word 'Muslim' with the word 'Arab'. This is misleading, for although Islam has its roots amongst the Arabs, there are now millions more non-Arabic than Arab Muslims.

The spirit of Islam is totally against acts of violence and oppression, although Muslims believe in defence of the weak and the constant battle against evil. Islam is a religion that offers God's compassion and guidance to all people, a spiritual system based on mercy, peace, forgiveness, modesty and happiness.

'He is not a believer whose
neighbour cannot feel safe
from his harm.'

(Hadith)

(A **Hadith** is a saying or tradition of Muhammad.)

This book aims to

- give an outline of what it means to be a Muslim
- help you to understand what Muslims believe, and why they believe it
- help you to realize that Muslims see many things in exactly the same way as other people who believe in God, i.e. Jews and Christians, but have certain beliefs and practices which are special to them

- enable you to develop and express your own views on these issues and beliefs.

    *'God does not look upon your
    bodies and appearances;
    He looks upon your hearts
    and deeds.'*

    (Hadith)

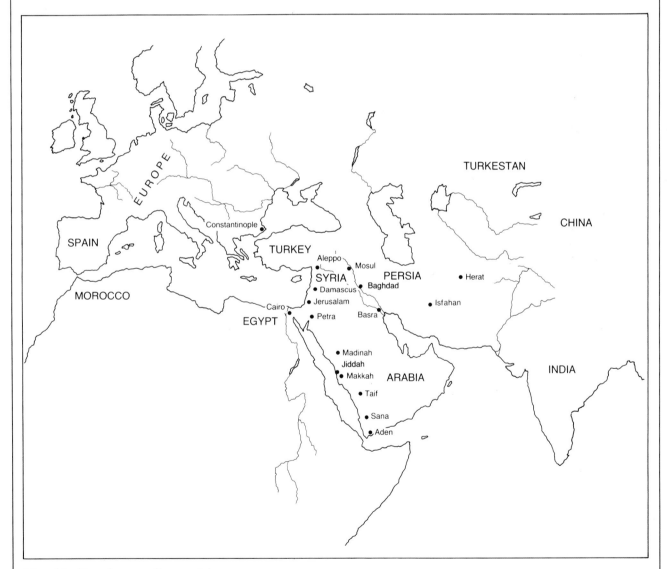

Map of Arabia and surrounding countries

2 THE LAND AND THE PEOPLE

The land

The Prophet Muhammad (peace be upon him) was born in **Makkah** in the land of Arabia. Much of Arabia is desert – vast, silent, barren regions where the stars loom large at night and where people are dependent on shade, water and each other's goodwill for survival.

Makkah was one of three major towns, the others being **Yathrib**, a huge oasis, and **Taif**, a cool refuge in the mountains famous for its grapes. Makkah, by contrast, lay in a barren valley, but it was important because of its position at the junction of many important trading routes.

The Ka'ba

Makkah was famous as a sacred city, because it contained an ancient temple known as the **Ka'ba** or 'Cube' because of its distinctive plain cube shape.

There is a tradition that the original Ka'ba was built by **Adam**, the first man, and was therefore the first house of God on earth. According to Islam (see surah 2:125–7) its known history began when it was rebuilt by **Ibrahim**, and his son **Isma'il**, two tribal chiefs whose lives were particularly devoted to God, and who became prophets – people through whom God gave messages to humanity (see p. 42).

At the time of Muhammad, the Ka'ba contained a collection of over 360 altars, statues and cult objects of various gods.

Many idols were meteorites, slabs of rock, or pillars. Some were worshipped as gods, but most were considered to be focal points that somehow contained the 'home' or 'power' of a god. Many were symbolic – for example, pyramid shapes symbolized the sun breaking through the clouds, and therefore the power and blessing of the Supreme Force reaching earth. Deeper thinkers said they symbolized spiritual awareness breaking through the 'blank' world of matter, touching the soul and bringing it to life.

The gods

In the Ka'ba, the most important gods were **Allah**, the 'Strong One' or 'Most Powerful', and three goddesses said to have been his daughters – Al-Lat the sun (the life-force); Al-Uzza the planet Venus or Evening Star (the force of purity and love); and Manat or Fortune (the decider of fate).

A pre-Islamic stone idol

The Quraish

The most important tribe living in and around Makkah was the **Quraish**, merchants who organized and gave protection to the vast numbers of traders who came through Makkah from many countries. The Quraish had control of the Ka'ba and the water supply of Makkah, and so made a profit not only out of the traders, but also by supervising provisions for the thousands of pilgrims who came there to see and worship the gods.

The hanifs

With so many visitors coming to Makkah, the Quraish became extremely wealthy, but many honourable tribesmen were not entirely happy with the greed, selfishness and corruption that seemed to come with the money.

These pious ones, known as **hanifs**, would often go off alone to pray and refresh their longing for purity in the silence and solitude of the desert and mountains. On the whole, hanifs also disapproved of the paganism of the Ka'ba, with its many idols of stone and wood.

They believed that there could only be one Supreme Power, who must have created the universe. Since He created it He must therefore be quite separate from it and exist outside it. This Almighty God, who had sent revelations many times in the past to such prophets as Moses and Jesus, was a spiritual power that could not have physical sons and daughters. He entered the heart, and was not to be found in rocks. The Ka'ba collection, therefore, was seen as just a museum of oddments to the hanifs, and in itself quite powerless.

One hanif, a man highly respected for his devout life of prayer and fasting, who often used to spend an entire month praying in a cave near Makkah, was **Abd-al-Muttalib**.

Abd-al-Muttalib was famous for his visions. According to tradition, in one of these visions an ancient water supply which had been lost for centuries was revealed to him. This was said to have been the spring which God's angel had shown to Ibrahim's wife **Hagar**.

In the year 570 CE Abd-al-Muttalib's son **Abdullah** died suddenly, shortly after marrying, leaving his young wife **Amina** pregnant. The boy who was born in due course was to change the whole history of the world. That boy's name was Muhammad.

FOR YOUR FOLDERS

▶ Copy the map on page 5 carefully, and underline Makkah Madinah, Jerusalem and Damascus.
▶ Join with dotted lines these trading routes:
  a India – Aden – Sana – Makkah – Madinah – Basra – Isfahan – Herat – China
  b Makkah – Jidda – Petra – Cairo
  c Makkah – Madinah – Petra – Jerusalem – Damascus – Aleppo – Constantinople – Europe
  d Makkah – Madinah – Basra– Baghdad – Mosul – Aleppo.
▶ Why do you think that the hanifs disapproved of life in Makkah?
▶ Explain how the belief of the hanifs differed from that of the pilgrims coming to the Ka'ba.

THINGS TO DO

▶ Imagine you are taken to meet:
  a the Quraish supervisor in charge of water
  b the Quraishi guide at the Ka'ba
  c a Quraishi hanif.
    Write a brief diary entry recording these three meetings, and the impression each one made on you.
▶ Imagine you are a young trader travelling with a camel train. Write a letter home describing your arrival in Makkah and what you see and experience there.

QUICK QUIZ

▶ Name the three major towns of Arabia.
▶ Why was Makkah important?
▶ Who was said to have built the first Ka'ba?
▶ Name the most important tribe in Makkah.
▶ What was a hanif?
▶ Name Muhammad's father and grandfather.

FOR DISCUSSION

▶ Does ownership of property and possessions *always* make people selfish? If a rich man lives alongside a poor one, what might this suggest about the character of the rich man?
▶ Why do you think people worshipped stone pillars and statues, or the sun, moon and stars? What did these things represent?
▶ Is it possible for a person to understand prayer, solitude, or fasting without actually experiencing them?

Arab shepherd

'By the glorious light of morning, and by the
stillness of night! Your God has not forsaken you,
and He is not angry with you.
Surely your future will be better for you
than your past, and in the end
God will be kind to you, and you be satisfied.
Did He not find you an orphan, and gave you a
home?
Did He not find you lost and wandering,
and showed you the way?
Did He not find you in great need,
and took care of you?
As to you, therefore, do not wrong the orphans,
do not turn away those that ask your help,
spread and increase your Lord's blessings.'

(surah 93)

Legends

There were many legends about the birth of
Muhammad. One said that before his birth his
mother Amina heard a voice telling her the child
would be a great leader. Another told of a heavy
shower of rain, a blessing that ended a long
drought.

Yet another legend was that two angels removed
Muhammad's heart, washed it clean, then weighed
it against first one man, then ten, then a hundred,
then a thousand. Finally they said: 'Let it be. Even if
you set the whole community in the scale, he would
still outweigh it.'

Muhammad himself disapproved of all untruths,
especially the spreading of any stories suggesting he
had miraculous powers other than the ability to
receive the Qur'an. He insisted that it was the
Prophet Jesus who was the miracle worker, and not
himself. He was no more than a simple and devout
man, through whom God had chosen to speak (see
surah 7:188). It is hard for us now to know which
stories about him are true, and which are just
legends – so much depends on whether we accept
the existence of such things as God's guidance and
signs, and angels, or not.

Early tragedies

It was customary for Quraish women to entrust
their babies to **Bedouin** women (wandering
tribespeople), to take them away from the towns
and raise them in the desert where the air was pure
and free from disease. Muhammad was taken by
Halima the Bedouin until he was six, when he
returned to his mother.

Sadly, she died that year, and he became an
orphan. He was not abandoned to the streets,
however; his devout grandfather, now an old man
of eighty, took him in.

Two years later he also died, and Muhammad
passed into the protection of his uncle **Abu Talib**, a
wealthy merchant.

Muhammad grows up

Muhammad first worked as a shepherd. When his
uncle found him to be trustworthy and
hardworking, he began to take him on business
journeys. At this time Muhammad earned the nickname Al-Amin, the Trustworthy One.

According to tradition, Muhammad was
recognized as a future prophet while still a child. At
the age of nine, while going with Abu Talib to
Damascus, Muhammad had to pass the place where
the prophet Aaron was buried (Jebel Harun, near
Petra). The grave was guarded by a Christian hermit
called **Bahira**. Muhammad was left in charge of the

camel train while his uncle climbed up the mountain to pay his respects.

But the monk had seen a vision of trees bowing down to a person with a certain mark between his shoulder blades. He sensed this person's presence, and asked if there was anyone else with Abu Talib. He replied, 'There is my nephew, but he is only a boy.'

Muhammad was sent for, and as soon as Bahira saw him he recognized the person of his vision. 'Guard him well,' he said, 'for the future welfare of mankind rests on his shoulders.'

Muhammad grew up to be a fine man, with dark eyes and hair, a piercing expression, a thoughtful intelligent face, and a decisive manner. He was very kind and had a lively sense of humour.

Muhammad gets married

Muhammad continued to impress the merchants by his hard work and fair dealings. One of these was **Khadijah**, a wealthy widow who employed young Muhammad to supervise her caravan (camel train) trade.

When she was about forty years old, she found the courage to ask Muhammad – who was then only twenty-five – to consider marriage to her. He was young, handsome and devout, and no doubt any woman would have been honoured to marry him, so she may have been afraid he would reject her, or feel embarassed because of her possessions.

However, she became his only love until she died twenty-five years later, standing by him through all his trials and persecutions, and even after her death she remained close to him in his mind and heart.

They had six children – two sons, Qasim and Abdullah, and four daughters, Zainab, Ruqaiyya, Umm Kulthum and **Fatimah**. The two boys died in infancy.

Ali and Zaid

Muhammad's uncle Abu Talib fell on hard times, and Muhammad repaid his kindness by taking on his little son **Ali**.

Another child in the house was **Zaid ibn Haritha**, a slave boy given to Khadijah as a present. One day Zaid's father, who had been searching for him for years, discovered where he was and offered to buy him back. Zaid was asked what he wished to do, and chose to stay with Muhammad. Muhammad was so moved that he freed the boy instantly, and adopted him as his own son.

THINGS TO DO

▶ Look at the Hadith (sayings of Muhammad) given below. What do they tell us about his character?
▶ Explain what parts were played in the early life of Muhammad by – Halima, Abu Talib, Bahira and Khadijah.

TALKING POINTS

● **Muhammad's feelings would have been quite different if he had not suffered himself, and if people had not been kind to him.**
● **What does surah 93 teach us about God's feelings towards those in trouble? What kinds of people stirred God's compassion?**

'Everyone begins the morning by trading with his soul; he either wins it or ruins it.'

*'There are four qualities in a hypocrite:–
when they are trusted they cheat;
when they talk, they lie;
when they give promises, they break them;
when they argue, they are abusive.'*

'Those who show the most perfect faith are those who are kindest to their families.'

(Hadith)

FOR YOUR FOLDERS

▶ Imagine that you are the father of Zaid, finding your son again after years of searching. Describe your feelings:
  a on finding him
  b on discovering he chooses to stay with Muhammad
  c when Muhammad frees Zaid and adopts him as his own son.
▶ In what ways do you think Muhammad proved he was a fine man, worthy to be used by God as a prophet? What do his sayings reveal about his character?
▶ Why did Muhammad disapprove of flattering legends about himself?

4 THE NIGHT OF POWER

*'Truly, We caused the Qur'an to descend
on the Night of Power. The Night of Power
is greater than a thousand months; on that night
the angels and the spirit (Jibra'il) descended
by permission of God, and
all is peace till the breaking of the dawn.'*

(surah 97)

The preparation

Muhammad spent more and more time in solitude and prayer, often going to the hills to be alone. Sometimes he stayed out all night, and like his grandfather, he liked to spend the whole month of Ramadan in prayer (see p. 7).

He was respected as a man who was close to God, who thought deeply and was kind and wise. Muhammad had known the Ka'ba all his life, with its many shrines and altars. He had also known the greed, exploitation, lack of compassion and corruption of the rich merchants. Oppressed people prayed hopefully to their idols, but how could objects of stone help or understand?

Muhammad spent his life searching for spiritual guidance, drawing ever closer to God.

The revelation

One night, when Muhammad was forty years old, something happened that changed his life. This night became known as the night of power, or **Lailat ul Qadr**. It was the year 610 CE, in the ninth month (Ramadan). Muhammad had gone to pray alone in a cave on Mount Hira (later called **Mount Nur**, or Hill of Light). Suddenly he heard a voice calling his name, and the command **'Iqra!'** which means 'Recite!'. He saw a roll of silk with writing on it in fiery letters, but he could not read what it said.

There is a tradition that Muhammad could not read or write, although many believe that if he worked as a merchant he must have done. (Surah 7:157–8 calls him 'unlettered'.)

Three times the voice ordered him to read aloud, and each time he replied that he could not do so. A tension or pressure began building up inside him, then something seized his body and throat, gripping him so tightly that he felt he would die.

Suddenly Muhammad knew in his heart what the words said, and began to utter them. The message shook him.

The message

*'In the name of your Lord,
who created all humanity from
a single drop of blood,
speak these words aloud!
Your Lord is the Most Generous One –
He who has shown the Pen,
who reveals directly
things from beyond human knowledge.'*

(surah 96: 1–5)

The angel

The angel which appeared to Muhammad was **Jibra'il**, who stood in the presence of God – the same angel who had appeared to the prophet Ibrahim and to Mary the mother of Jesus, the founder of the Christian religion. Now Muhammad had also been chosen to be God's messenger.

The vision faded, and Muhammad was alone in a state of tremendous fear and excitement. What had happened to him? Was he going mad, or being possessed by a demon? The words had been so vivid they were stamped on his heart. But he was terrified of what had happened, and fearing for his sanity, even thought of killing himself by jumping off the edge of the mountain.

The Pen

The Pen referred to in this passage (see also surah 68:1) was the symbol of the eternal plan of God, the law that brings order out of chaos and without which the universe could not exist (see p. 43). Muslims believe the record has always been there, and sometimes humans discover it in flashes of insight or intuition.

The waiting

After this shattering experience came the temptation of doubt. Muhammad struggled home to Khadijah, trembling with shock. He had always been a good man, but how did he know what he had seen was not some trick of the devil, trying to make him claim something about himself that was

10

not true, something he was unworthy of?

He told Khadijah everything. She wrapped him in the thick cloak he used as a blanket and helped him sleep. She had a cousin called **Waraqa Ibn Nofal** who had always been a seeker after truth. He had become a Christian and produced a translation of the Gospels in Arabic. He was now nearly 100 years old, and blind, but she respected his judgement above all others. Waraqa was quite sure that this was no evil demon, but that God had indeed spoken to Muhammad.

Knowing him so well, and seeing the utter change that had come over him, Khadijah became Muhammad's first convert, the first to accept that what he said was true. The second convert was little Ali, then only ten years old, and the next was Zaid. Soon Muhammad's friend **Abu Bakr** was also convinced, but at this stage Muhammad did not talk about his experiences openly.

Some months later Muhammad had another vision. Suddenly he heard the voice again, and this time saw a huge pair of eyes staring at him, which became a gigantic figure whose feet straddled the horizon. He shut his eyes and turned away, but no matter what he did he could still see the angel. There was no escape.

Once again he rushed home in shock. Khadijah noticed this time that when she wrapped him up he began to breathe deeply and sweated profusely. He was seeing the angel again. It said:

*'O you who lie wrapped in your cloak –
arise and warn! Glorify God! Make yourself pure!
Give up all uncleanness. For the sake of your Lord,
endure with patience!'*

(surah 74:1–7)

The wait

Now Muhammad's faith was tested. He saw no further visions for about two years, and became fearful and anxious of what it might mean. At last the angel came again, with the moving message:

*'Your Lord has not forsaken you, and
He is not angry with you.'*

(surah 93:3)

(The full text is given on p. 8.)

From that time on, for the rest of his life, Muhammad continued to receive messages and instructions from God.

FOR YOUR FOLDERS

▶ Muhammad had always been a devout man. In what ways, therefore, do you think his life was different after the Night of Power from his life before?
▶ Imagine that you are one of the characters in this unit. Write a brief account of what happened on the Night of Power, and what convinced you that what Muhammad told you was genuine.
▶ In what ways could doubt have tempted or discouraged Muhammad? What would have been the outcome if Muhammad had given in to doubt?

'Say – "O people, your companion is not one possessed. He saw him without any doubt in the clear horizon; he keeps back nothing of what was revealed to him; it is not the word of an accursed spirit."'

(surah 81:22–5)

THINGS TO DO

▶ Write out the surahs given in this unit and explain what they teach about God and His relationship with Muhammad.

QUICK QUIZ

▶ What age was Muhammad when he received the first revelation?
▶ What was the name of the angel?
▶ What is the meaning of the command 'Iqra!'?
▶ What was the name of Khadijah's Christian cousin?
▶ Who was Muhammad's first convert?
▶ Who was the first male convert?
▶ How did Khadijah know when Muhammad was receiving a revelation?

5 THE REVELATIONS

Muhammad was not a theologian, or a learned man. He did not have a set of rules or theories about God. He was simply a very devout person to whom God had chosen to make Himself known.

Revelation

The closest experience a non-religious person can get to religious awareness is probably love. Imagine you have been happy and contented as a child, enjoying life and play. Suddenly you fall desperately in love, and discover a new range of overwhelming joy, belonging, and agonized suffering that you never knew existed. Your whole life takes on a new meaning, and you can never go back to being unaware and contented as you were before. A door has opened, and you have gone through it. You cannot explain your experience to a child who has no awareness of it.

There are other moments of truth in life: the realization that you are totally alone and no one can help you but yourself (and God); childbirth; the discovery that you are going to die. All these moments are flashes of enlightenment, and after experiencing them your life is totally changed and you can never go back.

Discovery or awareness of God is the most shattering moment of all, and is often spoken of as being 'born again', because the experience is so devastating. Everything becomes different, everything has a new meaning, everything falls into place. New believers look at everything in a completely new light, and the whole motivation and interest of their life changes.

Conviction

You can be good and honourable and kind without ever experiencing this awareness, but when it comes, perhaps the most obvious change that comes over a person is conviction.

To know God is to submit. To accept Him is to hand over ordinary life and begin to live a guided life. It is conviction that is the mark of the prophet.

'Wait with patience for your Lord's commands; and don't be like the prophet Jonah who cried out in agony. If grace from his Lord had not reached him he would indeed have been cast off on the naked shore, in disgrace. But your Lord chose him, and placed him among the righteous. Unbelievers might well stare at you and abuse you, and call you mad – but you have nothing less than a message to all the world.'

(surah 68:48–52)

Muhammad related the messages to his friends, whose duty it was to memorize them and write them down, so that nothing of the message might be lost. It is important to realize that all Muslims accept without question that these messages were not just the thoughts and teachings of Muhammad, which were a different matter altogether, but the words of God revealed through the angel Jibra'il.

- The special revelations were always attended by dramatic phenomena, like shaking or trances.
- Muhammad always knew when they were about to happen.
- Normally he lay down covered in his cloak.
- Sometimes he seemed to lose consciousness.
- Sometimes he became very hot and would be soaked in sweat, even in cold weather.
- Sometimes the voice did not come through clearly. One tradition claims that on these occasions his head seemed to be ringing with noises like muffled bells, a painful and frustrating sound, for he could not work out what the voice was saying. At other times the revelation was quite clear, and he heard the words plainly.
- Sometimes the message came instantaneously, while he was out riding, or being questioned by the public.
- On a few occasions God spoke to him through Jibra'il, the angel who appeared in the form of a man.

Muhammad's visions always appeared to make him feel close to death, and that he was leaving his body and might not re-enter it. At the end of the experience he would appear as usual again, sit up, and repeat the message.

'Not once did I receive a revelation without thinking that my soul had been torn away.'

(Hadith)

- Muslims believe, therefore, that the Qur'an is not a book written by Muhammad, but the word of God exactly as he received it. Muhammad was simply the instrument by which the words were revealed.
- The Qur'an is not a book *about* Muhammad, although sometimes, when the events and problems of Muhammad's personal life caused difficulties, a revelation would come to him with specific instructions for dealing with that problem.

- Muhammad faced many people in his lifetime who did not believe in him. They challenged him to work a miracle like the prophet Jesus in order to prove that God had really spoken to him. This he could not do. He retorted that it was quite unnecessary, as the Qur'an itself was the supreme miracle. If anyone doubted it, let them try to compose ten verses that would bear comparison with it (see surah 11:13).
- Those who do not believe in God or His desire to communicate in this way still explain the messages as being no more than the product of Muhammad's mind, and even suggest that he suffered from some sort of illness.

Certainly the messages had to pass through Muhammad's mind. His mind and body were 'receiving equipment', and there is no way of proving whether or not that equipment was 'faulty' other than by examining the content of the messages and the life and influence of the prophet.

If, for example, Muhammad had suffered from epilepsy, you would want to compare revelations received in this way over a span of twenty-two years by other epileptics.

Certain individuals have claimed 'divine guidance' who have been either quite mad, or deluded by evil influences. When you examine their words and actions, it is immediately obvious that what they did or said was not 'from God'.

'Those without knowledge say "Why doesn't God speak to us, why can't we have a sign?" . . .
But the signs are clear to any people who hold firmly to faith in their hearts.'

(surah 2:118)

'You are not mad or possessed.
Your character is above the standard that can be slandered. Soon everyone will see which of you is really mad . . . . Take no notice of despicable slanderers.'

(surah 68:2–6, 10)

'Nothing is said to you that was not said to the messengers before you.'

(surah 41:43)

'You are to keep the same revealed religion as that revealed to Noah and Ibrahim and Moses and Jesus. God chooses those whom He will.'

(surah 42:13)

If a later revelation seemed to contradict an earlier one, this did not worry Muhammad. God was entitled to do as He wished. All Muhammad did was to faithfully pass on the words as he received them.

'Say – "Whenever He suppresses a verse, or causes it to be forgotten, we bring one which is better or similar. Do you not know that God can do anything?" '

(surah 2:106)

FOR YOUR FOLDERS

▶ List the kinds of things Muhammad's family and friends observed when he was receiving revelations.

▶ Explain why believers became irritated if too much stress was laid on such things as these phenomena, or the desire to see miracles.

▶ Construct an argument for and against the theory that Muhammad may have suffered from a disease such as epilepsy. You could do this as a play script using as your characters either modern twentieth-century critics, or characters from the time of Muhammad.

FOR DISCUSSION

▶ How might a person judge whether their conviction that they are doing God's will is really right, not wrong?

▶ God cannot be 'seen' or 'proved'. Neither can the existence of love. What evidence would you use to prove that love exists?

▶ Why is it impossible to give a 'sign' to someone who is not ready to believe?

6 PREACHING IN MAKKAH

The message

As soon as Muhammad was ordered by the voice to go out and preach in public he began to do so with great urgency. He had to make people realize not only that there *was* a True God, but that life after death was real too, and there could be a time of judgement when they would be rewarded or punished according to how they had lived.

Muhammad tried to convince everyone that even if they did not believe in life after death, they would be forced to do so once they had experienced it. When that happened, they would be sorry for all the things they had done wrong and would beg for forgiveness – but it would be too late. Their lives were tests, and if they failed, they failed.

God was indeed merciful, and knew everyone's background and motives – and if people were truly sorry for their bad thoughts and actions they would be forgiven. But God was also perfect justice – if people who had passed a lifetime doing bad things were still not sorry about them when they died, they would not be forgiven. That was not fair, and God was always fair.

The prophets, like Ibrahim, Moses and Jesus, had all given the true message, and now he, Muhammad, was also putting God's commands before them. People had the freedom to choose whether to listen and obey or not, and they had been told what the outcome would be. If they refused to listen, it was their own fault.

Muhammad insisted that their duty to God, who saw everything, was much more important than any links with family or tribe – and their first duty was to become aware of the difference between God and the useless idols that had no powers.

Muhammad taught that God required dignity for all people, including women and slaves – two groups who had very few rights in those days and were often badly treated.

The reaction

It must have been very difficult for Muhammad to go out for the first time to the people of Makkah, who knew him well, and preach openly. Everyone was amazed. His kindness and gentle wisdom had shown him all his life to be a noble and devout man – but now he was claiming that he had received messages from God, and that he had been sent to change their lives.

Crowds gathered, but most people didn't take him seriously, and ridiculed him. Few wanted to give up their selfish ways. Muhammad's own tribe was in charge of the Ka'ba with its idols, and when they realized that he was trying to stop people worshipping there they were furious because they thought their profit was in danger.

They did not hurt Muhammad, but they threatened, ridiculed and insulted him. When this had no effect, they accused him of being a sorcerer, insulting the gods, and trying to split up families by making young men rebel against their fathers. Muhammad's uncle **Abu Lahab**, one of the tribal chiefs, tried argument, bribery and threat against him, but nothing would make him give in.

The people who braved the opposition and joined Muhammad became known as 'Muslims'. Many of them were hurt, including a negro slave **Bilal** who was left to die in the sun with a huge rock on his chest. He was rescued by Abu Bakr.

The bravery of the Muslims impressed others, however, including people like Muhammad's uncle **Hamza**, a famous and highly respected warrior, who decided to join them. Muhammad's enemies grew more worried when they realized that important people were beginning to believe his message. (For other stories of the early converts see pp. 130–135.)

> 'By the star when it sets,
> your fellow man [Muhammad] is not mistaken,
> neither has he been misled.
> He does not speak from mere impulse.
> The Qur'an is nothing less
> than that which was revealed to him.
> One terrible in power taught it to him,
> one full of wisdom.
> He revealed to his servant
> what he revealed.
> The servant's heart did not
> falsify what he saw.'
>
> (surah 53:1–11)

THINKING POINTS

- Why do you think the Quraish merchants of Makkah were so against their kinsman Muhammad and his message?
- Why do you think Muhammad's message was particularly successful with poor people, women and slaves?

Abu Talib's protection

Muhammad was under the protection of Abu Talib. Abu Talib's brother Abu Lahab tried angrily to make him disown Muhammad. Abu Talib was very distressed by the rift growing in his family, and begged Muhammad to go back to private life, and spare him this embarrassing situation.

Muhammad turned away in tears, saying that his first duty was to Allah, the only true God, who had called him. He could never abandon God. Abu Talib was deeply moved, and swore he would always protect him, come what may.

One day he caught Muhammad and the two boys praying. Muhammad urged him to join them, but to the prophet's sadness, the proud old man would not pray in the undignified position with his backside above his head (see p. 65).

At prayer

THINGS TO DO

▶ Write an argument between Abu Lahab and Abu Talib, taking sides for and against Muhammad.

▶ In the word square, find the first Muslims: Khadijah; Ali; Zaid; Abu Bakr; Bilal; Hamza.

K	I	E	U	Q	S	H
H	R	A	D	Y	K	A
A	U	H	O	Z	M	M
D	B	I	L	A	L	Z
I	K	U	M	I	O	A
J	A	X	B	D	T	K
A	L	I	M	A	N	O
H	L	O	D	J	K	Q
V	A	C	B	D	O	R

THINKING POINTS

● 'I have no control over what may be helpful or hurtful to me, but as God wills. Had I the full knowledge of His secrets, I should revel in the good and evil should not touch me. But I am only a warner, and an announcer of good tidings to those who believe.'

(surah 7:188)

● Muhammad's critics claimed that if he was a genuine prophet God would protect him, or at least he would be able to see suffering coming and avoid it. How does this passage answer this criticism?

FOR YOUR FOLDERS

▶ *'Ridicule is one of the most destructive forms of torture, but it is also a refining fire.'* Discuss the truth of this statement, with particular reference to Muhammad's experience.

▶ How true do you think it is that the most difficult people to impress are those in your own family? Why do you think this is so? Is it a good thing?

▶ Read surah 53. Why do you think Muhammad received the revelation in this surah? What effect do you think it had on him?

Jerusalem – the al-Aqsa Mosque (left) and the Dome of the Rock Mosque (right)

The year of sorrow

Ten years after he had received his call, when Muhammad was fifty, his uncle Abu Talib died. Immediately Muhammad lost his strong protector and his life was in danger. At the end of the year, his beloved Khadijah also died at the age of sixty-four. Without their support, Muhammad went through a time of bleakness and despair, though he accepted, of course, that death must come to all.

The persecutions got worse, his enemies taking advantage of Muhammad's difficult time. Muhammad was despised and humiliated by those who did not believe in him. Abu Lahab's wife used to take sharp thorns and rubbish and throw them down outside his house every day. (Later, she was taken ill, and Muhammad did housework for her until she recovered.)

Rejection at Taif

As much as three years before, some of Muhammad's followers had found the persecution too much for them and had moved away to Abyssinia, which was a Christian country. Muhammad now moved to **Taif**, but the people there just laughed at him and incited the youths to throw stones at him. Muhammad said this was the saddest day of his life.

Lailat ul Miraj

It was probably during this period of persecution that Muhammad had his next extraordinary experience. It is known as the Miraj. This means 'ladder' or 'ascent', and refers to what Muhammad saw on his Night Journey, or **Lailat ul Miraj**.

The Qur'an does not reveal much about this incident. It states only that glory should be given to

'Him who made His servant travel by night from the sacred place of worship to the farthest place of worship.'

(surah 17:1)

The meaning of the words is ambiguous, and some think they really refer to the vision that caused Muhammad to start his career as a prophet. The 'farthest place of worship' is taken to mean either the holy city of Jerusalem, or the presence of God in heaven.

Later, tradition added many details. Since it was a miraculous journey, it is not clear whether the event was supposed to have really happened physically, or was a vision or dream. In one tradition Muhammad's body remained in Makkah while his spirit journeyed to heaven. However, like the first revelation, the things Muhammad experienced on the Night Journey were a profound influence on the rest of his life.

The journey

As Muhammad lay sleeping by the Ka'ba, the angel Jibra'il shook him into wakefulness and took him to Jerusalem on a strange animal like a horse with wings, named al-Buraq, the Lightning.

In one tradition the story of Muhammad's miraculous purification by angels came first. His heart was taken out and cleansed of doubt, idolatry, ignorance and error, and his body filled with faith and wisdom.

From Jerusalem he was taken through the seven heavens and was shown paradise and hell. In each of these heavens he met and spoke to earlier prophets, including Aaron, Moses, Ibrahim and Jesus the Messiah. Muhammad was particularly surprised when he met Ibrahim: 'Why, I never saw a man who looked so much like myself!' Jesus, apparently, was notable for his freckles.

The prayers

One very important detail Muhammad was given was the number of times per day a devout Muslim should pray. Muhammad thought fifty times to be about right, but Moses said the burden would be too great for ordinary humans. The number was finally settled at five, and that has remained Muslim practice ever since.

The light

Gradually, Muhammad and the angel approached the highest heaven and the throne of God. Muhammad was aware only of great peace and the brilliance of pure light. Neither he nor the angel could approach any closer. Time, thought and feelings were all stilled as Muhammad experienced the overwhelming blessings of the presence of God, an experience that he could never put adequately into words, for it was beyond all human knowledge and understanding.

   All too soon the experience drew to a close, and Muhammad was brought back to earth. To his amazement, when he finally arrived back in Makkah he found that the place where he had lain was still warm, and a cup he had tipped over was still emptying. It had all happened in a flash.

   *'No vision can grasp Him, but His grasp
   is over all vision; He is above all comprehension,
   yet Himself knows all things.'*

   (surah 6:103)

   *'Those round the throne of God sing glory and
   praise to the Lord and worship Him, and implore
   forgiveness for those who believe. Our Lord, Thy
   reach is over all things in mercy and knowledge.'*

   (surah 40:7)

   *'It is God who is in the splitting of the seed-grain
   and the sprouting of the date-stone, who causes
   the living to come from the dead . . . who splits
   the daybreak from darkness.'*

   (surah 6:95–6)

The meaning

The real meaning of this night was not the making of a journey from Makkah to Jerusalem, but the inward and mystical experience of Muhammad's spiritual ascension from earth to heaven.

   Sufi mystics (see p. 140) stress that it is an experience that can be shared by all believers – the soul's journey to God as it abandons the weakness and corruption of the human body and rises to the heights of mystical knowledge and ecstasy in union with God, a state of pure spirituality.

   The experience brought great comfort and strength to Muhammad, and convinced him that God was with him always.

TALKING POINTS

- Many believers experience a time they describe as a 'dark night of the soul' before times of great spiritual awareness. Is it necessary to go through the depths of sorrow and helplessness before one can fully know joy?
- Believers are often described as having seen the light. What do you think is meant by the 'darkness'?
   After experiencing something like this, do you think the 'darkness':
   a would seem darker;
   b would not matter at all; or
   c would be regretted, but would no longer affect the believer?

THINGS TO DO

▶ Write and act out a short play script about 'the day after the Miraj'. Your characters could include Ali, Zaid, Abu Lahab and his wife, and Abu Bakr.
▶ Copy out surah 6:103 or 6:95–6, and explain why one of the names of God is al-Latif – the One unable to be imagined or understood.

FOR YOUR FOLDERS

▶ Why was the night of the Night Journey regarded as the second most important time in Muhammad's life?
▶ What was the inner meaning of the Night Journey? In what way do all Muslims believe they can share in it?
▶ Why would a Muslim be suspicious of anyone who claimed direct knowledge of God, or to be able to describe God?

8 MUHAMMAD IN MADINAH

The converts of Yathrib

Muhammad returned to his preaching in Makkah. One day he was heard by some pilgrims from **Yathrib**, a town inhabited by three Arab and two Jewish tribes. The visitors were very impressed by what Muhammad had to say, and invited him to go to their town and judge their disputes.

They made a pledge in which they agreed:

- to obey none but Allah
- never to steal
- never to commit adultery
- never to do evil
- to protect the Prophet against all odds.

Muhammad warned of the dangers they would face if they responded to his call. They said:
'We take the Prophet, despite all threats to property, wealth and life. Tell us, O Prophet of Allah, what will be our reward if we remain true to this oath?'
The Prophet answered:
'Paradise'.
Muhammad eventually agreed to leave Makkah, and go to their town.

The Hijrah

Muhammad's followers were sent on ahead, and he stayed behind, still waiting for the final guidance from God that he should leave. Everyone knew that once he started out and was isolated in the desert, he could easily be ambushed by the enemies who wanted to kill him. According to tradition, there was a plot that one member from each tribe should stab him, so that no individual could be blamed.

Ali insisted on staying behind as a decoy, while Muhammad left the city. Muhammad doubled back and hid in a cave on **Mount Thawr** for four days. His enemies were soon on his trail, and at one point they came right to the mouth of the cave; but a spider had woven its web across the front, and a pigeon was nesting there, so they suspected nothing.

The arrival

When Muhammad arrived at Yathrib he was amazed and delighted at the welcome he received. Here he was accepted as an honoured and respected prophet. Everyone wanted to take him into their homes.

Not wishing to give offence, he said that he would leave the choice to his camel, al-Qaswa. The animal knelt at the place where the dates were dried out. Here Muhammad bought land and built a house. It is preserved to this day as the first **mosque** or **masjid** (see p. 122).

The calendar

Yathrib took the new name of Madinat-an-Nabi or **Madinah**. The year was 622 CE, and this became year one in the Muslim calendar.

The journey to Madinah was known as the **Hijrah** or Hegira, meaning migration. The Muslim calendar therefore makes all its dates **AH** – after Hijrah.

The ansars

The Muslims who had gone with Muhammad were refugees. They had left everything behind them and had no homes, little money and no employment. Muhammad asked the people of Madinah to share their belongings with the new arrivals from Makkah, and they did so without hesitation. These kind people were known as **ansars** or helpers. Many 'adopted' a stranger, or a complete family.

Organization

Muhammad became the city's political chief as well as its religious adviser. For the next ten years he worked to unite the tribes under the rule of God. Faith in God had to come before loyalty to the tribe or family.

- He drew up a written constitution outlining all the rights and duties of Muslims.
- He built the first mosque, or meeting-place for the faithful, on his own premises.
- He taught the regular prayer times.
- He organized collection of money for the poor, and taught regular fasting.

Conflicts

Muhammad's life was still in danger from the Makkans, who demanded that he should be handed over, and also from some Jews who were angry because part of his revealed message disagreed with their own holy books.

Muhammad accepted that all the Jewish prophets had received revelations from God just as he had, and expected the Jews of Madinah to accept his message and become Muslim. He respected their customs by praying facing Jerusalem, keeping the fast on the Day of Atonement, and summoning the faithful to prayer with a ram's horn trumpet as they did.

'Say – "We believe in the revelation which has come down to us and also in that which came down to you;
Our God and your God is one,
and it is to Him that we bow."'

(Surah 29:46)

But Muhammad could never deny what God revealed to him, and therefore when his revelations disagreed with the Jewish holy books he had to believe that the Jewish books must be at fault.

He received the revelation that Muslims should turn towards Makkah for prayer (surah 2:142–50), that the fast on the Day of Atonement was to be replaced by a month-long fast in the month of Ramadan, and that the powerful voice of his friend, the converted Ethiopian slave Bilal, should call them to prayer.

This tested whether or not the Jews really believed in Allah, and whether they were willing to obey the voice that spoke to Muhammad, or their own traditions. Many Jews would not accept the new revelation, so there was conflict between them and the Muslims.

FOR DISCUSSION

▶ Muslims believe that they should place loyalty to God before loyalty to their families. How could this
  a split families up
  b bind them more closely together?

THINGS TO DO

▶ Write out the promises made by the converts of Madinah (Yathrib).
▶ Make a list of the ways in which Muhammad began to organize the Muslims of Madinah.
▶ Write and act out a short play script about Muhammad's arrival in Madinah.
▶ Copy the table, and fill in the blanks:

Activity	Original instructions	Muslim instructions
1 Direction of prayer	Facing Jerusalem	Facing _____
2 Name of the fast	Day of _____	Month of _____
3 Length of the fast	One _____	One _____
4 Summons to prayer	By ram's horn trumpet	By the voice of ____

THINKING POINTS

● Why do you think Muslims decided to count the year of the migration to Madinah as year one of their calendar?
● Why do you think Muhammad might have expected the Jews of Madinah to suport his mission? Why do you think they finally decided against him.

FOR YOUR FOLDERS

▶ *'Say not of a thing "I will surely do it tomorrow" without adding "if God wills it".'*
(surah 18: 23–24)

What does this teach us about Muhammad's attitude to life? How did Muslims feel Muhammad's attitude differed from that of the Jews of Madinah?

9 MUHAMMAD THE RULER

Simple Arab house

Although Muhammad was now the ruler of Madinah, and eventually became the supreme head of a nation commanding the loyalty of thousands of believers, he continued to live like a poor man. He used to work alongside his friends, mend his own clothes, repair his shoes, do the shopping and milk the goats.

He could have lived like a king, taking taxes and tribute from all his subjects and using them to build palaces to keep himself and his friends in luxury. He could have worn a golden crown and dressed himself in the finest garments – but he believed with all his heart that there was no king but God, and that to keep more for himself than he needed was a sign of greed, deprived somebody else, and showed a lack of faith in God the provider.

Everything belonged to God, not to any individual; therefore when Muhammad was given money or goods, they were instantly given away again, to be shared amongst the needy.

God must come first, before any earthly possessions; a Muslim had to be willing to give up all material things for the sake of God and keep nothing back. To do less meant that love of another thing came before love of God. This was not true submission; that person had not truly found God.

Muhammad taught that self-discipline was not a matter of 'going without' or 'giving things up' – that was the wrong attitude. It should never be a burden, but be done out of great love for God.

Muhammad's 'kingdom' was one in which God was king, and all the subjects agreed to accept His laws and not the wishes of any human ruler. Some of the laws are given here:

- Control your anger, then forgive your brother. Do you not wish to be forgiven?
- Do not hate each other, envy each other, or provoke each other.
- Do not spy on each other, or betray each other's trust.
- Do not speak ill of your friend behind his back.
- Give the labourer his wages before his sweat dries.
- Do not drink alcohol, and do not gamble – it opens the door to the devil.
- Do not steal the property of another.
- Do not cheat each other.
- Do not defile the honour of a woman.
- Do not charge interest on money loaned to those who have need of it.
- Do not take part in corrupt practices, or do anything of which you would be ashamed if it became known.
- Do not reveal your friends' weaknesses. Cover their failings if you wish God to cover yours.
- Do not pay bribes to get what is not lawfully yours.
- Do not commit adultery, or practise homosexuality.
- Do not be cruel to slaves, or forbid them to marry or buy their freedom.
- Do not force slaves into sexual relationships they do not desire.
- Do not kill unwanted babies, either before or after birth, because of poverty.
- Do not be cruel to animals.
- Gladden the heart of the afflicted, feed the hungry, give comfort to the sorrowful, and remove the wrongs of the injured.

Slavery, as such, was not forbidden, for it was accepted by many poor people as a way of saving themselves and their families from debt, or even starvation. People could put themselves into slavery for agreed lengths of time in order to pay off what they owed. Muhammad did, however, look forward to a time when slavery would no longer be necessary, because no one would take interest on money lent, and all the needy would be taken care of by the community.

Muhammad's life was extremely simple. He regarded it as a weakness to give in to urges to comfort the body. He would never allow his stomach to become full, and existed mainly on a diet of dates and parched barley. He sometimes went without lighting a fire in his hearth for days, and ate raw food only. Some days he took nothing but water.

He owned only one change of clothes, carefully mending and patching them, and using his only cloak as his blanket at night. One story tells of a cat which brought her kittens and settled down on the corner of his cloak. Rather than disturb or deprive them, he cut off the piece of material, and made sure they stayed warm and cosy.

It was quite usual before Muhammad's time for men, including prophets, to have as many wives as they liked. The prophet **Dawud** (King David of Jerusalem) had ten; his son **Suleiman** (King Solomon the Wise) maintained 1000 women. In practical terms, most men took as many women as they could afford, and if they were not pleased with them, they could just throw them out. Under guidance from the Qur'an, the marriage laws were changed to care for the many defenceless women who had lost their families and protectors.

 After the death of Khadijah, Muhammad took into his household thirteen other women – daughters of his friends, widows of his close warriors and daughters of defeated enemies. Other Muslim men were allowed to support up to four women, but only if all were willing, it did not cause hurt, and they were treated equally (see p. 110).

Muhammad's dwelling was no more than a row of tiny rooms for himself and his wives, alongside the place of prayer. The only furniture in Muhammad's bedroom was a leather sack filled with twigs and palm branches to lean against when sitting, and a rush mat to sleep on. Muhammad never slept in a bed. He often spent the whole night standing up in prayer, sometimes accompanied by his youngest wife **Aisha**.

Muhammad's wives were devout women, able to accept this life of extreme simplicity, and total devotion to God. They were known for their kindness, unselfishness and generosity, and were held in very special regard by the Muslims as 'mothers of the faithful'.

Muhammad loved children. Another story tells how his two little grandsons ran up to him while he was kneeling in prayer, climbed up on to his back, and rode him like a horse. Instead of being angry, he allowed their game, and continued his prayers afterwards. Sometimes, when he saw them coming, he would interrupt his prayer to go and fetch them.

Muhammad's words, actions, and way of life reveal him as a man of gentleness, kindness, humility, good humour, and excellent common sense, who had great love for all people, especially for his family. Muhammad's way of life, or example, is known as the **Sunnah**, and Muslims who take the Qur'an and Sunnah as their only guides are known as **Sunni** Muslims (see p. 136).

FOR YOUR FOLDERS

▶ Explain what is meant by the Sunnah. Why do you think Muhammad did not take advantage of all the riches and luxuries he could have had? Do you think his attitude is to be admired?

▶ Look at the list of laws Muhammad expected the Muslims to obey. What would you say were the main principles that Muhammad revealed to be the will of God?

THINGS TO DO

▶ Make a list of the commandments given here that you think would be particularly difficult to keep:
a for a nosy, bad-tempered person
b for an employer
c for a wealthy business person
d for you.

FOR DISCUSSION

▶ In what way would a love of material comforts and possessions reveal that a person was not truly Muslim?

The new Islamic state of Madinah made no distinction between its ruler and subjects. Every citizen belonged to Allah and had equal rights. There was no discrimination on the grounds of colour, class, sex or family. God judged a person's worth or nobility according to his or her heart.

'The most noble among you in the sight of God is the one who is the most virtuous.'

(surah 49:13)

Few in the community were wealthy, because the migrants from Makkah had arrived with nothing. The people of Madinah took them into their homes and shared their possessions with them. But Muhammad was full of hope and confidence – what mattered was the strength of their faith, not their wealth.

The Battle of Badr

The Makkans were still determined to harm Muhammad. They tried to bribe the Madinans to hand him over. They persecuted the relatives of the Muslims that remained in Makkah, and took away' their property. In 623 CE a small group of Muslims raided a camel train in the old pagan month when warriors usually kept a truce. Although Muhammad had not sanctioned this attack, he understood their grievances. Sadly it provided the Makkans with an excuse to attack Madinah with a full army.

In 624 CE Muhammad's relative **Abu Sufyan** set out with a force of 1000 men. Muhammad only had 313 warriors, including young boys. They marched out of the city expecting to die, and camped at **al-Badr** – determined to die for God if they must.

To everyone's amazement, their faith and courage won the day. The Makkan army fled, leaving 70 killed and another 70 prisoners. In those few hours the Muslims changed from being a despised and persecuted group into a victorious military power, whom Allah had protected.

The Battle of Uhud

The Makkans longed for revenge, and a year later a much larger army attacked the Muslims at **Mount Uhud**. This time the Muslims were confident, but things went wrong. There was lack of discipline and confusion over tactics, and the Muslims lost the battle. Muhammad was wounded – he lost two teeth.

Now the Muslims were depressed, and wondered if God had deserted them. Later, however, it was seen as additional proof of Muhammad's mission.

'Your courage failed, there was chaos, and they disobeyed the Prophet. God allowed you to be defeated in order to test you.'

(surah 3:152)

When Muslims acted on revelation, they were always right, but when they acted on a human level, mistakes were made (see surah 3:152). It was revealed to Muhammad that:

- Defence against those who were challenging the faith was acceptable.
- Muslims who died fighting for God would go straight to paradise.
- The wars were God's will and the Muslim soldiers were God's army.

'Fight in the cause of God those who fight you, but do not go beyond the limits. Slay them whenever you find them, and remove them from the places they forced you to leave; for tyranny and oppression are worse than murder. Don't fight at the sacred mosque unless they fight you there first – but if they do, then slay them, for they are oppressing the faith. But if they stop, remember God is the Forgiving, the Merciful. Fight only until there is no more tyranny and oppression, and justice and faith in God prevail: if they stop let there be no more hostility – only to those who are tyrants.'

(surah 2:190–3)

After several other battles, in 629 CE Muhammad had a dream telling him to go unarmed on a pilgrimage to Makkah. He went with 1400 men, and the Makkans came out to fight. When they realized he came in peace they settled for a ten-year truce known as the Treaty of Hudaibiya. However, the next year, when Muhammad returned with 2000 followers, the truce was broken by the Makkans.

Muhammad takes Makkah

In 630 CE Muhammad marched on Makkah with a force of 10000 men. No one could withstand him. He rode into the city on his camel, circled seven times round the Ka'ba, touched the Black Stone set in a corner of the Ka'ba (see p. 82), and then called everyone to midday prayer. Entering the Ka'ba, he destroyed all the idols, and ordered all the pictures to be rubbed off – except, according to tradition, those of Jesus and Mary. He had conquered in the name of Allah, and Makkah was his.

As a conqueror, he was lenient and forgiving, and declared a general amnesty. Soon everyone in Makkah accepted the faith and became Muslim. After this, Makkah became the holy city dedicated to Allah, and anyone who was not a Muslim was forbidden to enter it. This ban is still in force today.

Out of the chaos and wickedness he had known when he first started his mission, Muhammad had created a well-disciplined state in the name of Allah. There was justice instead of oppression and compassion for the poor instead of callousness. The energies of the Muslims were directed into longing for the submission of the whole world to Allah.

'Permission is given by God to those who are fighting because they have been wronged . . . . Those who were driven from their homes for no reason other than saying "God is our Lord."'

(surah 22:39–40)

'You shall not enter Paradise until you have faith, and you cannot have faith until you love one another. Have compassion on those on earth, and God will have compassion on you.'

(Hadith)

TALKING POINTS

- Belief in peace at all costs might be no more than a temptation to cowardice.
- Humans are the only animals which wage war on each other.
- Defence is not the same thing as attack.
- Being prepared to sacrifice yourself because of your beliefs in non-violence is not the same thing as bringing about a just peace.

THINGS TO DO

- ▶ Explain what lessons the Muslims learned from the battles of Badr and Uhud.
- ▶ Is it ever morally wrong *not* to fight? Make a list of occasions on which you think this might be so.

FOR YOUR FOLDERS

- ▶ Muslims do not believe in peace at all costs, but accept that people should fight in order to establish a 'just peace'. What is meant by the phrase 'just peace'? Under what conditions do Muslims accept that war is justified?
- ▶ The battles of holy war are not against people, but against evil. How far do you think this is true?
- ▶ Muslims cannot be expected to fight for Allah if they are ill, old, infants or disabled – and yet they would like to think they are not left out of the fight against evil. How might such people show that they, too, were 'warriors for God'?

THINKING POINTS

- People often talk of total pacifism as if it is a good and noble thing, but Muslims consider it is sometimes wrong *not* to fight. Here are some examples of when action would be thought necessary:
- someone was beating up an old woman or a child
- someone was attacking your mother or brother
- a teacher was watching a bully torment a child.
  What principles do you think lie behind Islamic action?

11 THE FAREWELL

The burial place of Muhammad in Madinah

'Today I have perfected your religion for you, completed My favour upon you, and have chosen for you Islam as the way of your life.'

(surah 5:3, the last revelation given to Muhammad)

In 632 CE Muhammad became aware that his great mission was drawing to a close. He went back to Makkah on a pilgrimage along with a vast crowd of some 140 000 people. Going up to the Mount of Mercy he addressed them in a sermon charged with high emotion.

The sermon

'O people, listen to my words carefully, for I do not know whether I will meet you again on such an occasion as this. You must live at peace with one another. Everyone must respect the rights and properties of their neighbours. There must be no rivalry or enmity among you. Just as you regard this month as sacred, so regard the life and property of every Muslim in the same way. Remember, you will surely appear before God and answer for your actions.

All believers are brothers . . . you are not allowed to take things from another Muslim unless he gives it to you willingly. You are to look after your families with all your heart, and be kind to the women God has entrusted to you.

You have been left God's Book, the Qur'an. If you hold fast to it, and do not let it go, you will not stray from the right path. People, reflect on my words . . . I leave behind me two things, the Qur'an and the example of my life. If you follow these you will not fail.

Listen to me very carefully. Worship God, be steadfast in prayer, fast during Ramadan, pay alms to the less fortunate.

People, no prophet or messenger will come after me, and no new faith will emerge. All those who listen to me will pass on my words to others, and those to others again.'

(Hadith)

At the end of the speech he looked round at the vast array of people. 'Have I fulfilled my mission?' he cried. The crowd roared their approval. 'You have fulfilled it, O messenger of God.'

Muhammad raised his eyes to heaven and called out three times, 'O God, You are Witness, You are Witness, O God You are Witness.'

There was a moment's silence broken by the call to prayer from the powerful voice of Bilal. Shoulder to shoulder they joined in worshipping God.

'If all the waters of the sea were ink with which to write the words of my Lord, the sea would surely be drained before His words are finished, even, if we were to add to it sea upon sea.'

(surah 18:109)

Death of Muhammad

When Muhammad returned to Madinah he fell ill with a fever and violent headaches. Becoming weak, but still mindful to the last of fairness to his household, he asked permission of all his wives to move into Aisha's room to be nursed until he died.

He still tried every day to reach the praying place outside, but he knew his death was not far off and asked Abu Bakr to lead the prayers in his place.

On his last day, after the dawn prayer, he was helped back exhausted, and lay in Aisha's arms. She felt his head grow heavy, and heard him say, 'Lord, grant me pardon'. His last words were said to have been, 'I have chosen the most exalted company, in paradise'.

With his head in Aisha's lap, the Prophet died.

Instantly, there was shock and panic. **Umar**, a friend of Muhammad, refused to believe that it was possible Muhammad could die. He thought he would live for ever, and began to raise false hopes.

Abu Bakr took control. 'O people,' he cried, 'don't worship Muhammad, for Muhammad is dead. Know that God is alive and never dies!' He then recited the verse of the Qur'an:

'Muhammad is but a messenger; there have been prophets before him, and they all died. Will you now turn back?'

(surah 3:144)

Muhammad was buried where he died, in Aisha's room, and his grave is still a place of pilgrimage to this day. Muslims regard him as the greatest of all men – the seal of the prophets, the servant and messenger of God.

May God's blessings and peace be upon him.

Tradition suggests Muhammad died on 8 June 632 CE (12 Rabi'ul-Awwal 11 AH) at the age of sixty-three.

THINKING POINT

- **Why do you think Muhammad was called the 'seal' of all the prophets? (A seal is the 'stamp of approval', or the guarantee that everything in a document is in order.)**

FOR YOUR FOLDERS

▶ What do you think are the qualities of truly great people? To what extent to you think Muhammad possessed those qualities?

▶ Why were Abu Bakr's words after the death of Muhammad important? How did this incident show that he was worthy to succeed Muhammad as leader of the Muslims?

TALKING POINT

- **Do you think Muhammad would have been equally successful if he had lived in our time instead of when he did? Give reasons for your answer.**

God is often compared with light

The light

'God is the light of all worlds;
His light may be compared to a shrine
in which there is a lamp;
the lamp is in a crystal;
the crystal is, as it were,
a glittering star
kindled from a blessed olive tree.
The oil would burst into flames
even though fire had never touched it:
Light upon Light!'

(surah 24:35)

'O Lord!
Illumine my heart with light,
my sight with light and
my hearing with light.
Let there be light
on my right hand and on my left and
light behind me and
light going before me.'

(Hadith)

'O God, who knows the innermost secrets
of our hearts –
lead us out of the darkness
into the light.'

(Hadith)

The recognition

To be a Muslim, you must have thought about the vital question – is there or is there not a God? Either God does exist, or He doesn't. Many people seem to pass their entire lives without ever thinking about the reason for their existence, or whether there is any point to their lives, or any goal to be aimed for. They think this universe is all there is, and there is nothing beyond it. Their lives are just chains of happenings until everything stops at death.

Muslims think it is impossible for anything to come into existence from nothing, or exist without being caused. They believe that certain people (the prophets) have been given 'insights' from God, and guidance, throughout history. Muslims acknowledge the urge to improve themselves and to stop themselves doing wrong that is triggered off by conscience. From all this, they conclude that *there is a god*.

To recognize that God does exist, and is unique – above and beyond all the things He has created – is the recognition that Muslims believe will bring a person to paradise. Without this awareness, you cannot be admitted to paradise. It is not that God refuses to forgive a person, but if a person refuses to accept God's loving presence and 'puts up a wall', then nothing can be done until the 'wall' is taken away.

Anyone who believes in God, and submits to His will, is 'Muslim', a 'surrendered person'.

Since the time of the prophet Muhammad, however, it is usual to think of Muslims as those who accept that the revelation made to him was the last revelation, which they believe corrected and took the place of all earlier messages from God.

'Those who believe in the Qur'an
and those who follow the Jewish scriptures
and the Christians and the Sabians
and any who believe in God
and the Last Day
and work righteousness
shall have their reward
with their Lord; on them
shall be no fear,
nor shall they grieve.'

(surah 2:62)

'It is He who sends down
blessings upon you, as do His
angels, that He may bring you
out of the darkness into the light.
He is full of mercy to
those who believe;
on the day they meet Him
the cry will be "Peace".'

(surah 33:43)

'He is the Light by which you
will walk straight on your path;
If you come to the light and walk in it
He will forgive your past,
for He always forgives and is
merciful.'

(surah 57:28)

'The light shines into many
courtyards, all separated by walls.
Take away the walls, and you will see
the Light is the same.'
(Jalal ud-Din Rumi, a Muslim
teacher)

FOR YOUR FOLDERS

▶ Why do you think some people never think about God, or the possible reasons for their existence, while others are quite convinced that God exists? Are certain types of people more 'religious' than others?

▶ What sort of events or experiences do you think lead certain people to an awareness of God?

▶ Read 'The recognition' and the words from surah 2 in the introduction. What is it that qualifies a person as a Muslim?

THINGS TO DO

▶ Read the words about light. Why do you think God is so often compared with light?

▶ Make a list of events, experiences or emotions that could come under the headings 'light' and 'darkness'.

▶ Copy out one of the sayings about light, and make a decorative border for it.

The most basic Muslim belief about God is **Tauhid**. This means 'one-ness', 'unity', 'the absolute' or 'the alone'. This is one of the hardest concepts to grasp of all. It means accepting that God by definition is supreme. If God exists at all, there can be nothing that can rival Him as a source of power or love. It means there is nothing remotely like Him.

> 'He is Allah, the One,
> Allah is Eternal and Absolute.
> None is born of Him,
> He is unborn.
> There is none like unto Him.'
>
> (surah 112)

Tauhid means that God alone is the creator, the power behind the universe and the sole source of its guidance. He knows everything, sees everything and is able to do anything.

As creator, God exists outside and beyond everything that He created. God is outside time, whereas all created things are part of time. Things which are part of time have beginnings and ends, but this is not true of God.

When Muslims talk of God being 'eternal' or 'infinite', they are admitting that He is beyond human knowledge and reasoning.

> 'No vision can grasp Him,
> but His grasp is over all vision;
> He is above all comprehension,
> yet is acquainted with all things.'
>
> (surah 6:103)

Tauhid does not mean that God is so far away He cannot possibly know or care about people.

> 'I am close to them; I listen to the prayer of every suppliant who calls to Me. Let them listen to my call and believe in Me, that they may walk in the right way.'
>
> (surah 2:186)

> 'It was I who created man, and I know even the secret suggestions his soul makes to him; for I am nearer to him than his jugular vein.'
>
> (surah 50:16)

To think that you own any object, or any person, breaks Tauhid. Everything in the universe belongs to God. You may only 'borrow' possessions, or even your own bodies, for as long as God wills.

Pride or arrogance breaks Tauhid. You were given your talents or brain capacity before birth, and did not choose them for yourself.

Ignorance of God's supremacy breaks Tauhid. No other power in the universe can act except as God wills it. Superstition breaks Tauhid.

Complaining to God, or begging for favours, or trying to change His will as if your own was better, breaks Tauhid. God already knows everything and is supreme compassion. If tragedy strikes it is for a reason, even if we do not understand it.

Thinking God can be fooled or deceived breaks Tauhid. He knows even the thoughts you conceal from yourself in your subconscious mind.

A false pride, or sense of holiness, breaks Tauhid. God is not fooled by hypocrisy. He knows all our weaknesses, our lack of faith.

Shirk

When a person tries to liken God to any created thing, or to suggest that other things in the universe somehow share in God's creative power, or have His knowledge or ability to guide or forgive – this is known as the sin of **shirk**.

God is beyond the world of matter, and the idea of His somehow mingling with matter to become the father of a human being, or produce a being that is half human and half divine, is blasphemy to a Muslim. For this reason Muslims think that Christians, who believe Jesus to be the Son of God, and that there are really three Gods in One (Father, Son and Holy Spirit) are making a terrible mistake.

To a Muslim, the Holy Spirit is the action of God and not a separate entity, and Jesus – the 'miracle worker' who even raised the dead – was in his humility a supreme Muslim and not in any way a divine being.

A prophet cannot *be* God. No prophet ever claimed this. Muslims insist that this is true of Jesus also, one of the greatest and humblest prophets. They think that the claims made about him by later Christians were not the claims made by Jesus himself. They believe that Jesus would have recoiled in horror from the suggestion that he was God. (If you have access to a Bible, you could look up such passages as John 20:17; Luke 18:19; Mark 12:25 to support the Muslim belief.)

The traditions that Jesus was born of a virgin mother and worked miracles are accepted by Muslims without question – for God revealed this to Muhammad in the Qur'an. But these two beliefs do not lead Muslims to assume that God has any equal or partner (see also p. 48).

THINKING POINT

- **A devout person could spend many hours in prayer, asking for God's help in connection with a particular problem or misfortune. Why might a Muslim regard this as a failing rather than something to be admired?**

FOR YOUR FOLDERS

▶ Why do Muslims believe it is impossible to describe God in human terms?

▶ In what ways do pride, envy, hatred or selfishness break Tauhid?

▶ Explain what is meant by the sin of shirk. Why is the highest expression of Christian devotion to Jesus regarded by Muslims as being a weakness and a misunderstanding?

Results

Belief in Tauhid results in:

- *faith*, and surrender to the will of Allah
- *self-respect* and *confidence*. No other power (king, employer, relative or friend) has any rights over Muslims. They depend on and fear no one but God
- *humility* and *modesty*. Whatever Muslims are or own is from God, so how can they be proud or boastful?
- *responsibility*, because Muslims know they are answerable to God for their actions
- *trust*, because they believe that everything must be God's will, and therefore planned
- *courage*, because they accept that they will face tests as God wills, and not die before the appointed time for them to do so
- *unity with the universe*, because they act for God in taking care of the planet
- *determination*, *patience* and *perseverance*, because Muslims have dedicated themselves to pleasing God, and it is no easy task.

'They do blaspheme who say that "God is Christ the son of Mary." For Christ himself said "O children of Israel, worship God, my Lord and your Lord." '

(surah 5:72)

'Of God speak only the truth. The Messiah, Jesus son of Mary, is only an apostle of God, and His word which He conveyed to Mary, and a spirit proceeding from Himself. Say not "Three". Do not do it. God is only one God. Far be it from His glory that He should have a son. The Messiah is not ashamed to be the servant of God.'

(surah 4:171)

THINGS TO DO

▶ Make a list of what Muslims believe are the most important results of Tauhid in their lives. You could do this as a diagram or table, using just the key words.

▶ Copy out one of the surah quotations given here and explain in your own words what you think it means.

Allah, the name of God

14 THE CAUSE

What do Muslims believe about God?

- Allah is the end, the final judge of everything.

- Allah is the only true God.

- He is the supreme being and can have no equal.

- Allah is always kind, and loves us.

- Allah is forgiving.

- No thing or person, even a great prophet, is equal to God.

- Allah is always just.

- Allah allows us free-will, but He controls our destinies.

- Allah is the beginning, the cause of everything that exists.

- You cannot think of Allah in human terms.

- Allah knows everything – nothing can ever be hidden from Him.

- No one can know Allah – unless He chooses to reveal Himself.

- Allah cannot be compared to anything.

- Allah is unique.

- No one can really know what Allah is like. He is beyond our understanding.

- Allah knows what is in our hearts.

- We know Allah always loves us, and He always forgives us if we are sorry.

- Allah 'sees' and 'hears' everything.

- Allah is nearer to us than the veins in our necks.

- Allah is perfect spirit; He created everything else.

- Allah made all the laws; He is beyond them and not ruled by them like us.

- Allah does not prefer any person or nation. He creates everyone equal.

Cause and effect

Every single thing in our universe is the effect of something that caused it – but the causes are not always instantly obvious. Suppose you did not know what an acorn was, and had never seen an oak tree. You could not possibly guess what the acorn would become. If you saw the tree, you could never guess what it had come from.

The whole universe is like that. We might happen to know a little bit about it, but we don't know much.

Think about yourself – who would have guessed that the whole 'programme' or 'package' that is you was once just a microscopic 'seed' and a 'seed receiver' in two separate bodies? And who knows how your 'self' – and the stage of life after this one – will compare to this?

Muslims believe the whole creation was caused by God. If it had no cause, it would never have existed.

*'Did you think that you were created
out of nothing, or were your own creators?
False gods cannot create a fly – nor could they ever
get back what a fly could take from them.'*

(surah 22:73)

*'The value of this world
in comparison to the hereafter
is like a droplet
in the ocean.'*

(Hadith)

Big Bang theory

This is the belief that the whole universe started expanding when a colossal first atom exploded. Think:
- What was this atom?
- Where was it?
- How did it get there?
- Why did it explode?
  Muslims believe the causes were already there.

FOR YOUR FOLDERS

▶ Work out the chain of cause and effect for the existence of a table. (The table exists because . . .)
▶ Love and conscience are known by their effects. Write down some of the effects of these two concepts that prove they really do exist, even though they are not physical things.
▶ The Big Bang theory is accepted by many modern scientists. Why do Muslims believe this does not contradict the idea of God as creator?

THINGS TO DO

▶ Choose ten of the statements about God which you most agree with, and write them out on a decorated scroll or a poster.

TALKING POINTS

- **Could a caterpillar ever understand what it is like to be a butterfly?**
- **Why do Muslims believe it is important to be aware of 'cause', and to be humble in our scientific knowledge?**

15 CREATION

'Nothing scientists discover is new – it has always been there'

Thinking about creation

Interviewer: Ali, why do you think Allah created all this? How can you prove it?

Ali: This universe did not just spring into being by chance or accident. Some scientists say that sort of thing because they do not want to believe in God. None of them can give the answer. They're only guessing.

Interviewer: But they know what they're talking about.

Ali: Look, isn't it possible that this whole universe might never have existed at all?

Interviewer: I suppose so.

Ali: Of course. *You* might never have existed. That table might never have existed. Nothing exists without a cause. Therefore, if the universe *does* exist, it must be because of a reason. If you take away the cause, how can anything happen?

Interviewer: We ought to be able to prove God exists, then, from the laws of nature. Couldn't God just have evolved?

Ali: How can God be under the same rules as that which He created? He is above and beyond them. There is this difference between Allah and everything else in the universe.

Interviewer: Don't you think the scientists will ever prove the existence of God, then?

Ali: How can a creature who sees only in black and white ever understand what is meant by blue? You can show a monkey all the rules of science, but it will never understand them. Likewise, a human being will never fully understand the universe, let alone Allah who made it.

Interviewer: Do you think the scientists are just wasting their time?

Ali: No, no. They make discoveries all the time. Allah wants us to be intelligent and to love Him. But look, everything the scientists discover – it is nothing new, is it? It has been there all the time, waiting to be found.

Science just suddenly sees what has always been there. But the true scientist realizes that he or she doesn't know very much.

Interviewer: I think that's true. Our great scientist Sir Isaac Newton once said that after the whole of his lifetime's study, he had been just like a boy playing with pebbles on the beach while a whole vast ocean lay before him.

Ali: And in any case, the universe contains far more than our earth and its solar system; it contains more than the whole of the 'space' that is waiting for the astronauts. There are whole regions of existence, whole 'heavens', which are quite beyond physical space.

Interviewer: Will we ever know the truth, Ali?

Ali: One day, one day – insha 'Allah [if God wills].

'There is no God but He, the Living, the Eternal. He neither slumbers nor sleeps. No person can grasp anything of His knowledge, except as God wills it.'

(surah 2:255)

'God has the key to all secrets. He knows whatever is on land and in the sea: no leaf falls without His knowing it; there is not a grain in the darkness of earth, or a green or dry thing, but it is carefully noted.'

(surah 6:59)

'If you think that you control your own destinies, then try to stop your souls leaving your bodies at the time of your death.'

(Hadith. See also surahs 3:168, 56:83–7.)

'To God belong the East and the West; wherever you turn, there is the Presence of God; for God is all-pervading, all-knowing.'

(surah 2:115)

The seven heavens

Muslims believe there are seven heavens beyond our universe. The Prophet Muhammad saw this revelation in his lifetime. In the heavens he met Adam, Abraham, Moses and Jesus, all still living.

As he approached nearer to God, he found himself surrounded by 'Oceans' of light, and felt a sense of perfect peace (see p. 16).

FOR YOUR FOLDERS

▶ Explain why a Muslim could never accept that:
  a the universe came into being by chance
  b there was no evidence for the existence of God.

▶ Read the surahs given here, and explain carefully in your own words what each one teaches about God.

THINGS TO DO

▶ Look up the meanings of these names of Allah, and list them carefully: Compassionate; Supreme; Omnipotent; Omnipresent; Omniscient; Beneficent.

▶ Fill in the missing words: Everything in our _____ has been _____ by something else that happened before it. Nothing just came into being by _____. All rules of science depend on this _____. Nothing, in our experience, can be created out of _____. Therefore, the Muslim believes that the universe itself has a _____, and a beginning. This cause is _____.

TALKING POINTS

● **Why do Muslims believe a created being can never understand that which created it?**
● **Does a living cell in your body know that you exist?**
● **There is no such thing as mind or conscience. These are just workings of the physical brain.**

*'We send forth guardians to watch over you,
and when death overtakes you,
the messengers will carry away your soul.'*

(surah 6:61)

*'Behold, two guardians
appointed to learn his doings,
one sitting on his right and
one on the left.
Not a word does he utter
but there is a sentinel
by him, ready to note it.'*

(surah 50:17–18)

*'Angels are appointed over you to
protect you; they are kind and
honourable, and write down your deeds.
They know and understand all that you do.'*

(surah 82:10–12)

Beings in the universe

Muslims do not accept that humans and animals made of matter are the only beings in the universe. They believe in at least two other kinds of beings, the **jinn** and the **angels**. Neither are human, and so they are beyond real human understanding. Muslims object strongly to any attempts to draw pictures of them based on imagination, as these can be very misleading.

Jinn are usually thought of as spirit forces, neither good nor evil and they are sometimes described as being made from fire.

Angels are the messengers of God, the channels by which humans become aware of Him.

Neither have physical bodies, but both can affect the world of matter and people with whom they come in contact.

Angels

The word 'angel' means 'messenger', and this is the chief function of these beings.

Muslims believe angels are creatures of light who pervade the whole universe. They are not far away, and are in constant contact with humans.

The presence

Muslims believe that angels are present all the time, especially whenever a person prays or thinks about God when they gather round and join in. Their presence can be felt as a sensation of peace and love, and it helps to build up the atmosphere of worship.

Humans only see angels on very rare occasions, but Muslims believe that they are sometimes seen by specially chosen people, or at times of great crisis. However, many sensitive people do become aware of loving and guiding presences watching over their lives, and those who become constantly aware take their presence almost for granted, so that it becomes quite hard to remember that other people do not share the same awareness.

An angel may take human shape, as Jibra'il did to the prophet Ibrahim, and to Mary the mother of Jesus – but this is not its true form. It can materialize in any shape it chooses. According to Hadith Muhammad first saw Jibra'il as a huge creature covering the horizon between heaven and earth with several thousand wings.

The record

Muslims believe that every person has two special angels, or guardians, who keep a record of their good or bad deeds. If you thought nobody saw you do a bad thing, and you have got away with it, you are wrong. It was seen and recorded. Likewise, if you thought no one had noticed your good deed and it was not appreciated, again you are wrong. Nothing a person ever does or thinks is ever unknown, unseen, forgotten, or left out.

At the end of formal prayers Muslims turn to the right and the left and bless their two angels as they hover near their shoulders (see p. 63).

(see p. 63)

> ## THINGS TO DO
>
> ▶ Think about flames of fire disappearing up a chimney. Try to describe what a flame of fire is, what it does, where it goes. Did you find it difficult?
> ▶ Think through the last two days. Make a list of some of your thoughts and actions that might have gone into your record book.

Angels

- **Jibra'il** – the messenger of God who gives revelations to the chosen ones
- **Azra'il** – the angel of death who is present at deathbeds to receive souls

There was an old superstition that hand prints warded off evil spirits

- **Israfil** – calls all souls on the Day of Judgement
- **Mika'il** – the protector of the faithful and guardian of places of worship
- **Iblis** – The chief jinn, regarded as the devil.

'Every person's judgement is fastened round his neck; on the Day we will bring forth a book which shall be shown wide open. Read your book; you have no need of anyone but yourself to work out your account.'

(surah 17: 13–14)

'On the Day of Judgement no step of a servant of God shall slip until he has answered concerning four things:
- *his body and how he used it*
- *his life and how he spent it*
- *his wealth and how he earned it*
- *his knowledge and what he did with it.'*

(Hadith)

TALKING POINTS

- Do you think the Muslim belief in guardian angels makes life easier or more difficult?
- The universe only contains the creatures proved to exist by science. The Muslim belief in angels is no more than imagination. Do you agree?

FOR YOUR FOLDERS

▶ Why do Muslims object to attempts to portray angels or spirit forces in art?
▶ Look at the saying of Muhammad about the Day of Judgement. What particular things are of great importance in a person's record?
▶ Why do Muslims believe in angels? How might a Muslim be helped in life by the belief in guardians?

THINGS TO DO

▶ Fill in the missing words:
Every human being is in close contact with two _____ or _____, whether they know it or not. These watchers keep a _____ of their good and bad _____ and thoughts. This record will be the basis for our _____ when we finally face God. The chief angel is _____ and the chief jinn is _____. Iblis is the Muslim equivalent of the _____.

35

'It is the soul, and not the body the soul lives in, that is the real person'

Soil

Muslims believe that all human beings are descended from one original couple, Adam and Eve, who were created by God. The word 'Adam' means 'soil' or 'dust', and 'Eve' comes from a word meaning 'living'.

The physical body is made of clay; the human aspect totally dependent on humus (the living part of the soil). We are what we eat. If we cease to take in matter from the soil, we die.

God's image

Muslims do not believe that God made humans to look like Him. There is no reason to suppose that the creator of the universe should have the form of *any* of the things He has created.

Muslims do not believe that humans have descended by evolution from apes or that both were descended from the same ancestor. Apes were created in their own image, and still exist, as apes. Humans were created as humans. They believe the modern 'theory of evolution' is only a theory, and not a proved fact.

Adam was created to be God's deputy on earth, to take care of it (see surah 2:30).

'We created Man from the essence of clay. . . . We made out of that lump bones and clothed the bones with flesh; then We developed out of it another creature. At length you will die; and on Judgement Day you will be raised up.'

(surah 23:12–16)

'O Mankind, be mindful of your duty to God, who created you from a single soul, and from it created its mate, and from the two created many men and women.'

(surah 4:1)

The soul

Human beings are the highest physical creations of God, with the most capacity for shaping their own futures. They have freedom of will and action. Like other species, they can reproduce themselves from their own living cells. However, although human bodies are living, they are not conscious.

Muslims believe that God gave to each reproduced human form a quite distinct individual soul, called **rouh**. It is the soul, not the body the soul lives in, that is the real person.

The time span

Muslims believe that God allows each soul to inhabit a body for a certain time, until it is taken away again. They believe that each soul remains the soul of that individual person, and does not travel into the body of another human, or animal, or live again on earth in a future reincarnation.

Although corpses break down after death, a person's soul and body will eventually be reunited when the Hour of Judgement comes.

All equal

During earthly life we all have different sets of experiences. Some are fortunate, others are not. Life is not a purposeless wander towards death, or a game. It is a test, in deadly earnest.

Because humans have conscious souls, they have the great ability to love and be kind – or to hate and be destructive. This means that humans do not remain equal.

The spiritual faculties of human beings raise them above the animal kingdom, and make them responsible for it. Some humans behave so badly, they sink below the level of the animal kingdom.

'We have honoured the sons of Adam,
provided them with transport on land and sea,
given them for food things good and pure,
and conferred on them special favours
above a great part of Our creation.'

(surah 17:70)

'Some say "There is only this present life;
we live and we die, and only Time destroys us."
In this they have no knowledge, it is
merely their own conceit. God gives you life,
then causes you to die; then He will
assemble you again on the Day of Resurrection.
There is no doubt of this – but most people
have not arrived at this knowledge.'

(surah 45:24)

'Be steadfast in prayer
and regular in charity;
and whatever good you
send forth from your souls,
you will find it with God;
for God sees all that you do.'

(surah 2:110)

THINKING POINTS

- **Think about the life cycle of a physical body. How is it kept alive? What happens to it after death? Is any part of it not dependent on the earth itself?**
- **How is it that a fat person can slim off pounds of weight, or an accident victim lose a limb, or a tiny baby grow into a huge adult – and yet still be the same person? What is it that makes a 'person'?**

FOR YOUR FOLDERS

- ▶ Explain what Muslims believe about the uniqueness of each species.
- ▶ Why do Muslims believe the physical body is not actually the real person?
- ▶ What do Muslims believe happens to a person after death?

THINGS TO DO

- ▶ Read the passages in this unit from the Qur'an. What do they teach about the beginning, lifetime and end of humans?

QUICK QUIZ

- ▶ Who was the first man?
- ▶ What do the names Adam and Eve mean?
- ▶ Why was Adam created?
- ▶ What was Adam made out of?
- ▶ What is the rouh?
- ▶ What is a soul's 'time-span'?
- ▶ When are soul and body reunited?

Suffering caused through human evil

'The Lord said to the angels – "When I have finished Man and breathed My spirit into him, then fall ye down and worship him." And all the angels bowed down in worship except Iblis, the Devil.'

(surah 15:29–31)

'"What prevented you from bowing down when I commanded you?" He said. "I am better than he. You created me from fire and him from clay."'

(surah 7:12)

'Iblis said: "O my Lord! Because you have put me in the wrong, I will make wrong seem a good thing to those on earth, and I will put them all in the wrong."'

(surah 15:39)

'Lead to destruction those whom you can! As for My servants, you shall have no authority over them!'

(surah 17:64)

The devil

Muslims believe that both angels and jinn existed before the human race at a stage when the universe was perfect and evil did not exist. The urge to do evil was caused when humans were created. God intended the first man, Adam, to rule the earth and look after it. He ordered all the angels to respect His decision, but the chief jinn Iblis refused to do this because he considered himself a superior creature.

For this he was punished, and therefore became the enemy of all humans. Since that time he has done his best to get revenge by leading people's hearts and minds away from God.

Instinct and mind

All humans are given an instinct (called **nafs**) which can be an influence for good or for evil. Everyone has the freedom to choose, and the part that makes the choice is the mind.

Muslims believe that God does not control anyone's mind by force, but has allowed *free will*.

Nothing can happen without the will and knowledge of Allah. He knows the present, past and future of all His created beings. Our destiny is already known. Whether we will obey or disobey His will is known to Him – but that does not affect our freedom of will. Humans do not know what their destiny is, and have the free will to choose whatever course they will take.

Free will

Freedom of choice brings enormous responsibility. It would be quite possible for God to make us all into robots, but He does not do so. We may choose how to act, how to respond to each challenge. It is usually quite obvious whether a particular deed is good or bad, and Muslims believe that if we deliberately choose to act *against* our consciences and do evil instead of good, then it is our own fault if one day we have to pay the penalty.

The devil and his followers are always eager to gain control of a person's mind, so people should be on the alert at all times. If we do not control our instincts, we are in grave danger – for the path towards evil is always attractive and tempting, and the path towards good is usually hard and full of difficult decisions and sacrifices.

DEBATE

▶ Why do Muslims consider God to be merciful and good if He does not rescue people from such things as floods, famine, earthquakes, disease, war, etc.

'It is not poverty which I fear for you, but that you might come to desire the world as others before you desired it and it might destroy you as it destroyed them.'

(Hadith)

THINKING POINTS

- **Why do Muslims believe that evil is possible in a universe created by a good God?**
- **Pride and disobedience are real causes of evil in the universe.**
- **If there was no such thing as evil, good would not exist.**

'Those who patiently persevere and seek God with regular prayers, and give generously – these overcome Evil with Good.'

(surah 13:22)

FOR YOUR FOLDERS

▶ Muslims do not believe it would be a better universe if we did not have free will, or the dangerous possibility of making wrong choices. Do you? Give reasons for your answer.

▶ Obeying without question might be unreasonable or even dangerous. Can you think of examples when it might be? In what ways do Muslims consider trust to be vital in their relationship with God?

Religion in action – famine relief in the Sudan

At home

When people become conscious of the existence of God it alters their entire attitude to life. The person no longer wanders blindly, but becomes aware that the universe has a meaning, and that each individual plays an important role in it.

Muslims believe humans are not lost in the universe, created by chance, but at home. They need not be overwhelmed by fears and superstitions, for they are loved, cherished, and all part of a plan.

Muslims think that to believe in God and live badly is a nonsense. Once we are aware that God knows all and sees all, how can we deliberately act in a dishonourable manner? It is meaningless to claim to love God and then lie, or cheat, or hate. This is what is meant by 'Islam' or 'submission'. Real awareness of God (called **taqwa**) brings with it the submission to Him of all your thoughts and deeds.

Nothing worthless

Humans are entrusted by God to take care of the planet. Everything and everybody matters – nothing is considered worthless. The poor, the humble and the oppressed are nearer to God than those who are mighty in their own eyes.

Nothing keeps a person away from God more than arrogance and worship of self.

A Muslim's responsibilities

- No Muslim may oppress women, children, old people, or the sick and wounded.
- Women's honour and chastity are to be respected and protected in all circumstances.
- The hungry must be fed.
- The naked must be clothed.
- The diseased must be treated.
- The wounded must be helped, whether friend or foe.
- Tyranny and evil must be challenged and defeated if possible.

Ummah

Muslims believe that we are all one family. There are no 'chosen races'. All people belong to God and are equal, whatever their colour, language or nationality. There should be no barriers of race, status or wealth, but a feeling of love and brotherhood between all people – helping each other out when in trouble, consoling each other when in grief, delighted when people are happy.

The word **ummah** describes this feeling of awareness, love and respect for others. The words used to translate it are usually 'brotherhood', 'family feeling' or 'kinship', but the word really implies the care and responsibility of motherhood. (See also p. 112.)

'To bring about a just reconciliation between two enemies is love, helping a person to mount his animal or load his baggage on to it is love, a good word is love, every step towards a mosque is love, to remove obstacles in the street is love, smiling upon the face of your brother is love.'

(Hadith)

'Who shall teach you what the steep highway is? It is to ransom the captive, to feed the orphan or the poor man who lies in the dust.'

(surah 90:12–16)

'He who has no compassion for our little ones, and does not acknowledge the honour due to our elders is not one of us.'

(Hadith)

FOR YOUR FOLDERS

▶ What is meant by ummah? How does the awareness of God lead to the awareness of ummah?
▶ Look at the passages from the Qur'an and Hadith given here and on p. 39. Make a list of the kind of responsibilities that a Muslim believes builds up the feeling of ummah.

TALKING POINTS

● Is there any evidence that God loves only good people and hates all bad ones?
● In what ways would the world be a better or a worse place if we were not allowed the possibility of making wrong choices?
● Should believing in a life after death make any difference to the way a person lives?

THINGS TO DO

▶ Copy and complete this word square.

1		D			■			E	
2			O		U				
3		U		U		■	■	■
4			U		■	■	■	■
5			D	G				T
6		A		■	■	■	■	■
7	F			■	W			
8	M					G		S
9		V		■	■	■	■	■
10			T	■	■	■	■	■

Clues:
1 The first human beings
2 The belief that one species is descended from another
3 The living matter in the soil
4 The Muslim word for soul
5 Soul and body are reunited at this time
6 The word for instinct
7 God allows this to everyone
8 They give warnings from God
9 He is always eager to control humans
10 Life is not without purpose, but is a _____

Some people become aware of the closeness of God and are chosen as prophets

God's duty

Muslims believe that it is a human's duty to love and serve God, and submit to His will. Obviously, no one can do this if God does not let them know what His will is. How is human life to be guided? How can a person decide whether an action is right or wrong?

Since God is just, it is obvious that He has a duty to reveal His will to us, and give us a code of conduct by which to live.

Risalah is this channel of communication between God and humanity. A **rasul** is a prophet. A message communicated directly to a prophet's mind in this way is called a revelation.

The messengers

Muslims do not believe that Muhammad was the first to receive such revelations, or that he was the founder of their religion. God Himself is the founder, and long before Muhammad had ever lived He had communicated with many other people.

Muslims believe the first prophet was the first man, Adam, and that between Adam and Muhammad there had been at least 124000 other messengers of whom at least twenty-four are mentioned in the Qur'an. In other words, God has always revealed Himself to those who had the necessary spirituality to understand His messages.

The messengers did not choose to do this work. On the contrary, God chose them – much to the surprise and reluctance of some of them! God did not pick the great and famous, the wealthy or influential – but those who lived virtuous and honourable lives.

The five major prophets before Muhammad were **Adam, Nuh** (Noah), **Ibrahim** (Abraham), **Musa** (Moses) and **Isa** (Jesus).

'God chooses for Himself whoever He pleases, and guides to Himself those who turn to Him.'

(surah 42:13)

The books

The holy books included the
- **Sahifa** – scrolls given to Ibrahim
- **Tawrat** – the revelation to Musa (the Torah)
- **Zabur** – the psalms given to Dawud (David)
- **Injil** – the teachings given to Isa (the Gospels).

Each of these was originally a complete revelation, but Muslims believe the books and teachings were not preserved properly. Some, like the Sahifa, were lost completely.

Others, like the Zabur, Tawrat and Injil, were changed in various ways. Bits were left out and forgotten, and many additions made.

Muslims do not believe that the Injil is the same thing as the Gospels now kept by the Christian Church, or that the Tawrat is the same thing as the present Torah of the Jews.

If you extracted all the specific teachings from God and laid aside all the comments, opinions, notes, legends and so on that were added afterwards by editors, you would get nearer to the truth, but even then Muslims do not accept that all the sayings are genuine.

'Those who say, "God does not send down revelations to humans", do not judge rightly. Who sent down the Book which Moses brought – a light and guidance for humanity? But you have made it into separate books for show, and you conceal much of its contents.'

(surah 6:91)

The Jewish and Christian scriptures, therefore, are accepted only as edited versions of the revelations, altered according to the beliefs or motives of the various writers and editors involved, and the guidance given in them – since it is no longer in its original form – cannot be relied on.

The seal

The Prophet Muhammad holds a very special place for Muslims, because he was the last of the long succession of prophets to whom specific revelations were made. He was the final seal of all who had gone before.

The Qur'an

What Muhammad saw and heard was quite different. It was the *complete guidance*, the last 'revealed book'.

When Muslims talk of the 'scripture', or the 'written record', they are referring to the concept of all the laws given by God for the guidance of the universe which were 'written by the Pen' before creation ever began – an eternal record (see p. 10).

This idea is rather like the whole history of scientific discovery which is gradually finding out what is already there – the laws that govern the universe existed before the universe did! Muslims claim the Holy Qur'an to be the eternal book giving guidance for human lives.

Therefore, the revelations given to Muhammad were to be preserved exactly, and were intended to put right any errors in previous holy books, and set the standard by which to judge all these earlier revelations – a message not just for Arabs but for the whole of humanity.

All the sections of the Qur'an were put into writing during Muhammad's lifetime and carefully checked on numerous occasions. The Qur'an still exists today in its original form, unaltered.

The order

The order of the surahs in the Qur'an is not the order in which Muhammad received them during his ministry. Muslims believe that the order set by God was specifically told to Muhammad towards the end of his life. Tradition states that in order to keep a check Muhammad was made to repeat all the surahs to the angel Jibra'il, in the order God required, once every year, and just before he died he had to repeat it twice.

So, to Muslims, the Qur'an is itself the greatest of miracles, the 'mother of books' or **Umm ul Kitab**, the exact message of God, and the words must never be altered. That is why they try to make all believers study it in Arabic, the original language, and not from a translation – since all translations differ, and none can give the exact meaning of the original.

'O people of the Book, you have no ground to stand on unless you stand fast by the Law, the Gospel, and all the revelation that has come to you from God.'

(surah 5:68)

'We believe in God, and in the revelation given to us, and to Ibrahim, Isma'il, Isaac, Jacob and the tribes. We believe in all that was given to Moses, Jesus, and all the other messengers from the Lord. We make no distinction between them. To God alone we surrender.'

(surah 3:84)

An ornamental bismillah (meaning 'in the name of God')

Some commandments

- Show kindness to your parents, particularly in their old age.
- Do not be either wasteful or mean – all your possessions belong to God.
- Do not commit adultery.
- Do not kill, except for just cause.
- Always keep your promises and agreements.
- In business and daily life be honest.
- Avoid gossip and slander.
- Whatever your life, remain humble.
- Do not take advantage of poor people or orphans.

(from surah 17)

The Qur'an has 114 surahs, or chapters. All except one of them begins '*In the name of Allah, the Most Merciful, the Most Kind.*'

The first surah in the Qur'an – the **Fatiha** or the opening – is given on p. 62. It was not the first message revealed to Muhammad, but he was told to put it first. The first surah Muhammad received was number 96.

Each surah is named after some striking incident or word in it, so some have very strange names, like the Spider, the Bee or the Cow. The Cow is actually about religious duties, divorce laws, and rules governing warfare!

The effect

The Qur'an was intended to be heard, and Muslims believe that blessings flow from the sound of it. From the beginning it made a profound impression on those who heard and believed. Some were overwhelmed with fear and trembling; warriors would burst into tears; some people would fall into a state in which they lost all consciousness of the world around them.

Many people, both men and women, learned all the surahs by heart and many still do. Such a person is called a **hafiz**.

Others wrote the messages down on pieces of paper, date leaves, shoulder blades, ribs, bits of leather, and tablets of white stone.

Muslims were taught to recite it, and it must still be learnt in Arabic. Although it can now be read in at least forty languages, all translations lose part of the inspiration and meaning, and are not treated with the same respect as the original.

The Qu'ran compiled

Muslims were involved in much persecution and warfare because of their beliefs, and after one battle about seventy hafiz died. Muhammad's friend Abu Bakr began to worry about how the accuracy of the

A Qur'an

messages would be checked after the prophet's death. On the advice of Muhammad's other great friend Umar, he asked Muhammad's secretary **Zaid ibn Thabit** to make a special book of all the revelations, in the order Muhammad had taught him. This was done in Muhammad's lifetime.

Zaid, who was himself a hafiz, did not attempt to shape the book into a connected sequence, or fill in gaps, or suppress details not flattering to Muhammad. No editorial comment was added to the text, nothing removed, nothing altered. Zaid accepted that every word was the word of God, the belief shared by every Muslim today.

Abu Bakr passed this volume to Umar, and it was kept by Umar's daughter **Hafsa**, who had been one of Muhammad's wives. Under the next caliph **Uthman**, the Qur'an began to be recited in different dialects, and this created confusion for new converts whose mother tongue was not Arabic. Uthman prohibited the variant readings and made sure that copies of Hafsa's book were sent to the chief places as the standard text.

Two of these very early copies still exist today, one in Istanbul (Turkey) and one in Tashkent (USSR). Modern technology has now taken over – the Tashkent original has recently been photocopied.

The Qur'an honoured

The Qur'an is considered to be so holy that Muslims treat it with enormous respect. While it is being read:
- you must not speak
- you must not eat or drink
- you must not make a noise
- you must not touch it unnecessarily.

Before reading or touching it:
- you must wash carefully, or take a bath
- you must be in the right frame of mind
- if you are a woman, you should not be having a period.

When not in use, it should be
- placed high up, so that nothing is put on top of it
- kept covered and free from dust.

During use, it is often placed on a special stool called a **kursi**, so that it is handled no more than necessary. It is never allowed to touch the ground.

The art of **calligraphy** (or beautiful writing) grew up because it was an honour to copy the Qur'an, and this task was done as beautifully as possible.

The boat calligraphy

THINGS TO DO

▶ If possible, listen to a tape recording of the Qur'an being recited. Do not do this surrounded by people who will laugh at its strangeness. Try to listen alone, for at least five minutes. Make a note of your impressions.

▶ Make a decorative card or poster, using the laws of surah 17.

▶ Explain why Muslims believe the Tashkent Qur'an (and all others) to be the exact words revealed to Muhammad.

QUICK QUIZ

▶ What is a hafiz?
▶ What is al-Fatiha?
▶ What is a kursi for?
▶ Why is calligraphy important to a Muslim?
▶ Who compiled the Qur'an in writing?
▶ Which woman kept the book?
▶ Where could you now find an original copy?
▶ Where is a Qur'an kept when not in use?

FOR YOUR FOLDERS

▶ In what ways do Muslims show their deep respect for the Qur'an by
  a their behaviour, and
  b the way they take care of the book?

*'He is not a believer who eats his fill,
while his neighbour goes hungry.'*

*'Do not shut your bag, or God will hold back His
blessings from you.'*

*'The warrior who truly fights for God's cause
is he who looks after a widow
or a poor person.'*

*'If you think of God, you will find Him
there before you.'*

(Hadith)

Hadith, often referred to as 'traditions', are the recorded words, actions and instructions of the Prophet Muhammad. After his death, many collections of reports about him appeared, accounts of things he had said or done. These are held in enormous respect, but are quite separate from the Qur'an.

There are actually two sorts of Hadith – sacred and prophetic.

The Prophetic Hadith are the wise words and teachings of Muhammad himself, who is loved and respected becuse of his outstanding character, and devotion to God and humanity. His sayings reveal him as a man of enormous compassion and kindness, and great practical wisdom.

The Sacred Hadith, or **Hadith Qudsi**, are so named because their authority is traced back beyond the Prophet to God Himself. They are further insights that God revealed to Muhammad, but which were not revealed as part of the Qur'an. Muslims hold these sayings in very great reverence.

Sources

The two main sources of reliable Hadith are the very early collections made by the scholars, Bukhari, which lists 2762 traditions, and Muslim, which lists another 4000.

The earliest biographies of Muhammad (i.e. stories of his life) were made by Zohri and Ibn Ishaq. Zohri knew Muhammad's scholarly wife Aisha, and Ibn Ishaq was Zohri's disciple.

When Muslims want guidance over a particular course of action – especially in today's complicated society – if there is no clear answer in the Qur'an, they turn to the Hadith to support their actions, or decide their differences.

However, by the third century after Muhammad there were some 600 000 Hadith in circulation, and many of these – although no doubt well-intentioned – were not genuine. One pious inventor, for example, admitted claiming Muhammad to be the source of no less than 4000 sayings of his own! This kind of fraud caused so much confusion and was taken to seriously that the writer was executed for his deception.

The chains

Muslims base their judgement of the reliability of the Hadith on the reputations of the people through whom the quotations can be traced back to someone who had actually been with Muhammad. Each saying is transmitted along a particular chain. Some are very complicated. For example:

'Abdullah ibn al-Awad told me that al-Fadl ibn al-Ala told us that Ismai'l ibn-Ummayya told us on the authority of Yahya ibn-Abdullah ibn-Sayfi, that he heard Abu Mabad the freedman of ibn-Abbas say: "I heard ibn-Abbas say – 'When the Prophet, the blessings of Allah be upon him and peace, sent Mudah to the Yemen, he said to him . . .'"'

Hadith Qudsi

Muslims accept that the Qur'an is nothing less than the Eternal Record, written before the beginning of creation, and revealed through the medium of the angel to Muhammad, unchanged (see p. 43). The Hadith Qudsi are different – insights about God communicated to Muhammad through revelations or dreams, but which the Prophet explained using his own words or expressions. In other words, the meaning is from God, but the words are those of the Prophet. Therefore they are open to interpretation and differences of opinion.

Muslims might choose not to accept the wording of a particular Hadith, and would not be held guilty of unbelief in the same way that they would if they repudiated any part of the Holy Qur'an.

On the whole, the Sacred Hadith are concerned with various aspects of belief, worship and conduct, and not the more practical aspects of everyday living, which are dealt with in the Prophetic Hadith.

The style is usually very moving, either commands direct from Allah to His servants, or through conversations with them.

Selection of Hadith Qudsi

'I am with him when he makes mention of Me. If he draws near to Me a hand's span, I draw near to him an arm's length.'

'O My servants, all of you are hungry except those I have fed: all of you are naked except those I have clothed.'

'Sons of Adam complain about the ravages of Time; but I am Time, and in My hand is the night and day. They said – "O Lord, among the pious people is a sinful person who was merely passing by, but sat down with them." The Prophet said, "He says – 'To him also I have given forgiveness.'"'

'On the Day of Judgement Allah will say: "O son of Adam, I fell ill and you did not visit Me." The man will answer, "O Lord, how could I have visited You when You are Lord of the Worlds?" He will say – "Did you not know that My servant had fallen ill, and you did not visit him? Did you not know that if you had visited him, you would have found Me with him?"'

'A man said of another – "By Allah, Allah will never forgive him!" At this Allah the Almighty said – "Who is this who swears by Me that I will never forgive a certain person? Truly, I have forgiven him already."'

'If I have taken to Me a person's best friend and he has borne it patiently for My sake, this faithful servant's reward shall be paradise.'

'If he has in his heart goodness to the weight of one barley corn, and has said There is no God but Me, he shall come out of hell-fire.'

'O son of Adam, so long as you call upon Me and ask of Me, I shall forgive you for what you have done.'

(from Ezzedine Ibrahim (ed.) *Forty Hadith Qudsi*, Dar al-Quran al-karim, Beirut, 1980)

FOR YOUR FOLDERS

▶ Explain what is meant by the word 'Hadith'. How do Muslim scholars decide which of the Hadith are reliable and which are not?
▶ What is the difference between Prophetic Hadith and Hadith Qudsi?

THINGS TO DO

▶ Look through the Hadith in this unit and choose any three of them. Write them out carefully on a decorated page.
Explain why you choose these three in particular.

THINKING POINTS

• How far do the Hadith Qudsi bear out the suitability of giving Allah the titles 'the Compassionate, the Merciful'?
• Although Muslims treat the Hadith with enormous respect, and refer to their teachings when a matter not covered by the Qur'an is in dispute, why do they nevertheless not regard them as sacred in the same way as the Qur'an?

Discussing Jesus (peace be upon him)

Interviewer: Tell me, Shakir, it is true that Muslims believe in Jesus?

Shakir: Yes, it is true, but not in the same way that a Christian does. We find it quite amusing, really, that Jesus does not seem to be reverenced as much in a so-called Christian country as he is in – shall we say – Libya?

Interviewer: What do you mean?

Shakir: Because of the revelations in the Qur'an about Jesus, no one would ever mock him, or doubt his miraculous birth, or treat his name lightly. You will never hear the name of Jesus used as bad language in a Muslim country.

Interviewer: You believe in the virgin birth of Jesus?

Shakir: Certainly. We believe in Mary. She is mentioned in the Qur'an more times than in the New Testament. The accusation that Mary was not a virgin is blasphemy to a Muslim. Such a charge is bad enough when made against any woman, but to make it against Mary brings into ridicule the power of God.

Interviewer: Why?

Shakir: God can do whatever He likes – there is no limit to His power.

Interviewer: And yet you don't believe that Jesus was the son of God, do you?

Shakir: Only in the sense that we are all God's children. Jesus is not God, but one of us, our brother. Don't forget that Adam had no father or mother, so his birth was an even greater miracle – yet no one claims he was equal with God or part of a Trinity.

Interviewer: Do you believe in the crucifixion?

Shakir: No. On that point we disagree. Some believe that Jesus died naturally, and others that God took him up to Heaven without dying at all. Either way we do not believe that God allowed the Jews to kill him or that he stayed dead.

Interviewer: So you don't accept that he died to save people from their sins?

Shakir: Certainly not. We reject this. It seems to us as though Christians might think that they will only be forgiven because Jesus has 'paid the price' for them. We do not accept this. God is the Compassionate, the Merciful – how can He be wheedled, or persuaded, or bribed to become more merciful than He already is? To us, such a thought is blasphemy. It means that the person pleading or sacrificing is more merciful than God! How can that be so? We say that if we turn to God for forgiveness, He will surely forgive us – He is our dear Lord. But if we die unrepentant, then we will have deserved our punishment. Justice requires it. That is why we have free-will – to accept or reject God as we choose. But we must pay the penalty ourselves. We cannot be bought off. How can God send Himself to earth and then kill Himself to save us? That does not make sense to us.

Interviewer: But what about the teachings of Jesus? Don't you accept them, if you believe in him, as you say?

Shakir: Yes, of course; but we believe the Christian holy books have been altered by editors. If there is a clear revelation in the Qur'an, we accept that – because it is straight from God. The Christian Gospels differ, and we think Saint Paul taught things about Jesus that Jesus never claimed for himself.

Interviewer: One of the sayings of Jesus is '*No man cometh to the Father except by Me*' (John 14:16).

Shakir: There is also the saying '*No man can come to me except it were given to him by the Father*' (John 6:65). This may perhaps have been the original saying, which was altered by a later editor.

Interviewer: I think I see what you mean.

Shakir: I like to read the prayer of Jesus best – '*Our Father, who art in Heaven*' – that is pure Islam. *Our* Father. We worship God *with* Jesus. He is our brother. You know Islam means 'submission to God'. That is how Jesus was – the most pure and holy Muslim, and one of the greatest prophets before Muhammad.

Jesus submits to God

'This is the most important commandment – "The Lord our God, the Lord is One. Love Him with all your heart . . . ."' (Mark 12:29,30)

'Why do you call me good? No man is good, only God alone.' (Mark 10:18)

'You shall worship the Lord your God, and Him alone shall you serve.' (Luke 4:8)

'Call no man 'father' on earth, for you have One Father, who is in Heaven.' (Matthew 23:9)

THINKING POINTS

- 'They love their prophet so much they have made him into a god, or a part of Allah.' Why is the greatest devotion of the Christian seen as misguided by a Muslim?
- Every time the devil tempted Jesus to call himself 'Son of God' he rejected this – yet Christians insist on going against his Islam. (See Luke 4:4, 8, 12; Luke 4:34–35).

Part 2 **BELIEFS**

'She said – "How, O Lord, shall I have a son,
when man has never touched me?"
He said – "Thus: God will create what He wills.
He says no more than 'Be!' and it is so."'

(surah 3:47)

'His name shall be Messiah Jesus,
the son of Mary, held in honour in this world
and the next; one of those who are
nearest to God.'

(surah 3:45)

'Jesus said: – "I have come to you with wisdom, in
order to make clear some of the points about which
you argue. Fear God, and obey me – for God is my
Lord and your Lord. Worship Him. That is the
straight path."'

(surah 43:63–4)

'And they crucified him not, but only one who was
made to appear to them like Jesus. . . . They did
not really kill Jesus, but God took him up to
Himself.'

(surah 4:157–8)

'We sent Jesus the son of Mary, confirming the
Law that had come before him; We sent him the
gospel, wherein was guidance and light, and a
confirmation of the Law, a guidance and a
warning to those who fear God.'

(surah 5.46, see also surah 57:26–27,
surah 2:87)

Parable

Jesus, on whom be peace, saw a blind leper who
was saying:
'Praise be to God, who has saved me from so many
things.'
'From what are you free?' Jesus asked him.
'Spirit of God,' said the wretched man, 'I am better
off than those who do not know God.'
'You speak truly,' said Jesus. 'Stretch out your
hand.'
He was instantly restored to health, through the
power of God. And he followed Jesus and
worshipped with him.

(Story preserved by the Muslim teacher al-Ghazzali
from *Elephant in the Dark* by Idries Shah, Octagon
Press, 1978)

FOR YOUR FOLDERS

▶ Why do Muslims not believe that Jesus'
death could have been a sacrifice for the
sins of humanity, or that Jesus should be
called Saviour or Redeemer?

THINGS TO DO

▶ Copy out these statements and tick the
ones Muslims would agree with:
- Jesus was miraculously born of the
Virgin Mary.
- Jesus was God made man.
- Jesus was the expected Messiah.
- Jesus died on the cross.
- Jesus died to save us from our sins.
- Everyone pays the penalty for their
own sins.
- Jesus ascended into heaven.
- Jesus was '*of one substance with the
Father, by whom all things were made*'
(from a Christian creed).
- Jesus was a pure prophet, the miracle
worker.
- Jesus prayed to '*Our Father in
Heaven*'.
- Jesus could have said, '*Not my will, O
God, but Thine be done*'.
- Jesus could have said, '*No man can
come to the Father except through
me*'.

FOR DISCUSSION

▶ Do you think God should be expected to
forgive everything? Why is the concept of
justice important? Can we ever have a
just system that does not involve
protection for the weak from the savage
and greedy, and punishment or deterrent
against the cruel and evil?
▶ How is it possible that some people do
suffer because of the sins of others? Is it
possible for one person to pay the
penalty for another?

24 AKHIRAH – LIFE AFTER DEATH

The test

All Muslims believe in **akhirah** – life after death. They accept that human life is divided into two sections – each individual's life on earth, and the eternal life that follows. Since our earthly lives are short by comparison to the eternal, it is obvious that eternal life is far more important.

If people wander aimlessly through this life, they are wasting it. Muslims consider that life on earth has a very important purpose – it is a test. We may be born

- wealthy or poor
- beautiful or ugly
- healthy or sick
- generous or mean.
- strong or weak

It is a complete waste of time moaning about our circumstances. We do not know the reasons why, or what we are intended to learn. We can be bitter or resentful, or we can accept. To a Muslim it is all God's will.

Muslims believe that nothing can happen that is not God's will, and nothing is ever an accident – but we have been given the free will to react to the things that happen to us in all sorts of ways. It is up to us to choose.

Is there a 'point' to it?

If – God can do anything He wishes, He could easily have made everyone exactly the same. Why didn't He?

If – wealth is not a reward for the rich, and poverty is not a punishment for the poor;

If – sickness and misfortune are not punishments either;

Is God unfair?

What is it that is tested?

- Our characters – are we greedy, selfish, lacking in sympathy, mean, spiteful or cowardly?
- Our reaction to misfortune – are we frightened, full of complaint, a burden to others, depressed?
- Our reaction to good fortune – are we selfish, conceited, arrogant, proud, miserly?
- Our way of life – are we dishonest, disrespectful, hurtful, unforgiving?

God knows

'A poor man owned nothing but a fine white stallion. One day, he found his paddock empty. "What terrible fortune!" said his friends.

"Maybe yes, and maybe no," he said.

The next day the stallion returned, fetching with him five beautiful wild mares. "What wonderful fortune!" said his friends, amazed.

"Maybe yes, and maybe no," he said.

The next day his only son tried to tame a mare, and was thrown down. He broke his legs and became a cripple. "What dreadful fortune," sighed the friends.

"Maybe yes, and maybe no."

The king came by, and took away all the young men of the village to fight in the army – all except the cripple. The army lost, and all the young men were killed. . . . '

(a Muslim story)

'On no soul does God place a burden greater than it can bear.'

(surah 2:286, 23:62)

'If God lay the touch of trouble on you,
no one can deliver you from it save God alone;
and if He wills good for you,
no one can prevent His blessing. He confers
them on His servants as He chooses.'

(surah 10:107)

The record

Muslims believe that:

- All people earn, or are responsible for, their own salvation.
- How we respond to our tests is our own business, and by our lives and actions we earn our place in the next life.
- Whatever we do will have a direct effect on ourselves alone.
- Our actions can neither help nor harm God, they only help or harm us.
- Everything we do or think is known by our guardian angels, who keep the full record on which our judgement will be based. This record is to show us, not God – who already knows everything.
- God cannot be bought or bribed.

'Your good actions will benefit only you, while evil harms only the person who does it.'

(surah 41:46, 45:15)

Judgement

There is a time limit for everyone. Muslims believe that the test takes place in this earthly life, and when it is over and they face God, it will be too late to beg for forgiveness.

After death comes judgement. No one else's love or sorrow can free another from their sins. All people stand alone before God, answerable only for themselves.

In every generation God sent witnesses or messengers to stir consciences and tell people what to do. If they chose to reject the warnings and not believe in them – when it was so obviously right to reject unkind and depraved living and do their best to live well – then that was their free choice from their free will.

Just as the people they hurt had to bear the consequences of their unkindness in this life, they must accept the consequences of their actions in the next life.

All a person has to do to gain God's forgiveness is to ask for it while there is still time, in this life. But if the person is determined to persist in evil and refuses to repent and accept God's mercy, then hell is the inevitable consequence.

'One burdened soul shall not bear the burden of another. And even if the heavy-laden soul cry out for its burden to be carried, not one bit of it shall be carried, not even by the next of kin.'

(surah 35:18)

'It is the Day when one soul shall be powerless to plead for another.'

(surah 82:19)

'To God belongs the mystery of the Heavens and the Earth. The Decision of the Hour of Judgement will be swift as the twinkling of an eye – for God has the power over all things.'

(surah 16:77)

'At evening, do not expect to live till morning, at morning, do not expect to live till evening. Take from your health for your illness, and from your life for your death.'

(Hadith)

THINGS TO DO

▶ Write out the following statements and put either a tick or a cross according to whether a Muslim would accept them or not.
  a Nothing can happen that is not God's will.
  b Sickness is a punishment for sin.
  c Good fortune is a sign of God's favour.
  d God loves the healthy more than the sick.
  e God loves the poor more than the wealthy.
  f God loves a good person more than a bad person.
  g God loves everyone the same, and watches over all.
  h God will let people off their punishment.

FOR YOUR FOLDERS

▶ What is the Muslim attitude to fate and free will? How does the way you exercise your free will affect your future eternal life?

▶ Choose two of the passages from the Qur'an or Hadith. Write them out and explain what you think each of them means.

▶ People in despair often cry out 'Why is this happening to me?' or 'What have I done to deserve this?'. How might a Muslim answer these questions?

TALKING POINT

● **Do you think God should always allow free will? Should He interfere with the laws of nature to protect people from such things as floods, earthquakes, famines, etc.? Why do you think God does not protect humans from such things?**

DEBATE

▶ It is harder to pass the test of life if one is born fortunate with little hardship to face.

▶ God intends us to accept everything without question, and do nothing about it.

▶ It would be a better universe if we did not have free will, or the dangerous possibility of making wrong choices.

'They of God's right hand shall ask of the wretched – "What has cast you into hell fire?" They will say, "We were not of those who prayed, or those who fed the poor, and we wasted our time with empty arguments, and we rejected as a lie the Day of Reckoning – till we were forced to accept the Reality." '

(surah 74:40–7)

Since Muslims believe they will be accountable after death, it affects the way they behave while living. It creates a sense of God-consciousness (taqwa, see p. 96), and helps them to live decent and generous lives on earth. If they act in a cruel, depraved or selfish manner, they know they will not escape God's punishment on the Day of Judgement.

Beliefs

- The knowledge that we will die makes humans different from all other animals.
- Death is not the end of existence.
- Once people die, they cast off the limitations of the body, and awareness is greatly increased.
- Even those who did not believe in God or life after death will have to accept it once they become aware of it.
- Unbelievers will beg for a second chance, to return to life and try again, but it will not be allowed.

Barzakh

For those who die before the Day of Judgement, Muslims believe that Azra'il, the angel of death, takes their souls to **barzakh**, a state of waiting that comes between the moment of death and the Day. The word 'barzakh' means 'partition' or 'barrier', and it may not be crossed by those who wish to go back and warn others (see also p. 114).

'When death comes, one may say "O my Lord, send me back to life in order that I might put right the things I neglected and did wrong." By no means! This is no more than an excuse. Before them is a Barrier until the Day of Resurrection.'

(surah 23:99–100)

The end of the world

Descriptions of the end of the world in the Qur'an

are vivid. There will be a blinding light, the sky will be cut through, the moon shall cease to appear and the stars be scattered, the mountains shall be reduced to dust, the oceans boil over with explosions of fire . . . all the contents of the tombs will come back to life, and people will be asked what kept them away from their God? (See surahs 81 and 82.)

The reward

The reward will be paradise, a state of joy and beauty, happiness and peace. The Qur'an describes it symbolically as a green garden, full of foliage and flowers and the sound of water and birdsong.

'In gardens of delight they shall enjoy honour and happiness, facing each other on thrones: a cup will be passed to them from a clear-flowing fountain – delicious to drink and free from intoxication or headaches: and beside them will be innocent women, restraining their glances, with eyes wide with wonder and beauty.'

(surah 37:40–56, see also surah 38:52)

'They will hear no unworthy talk there, or any mention of sin, but only the cry "Peace, peace".'

(surah 56:26, see also surahs 43:70, 48:5, 56:17–25)

The vision is of peace and purity, not sex and self-indulgence!

The punishment

Hell, or **jahannam**, is the reward for unbelievers. It is also described symbolically, in lurid terms – a horrible place of torment under the earth's crust, a place of scorching fire, where the damned will be chained amid hot winds, boiling water and black smoke (see surahs 14:16–17; 38:55–8; 56:42–4, etc.).

Many people find the idea of God punishing evil people hard to reconcile with His mercy – but no one will go to jahannam unless absolutely determined to do so.

'I warn you of the flaming fire. None shall be cast into it but the most wretched, who has called the Truth a lie and turned his back.'

(surah 92:14–16)

'If God punished people according to what they deserved, He would not leave on earth a single living thing.'

(surah 16:61)

The after-life

All the descriptions of the after-life, including such things as youth, beauty, dress, food, and so on are intended to be understood symbolically since in eternal life the faithful are not subject to physical limitations at all.

It is a completely different dimension, and we are created afresh in a form beyond our knowledge. Marital and family bonds do not necessarily continue, since individual eternal souls outside time are not bound by the relationships that belong to the world of time. Old relationships of the present world will be dissolved, and each soul will stand on its own merits.

'There will be no relationships between them that day, nor will they ask after another.'

(surah 23:101)

'We have created Death to be in the midst of you, and We will not be prevented from changing your forms and creating you again in forms you know not.'

(surah 56:60–61)

It may not sound very exciting, but that is because it is impossible for the real nature of heaven and the presence of God to be understood by human minds with their limited awareness, until the time comes.

'In Paradise, I prepare for the righteous believers what no eye has ever seen, no ear has ever heard, and what the deepest mind could never imagine.'

(Hadith, see also surah 32:17)

THINKING POINTS

- Is the idea of hell with its punishments compatible with the idea of God's compassionate justice? Could God be called just if there were no punishments, only rewards?
- Is it possible that certain people could become so depraved or evil that they could never be forgiven?
- Is belief in life after death a weakness or a strength?
- Does the burning fire suggest eternal punishment, or simply that the evil will be burnt up and cease to exist?

THINGS TO DO

▶ A comet flashes through the sky and hits the moon which then explodes, the fragments burning out or shooting off into space like stars. On earth, the fragile layer round the inner molten core is shaken and broken through as earthquakes and eruptions flatten everything out, and boil away the water.

Make a chart with two columns, and try to fit this possible sequence of events into the details given in the 'end of the world' description taken from the Qur'an on page 52.

FOR DISCUSSION

▶ *'The hands of Abu Lahab will perish. He is a doomed man. His wealth and property will not save him. He shall be thrown into the flaming fire of hell.'*

(surah 111:1–3)

Muhammad saw this vision about his uncle. Why do you think Abu Lahab was condemned so severely? (See pp. 14–16.) Do you think the merciful God should forgive everyone, no matter what they have done?

FOR YOUR FOLDERS

▶ Explain the idea of the Day of Judgement, and the ways in which this belief can:
  - a alter the character of an individual
  - b affect the way people treat each other, and
  - c affect the way a Muslim practises faith throughout an average day.

▶ What do the passages from the Qur'an given in this unit and the last unit reveal about
  - a individual life after death
  - b judgement
  - c the future state of existence?

▶ Explain why all descriptions of paradise and hell can be only symbolic, not literal.

53

All sane human beings are aware that they are not as perfect as they might be. Worship is based on this feeling – that above and beyond all humans there is a higher standard which they should be trying to reach in their lives. Those who believe in God feel that awareness of His presence changes the entire way they live – and it is a change towards good, not evil.

Turning to God in reverence, submission and wonder is called **Ibadah**, from the word **abd** meaning 'servant' or 'slave'.

Why worship?

If someone asks 'Why should I worship God?' it is like asking 'Why should I think this is beautiful?'. You cannot really give the answer to someone who is not aware of God, or of something's beauty. You may see beauty, and be lost in wonder and appreciation of it, or you may not see it at all. It is the same with awareness of God.

The failings

To a Muslim, pure worship has to be free of three 'sins', which are really matters of awareness:
- **kufr** – disbelief, ingratitude
- **shirk** – association,
- **tughyan** – arrogance, tyranny.

- If you choose to deny God, and are not aware of His existence by reason of intuition, feel no responsibility or obligation through conscience, and no purpose in life – that is kufr.
- If you question the nature of God, believe that He is not supreme or alone, or that some other entity or person shares His power and has the right to judge or forgive sins, and therefore no longer trust in God alone – that is shirk.
- If you become over-confident and arrogant, so 'religious' that your presence makes others feel small or uncomfortable or stupid, become oppressive or unkind, over-do your devotions and rituals to a fanatical extent or force your own laws or opinions on people in defiance of the Law of God – that is tughyan.

'You should worship Allah as if you are seeing Him; for He sees you, even if you do not see Him.'

(Hadith)

Turning to God in prayer

'God does not accept beliefs if they are not expressed in deeds; and your deeds are worthless if they do not back up your beliefs.'

(Hadith)

True worship

Ibadah, or worship, involves a complete way of life, and consists of:
- **iman** – belief
- **amal** – action, and
- **ihsan** – realization.

Realization is the heart of religion, and can begin even when faith is weak. No religious leader or teacher can *make* it happen, although they do their best to guide people towards God. When faith enters the heart it causes a certain mental state – a feeling of love and gratitude towards God.

You cannot be made to feel faith, any more than you can be made to feel love. It is a matter of awareness.

Muslims believe that we are created by God and belong to God, and to Him we shall return and give account of ourselves. Submission to God is not a passive, but a positive act of bringing all your likes and dislikes, attitudes and behaviour into harmony with God's will.

Therefore, whenever any act is done to please Him, it is worship. This covers everything – going to school or work, eating and drinking, enjoying all the pleasures of life, every aspect of our behaviour. Muslims aim to:

- reform their lives
- develop dignity
- develop patience and courage in face of hardship and difficulty
- enjoy and appreciate God's gifts to the full
- strive for good and try to defeat evil.

In extreme cases, the Muslim faith requires that they must actually fight in order to be a witness, and perhaps even die for what they believe in.

Someone who dies for the faith is called a **shahid** or martyr. The fighting of a war for the sake of God is known as **jihad**.

The word 'jihad' actually means 'striving'. It implies a readiness to give up everything that you have, including your own life, for the sake of Allah, but the real jihad is the struggle to keep on the pathway of God. It means putting in your full effort, exerting yourself to the very limit in order to live correctly, and working as hard as possible to see God's principles established in society.

'Those who do not believe take their comfort in this life, and eat as cattle eat; fire will be their future life.'

(surah 47:12)

Intention

Muslims believe your intentions are vital. People are not all saints, and often they fall short, or fail completely. It is easy then to get depressed, and give up. Muslims believe that God judges us by our intentions or **niyyah**, and is merciful, even when we do not succeed.

Nevertheless, our intentions should be honest, and our efforts as great as possible.

TALKING POINTS

- Is living as if God existed worth as much as actually being aware of His presence? Could it be worth more? Give reasons for your answer.
- History has given many examples of tughyan – people who have believed in God and yet acted badly or oppressively. Can you think of any examples? What do you think was missing from their faith?

THINGS TO DO

▶ Draw and decorate a poster to illustrate the theme 'every act done to please God is an act of worship', or 'every sincere act is a prayer'.

FOR YOUR FOLDERS

▶ Can belief in God really alter a person's life? Is it possible to be a good religious person by belief in God alone? What is wrong with worship that does not include all the elements of iman, amal and ihsan?

▶ Explain what is meant by
  a kufr
  b shirk
  c jihad
  d niyyah.

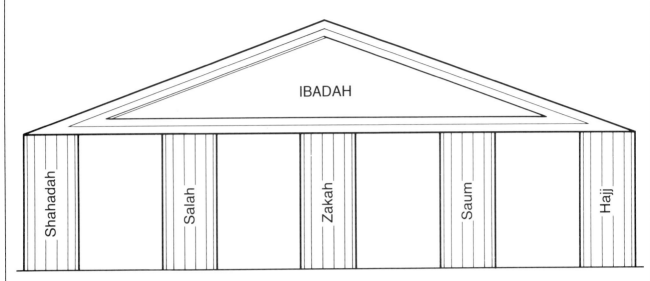

The five pillars or arkan

Pillars

Muslims often think of the practice of their faith as a kind of temple for God held up by five pillars, called **arkan**. These are the five basic duties which all Muslims must perform. They are:
- **Shahadah** – the bearing of witness, or declaration of faith, that there is truly one Supreme Being and that Muhammad was His genuine messenger
- **Salah** – prayer five times a day
- **Zakah** – the giving of money for the poor
- **Saum** – fasting during the month of Ramadan
- **Hajj** – making the pilgrimage to Makkah, at least once in a lifetime, if physically possible.

These pillars are not the whole of Islam, but without them Islam would not really exist. If any one of the 'pillars' is weak, the whole 'building' suffers.

Shahadah

Shahadah is the first pillar of Islam, without which the rest is meaningless. It comes from the word 'Ash-hadu' which means 'I declare' or 'I bear witness'.

Islam does not demand a great number of complicated things to believe. No religion, in fact, has a shorter or more dramatic creed. It states, quite simply:

'La ilaha illal Lahu
Muhammadur rasulullah.'

'There is no God but Allah,
and Muhammad is the Prophet of God.'

A longer declaration of faith is the Iman-I-Mufassal – the 'faith in detail'.

'I believe in Allah,
in His angels,
in His revealed book,
in all of His prophets,
in the Day of Judgement,
in that everything – both good and bad –
comes from Him, and
in life after death.'

The sacrifice

When people make this declaration and truly believe it in their hearts, they have entered Islam. But being a good witness involves far more than words – your whole life must back up what has been declared.

Muslims lay down their lives as sacrifices to God. Your life is your most precious possession; but if you are **shahid** (ready to die for your faith) you recognize that your life does not belong to you, but to God.

The call to prayer

Muslims repeat the shahadah first thing on waking and last thing before sleeping. They are the first words whispered into the ears of a new-born baby, and if possible, the last words uttered to the dying.

It was with these words that Bilal, the freed Ethiopian slave, first summoned the faithful to prayer, when the call to prayer was instituted by Muhammad after his arrival in Madinah in 623 CE.

The man who calls is the **muezzin** *(mu'adhdhin or mueddin);*
he calls the **adhan** *or* **azan**

'Allahu Akbar.
Ash-hadu an la ilaha illallah
Ash-hadu ana Muhammadur rasulullah.
Hayya alas salah
hayya alal falah
Allahu Akbar
La ilaha illallah.'

'God is Great! (said four times)
I bear witness that there is no God but God
(twice)
I bear witness that Muhammad is the Prophet
of God (twice)
Come to prayer! (twice)
Come to success! (twice)
God is Great! (twice)
There is no God but God (once)

THINGS TO DO

▶ If possible, listen to a recording of the call to prayer. Do you have any personal reaction to the sound of it? Try to imagine it piercing the sky at the break of dawn.

▶ Make a survey of your local area to discover what visible signs of Muslim commitment there are, e.g. mosques, special shops, people in Muslim dress (for instance prayer caps, veiled women, etc.).

FOR DISCUSSION

▶ Should a Muslim living in a non-Muslim community make his or her religion obvious to everyone, or not?

▶ Bearing public witness is too embarassing. Religion should be a private matter.

FOR YOUR FOLDERS

▶ Make a list of the seven sections in the Iman-i-Mufassal. You could present this as a diagram, or perhaps a flower with six petals, with 'I believe in Allah' at the centre.

▶ Do you think it takes courage to make a public declaration of faith, and if so, in what ways? How might commitment and bearing witness affect someone's life?

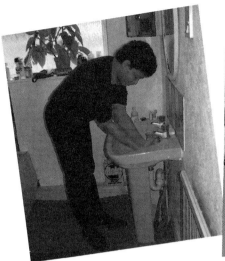

Hands washed to the wrists three times

Face washed three times

Arms washed up to the elbows three times

Head, ears and back of the neck washed

Ears wiped out with index finger

Feet washed up to ankles three times

The discipline

It is not easy to live all your life as a witness for God. People are very busy, they have lots of things to do. It is all too easy to forget God, and then disobey Him by either doing things that should not be done, or by not doing things that ought to be done.

Muslims believe that a deliberate conscious effort must be made, that is trained and disciplined.

The meaning

You can, of course, pray to God at any time and anywhere, but five times a day Muslims perform **salah**, a special kind of prayer that is not on the spur of the moment or spontaneous, but follows a deliberate preparation of the heart to receive God.

During salah, everything else in life is set aside for a few moments, and Muslims concentrate on God, praising Him, thanking Him, and asking for His forgiveness and blessing.

Salah is regarded as a duty that must be performed even if at work, at home, on a journey or even at war. If Muslims are too ill to stand or kneel, they can go through the motions in their hearts while sitting or lying down. It is not a burden to do this, but a great comfort.

Muslim children begin to practise salah around the age of seven; by the age of twelve it is expected of them as a duty.

Preparation

- The place chosen should be clean (a special mat is often used).
- The mind should be attentive.
- The body and clothes should be clean.
- A man's clothes should cover his body from the navel to the knees.
- A woman's entire body should be covered, except for her face and hands.
- A woman should not be wearing make-up or perfume.
- Prayer begins with the ritual wash, or **wudu**.

Wudu

Wudu (or wuzu) is part of the discipline. This wash is not because Muslims are dirty, but as part of the preparation for the prayer that follows. They may take a complete bath (called **ghusl**) or go through the procedure outlined below. If no water is available, as in the desert, then a wash with clean sand will do. This symbolic wash is called **tayammum**.

The wudu follows a set pattern:

1 Declaration of intent (**niyyah**). The heart must turn to God as a deliberate act.
2 The hands must be washed up to the wrists three times.
3 The mouth is rinsed three times.
4 Water is snuffed into the nostrils and blown out three times.
5 The face is washed three times.
6 The arms are washed up to the elbows three times.
7 The wet hands are passed over the top of the head and round the back of the neck. The ears are wiped out with the index finger, and the back of the neck with the thumbs.
8 The feet are washed up to the ankles three times. (See surah 5:6.)

This washing will do for more than one prayer, providing there has been no 'breaking' action in between. Wudu is 'broken' if anything has come out of the body (e.g. blood, wind or urine) or if the mind has lost conscious control (e.g. in sleep or unconsciousness). After a sexual act, or after a period, a complete bath is required.

Qiblah

After these preparations, Muslims face the direction of Makkah, standing on a prayer mat, or alongside other Muslims in orderly fashion at the mosque. They cover their heads, and pray.

The direction of Makkah is called **qiblah**. If you are in a mosque, there is a special alcove in the qiblah wall called a **mihrab** which locates the direction. Outside a mosque, many Muslims use a small compass in order to be accurate.

QUICK QUIZ

Explain what is meant by:
► wudu
► qiblah
► niyyah
► tayammum
► mihrab.

FOR YOUR FOLDERS

► If Muslims believe that a person can pray to God at any time and in any place, why do you think they go to such trouble for formal prayers?
► Which part of the washing do you think requires the most effort, and why?
► Give an outline of what preparations you would have to make if you were a Muslim about to perform salah.

THINKING POINTS

- How would praying at regular intervals affect someone's thoughts and activities during a normal day?
- Is making prayer an obligation for all Muslims over the age of twelve reasonable?

THINGS TO DO

► Draw a series of diagrams (pin-people will do) to illustrate wudu.
► Explain how the intention of salah is quite different from 'spur of the moment' prayers.
► Make a list of the sort of activities during the day that might stop a person thinking of God.

29 SALAH

The aims of salah

- to bring people close to Allah
- to combine soul and body in divine worship
- to keep them from indecent, shameful and forbidden activities
- to calm down dangerous passions and master the baser instincts
- to bring a sense of peace and tranquility
- to show equality, unity and brotherhood
- to promote patience, courage, hope and confidence
- to develop gratitude and humility
- to demonstrate obedience
- to train in cleanliness, purity and punctuality
- to develop discipline and will power
- to remind people constantly of God and His greatness
- to draw the mind away from personal worries and problems towards God – who could at any moment change the entire course of a person's destiny.

Times

The five set prayers have special names and are performed at special times.
- Salat ul-Fajr – between first light of day and sunrise
- Salat ul-Zuhr – after the sun has left the midst of the sky
- Salat ul-Asr – between mid-afternoon and sunset
- Salat ul-Maghrib – between sunset and the last light of day
- Salat ul-Isha – between darkness and dawn.

Salah should *not* be said at sunrise, noon or sunset as these times have pagan associations of sun-worship.

> ## THINGS TO DO
> ▶ Draw a clock face and mark on it the approximate times of the five prayers.

Women

Women usually pray at home, but mosques have a room or balcony set aside for them, should they wish to use it.

They do not sit among the men for worship – not because they consider themselves in any way inferior, but out of modesty, and because their presence might distract the men from worshipping. Minds have to be free of desire for the opposite sex, or worries about family matters.

When you see the description of the prayer positions (pp. 64–65) you will see why women prefer to sit at the back!

A Muslim place of prayer

Friday prayers

Salat-ul-**Jamaah** or 'communal prayers' take place at zuhr (midday) every Friday. The word for Friday is **jum'ah**, so sometimes they are called Salat-ul-Jum'ah.

   All adult male Muslims are expected to leave their work and attend. Women may come, but if they cannot get away from their household duties they are expected to pray at the same time, at home. In Islamic countries all shops and businesses close during the mid-day hour on Fridays.

'O ye who believe!
When the call is heard for the
prayer of the day of congregation,
leave your trading and
hasten to remember Allah'.

(surah 62:9)

Prayer mats are decorated with geometric patterns or pictures of the chief Muslim shrines such as the Ka'ba

بِسْمِ اللهِ الرَّحْمٰنِ الرَّحِيْمِ

اَلْحَمْدُ لِلّٰهِ رَبِّ الْعٰلَمِيْنَ ۞ الرَّحْمٰنِ الرَّحِيْمِ ۞ مٰلِكِ يَوْمِ الدِّيْنِ ۞

اِيَّاكَ نَعْبُدُ وَاِيَّاكَ نَسْتَعِيْنُ ۞ اِهْدِنَا الصِّرَاطَ الْمُسْتَقِيْمَ ۞

صِرَاطَ الَّذِيْنَ اَنْعَمْتَ عَلَيْهِمْ غَيْرِ الْمَغْضُوْبِ عَلَيْهِمْ

وَلَا الضَّآلِّيْنَ ۞

Bismillāhir raḥmānir raḥīm
Alḥamdu lillāhi rabbil 'ālamīn.
Arrahmānir raḥīm.
Māliki yawmiddīn.
Iyyāka na'budu wa iyyāka nasta'īn.
Ihdinaṣ ṣirāṭal Mustaqīm.
Ṣirāṭalladhīna an'amta 'alaihim,
Ghairil maghdūbi 'alaihim wa lāddāllīn. (Āmīn).

The al-Fatiha in Arabic

'All praise be to Allah,
the Lord of the Universe,
the Most Merciful, the Most Kind,
Master of the Day of Judgement.
You alone do we worship,
From You alone do we seek help.
Show us the next step
along the straight path
of those earning Your favour.
Keep us from the path of
those earning Your anger,
those who are going astray.'

(surah 1)

The **rak'ahs** are the sequence of movements, following a set pattern, that accompany salah. But the physical movements are not so important as the intention in the heart.

'Woe to those who pray, but are
unmindful of their prayer, or
pray only to be seen by people.'

(surah 107:6–7)

'When a person is drowsy during prayers,
let him sleep until he knows what he recites.'

(Hadith)

The Muslims may perform as many rak'ahs as they like, but the compulsory duties are:

- salat ul-fajr – two rak'ahs
- salat ul-zuhr – four rak'ahs
- salat ul-asr – four rak'ahs
- salat ul-maghrib – three rak'ahs
- salat ul-isha – four rak'ahs

There are eight separate acts of devotion (see pp. 64–65):

1 **Takbir** – shutting out the world and its distractions, delights and miseries. Muslims stand to attention, with their hands raised to the level of their shoulders, and acknowledge the majesty of God.

'Allahu Akbar' – 'Allah is Supreme'

2 They place the right hand over the left on the chest, and say:

'Glory and praise to Thee, O God; blessed is Thy name and exalted is Thy majesty. There is no God other than Thee. I come, seeking shelter from Satan, the rejected one.'

Next, they recite al-Fatiha, the first surah of the Qur'an (the words given at the start of this unit).

Now they may recite any other passage from the Qu'ran, e.g.

> 'He is God, the One; He is the Eternal Absolute; none is born of Him, and neither is He born. There is none like unto Him.'

3 **Ruku** – the bowing. Muslims bend their bodies forward, and place their hands on their knees. Their backs should be straight. This is to show that they respect as well as love God. They repeat three times:

> 'Glory be to my Great Lord, and praise be to Him.'

4 **Qiyam** – they stand up again, and acknowledge their awareness of God with the words:

> 'God always hears those who praise Him. O God, all praise be to Thee, O God greater than all else.'

5 The humblest position is called **sujud** or **sajda**, when Muslims prostrate themselves on the ground, demonstrating that they love God more than they love themselves. They kneel, touching the ground with their forehead, nose, palms of both hands, knees and toes, and repeat three times:

> 'Glory to be my Lord, the Most High. God is greater than all else.'

6 They kneel again, palms resting on the knees – a moment's rest before the next prostration. They may repeat three times:

> 'O my Master, forgive me.'

7 Sujud is repeated once again.

8 Muslims either repeat the rak'ah, or finish it. At the end of the sequence, they pray for the Prophet, for the faithful and the congregation, and make a plea for forgiveness of sins. The last action is to turn their heads to the right and left shoulders, to acknowledge the other worshippers and the guardian angels, with the words:

> 'Peace be with you, and the mercy of Allah.'

This final prayer is called the salam.

> 'The prayer said in Madinah is worth thousands of others, except that in Makkah, which is worth a hundred thousand. But worth more than all this is the prayer said in the house where no one sees but God, and which has no other object than to draw close to God.'
>
> (Hadith)

FOR YOUR FOLDERS

▶ What is the significance of the physical activities during salah? Do you think these movements make any difference to the way a Muslim feels?

▶ Read the Hadith of Muhammad given above. Try to explain what you think Muhammad meant by these opinions.

THINGS TO DO

▶ Copy out al-Fatiha, as a decorated poster or scroll. (If you have access to a Bible, you could look up the words of the Prayer of Jesus given in Saint Matthew's Gospel 6:9–15 and compare the two.)

▶ Copy out the following list of feelings, and tick which you think are expressed in Muslim prayer:
conceit
humility
pride
forgiveness
devotion
sense of togetherness
embarrassment
superiority
love
desire for forgiveness
desire to show off
putting God before self
union with God

1 Takbir

2 The right hand is placed over the left on the chest

5 Sujud

6 Kneeling with palms on knees

3 Ruku

4 Qiyam

7 Sujud is repeated

8 Salam

Muslims at prayer

Concentration

When prayers are being performed, Muslims
- should not talk, or look around
- should not make any movement or noise that would draw attention to themselves, or distract others
- should not try to look too holy – which suggests superiority and foolish pride
- should concentrate on the prayer alone and let nothing else enter their minds.

If they make a major mistake it can be put right by adding extra prayers at the end.

Du'a

Personal supplications, or requests, are called **du'a** prayers. These may be:
- private thanksgivings for some blessing received (e.g. recovery from sickness, birth of a child, release from worry)
- cries for help
- pleas for forgiveness
- general requests for God's guidance and blessing. These are not part of the formal or set prayers, but may be offered at any time and be of any length.

Congregation

It is not necessary to go to the mosque. Prayers can be said equally well at home, and in Muslim countries it is not uncommon to see people praying in the street, or wherever they happen to be when the call to prayer is sounded.

When Muslims pray together, they stand before God in a real sense of brotherhood, shoulder to shoulder in a line, facing the Ka'ba sanctuary in Makkah.

On Fridays Muslim men are expected to form a special congregation (**jamaah**) for the midday prayer. In Muslim countries the shops all close so that everyone can gather together.

TALKING POINTS

- If God knows everything, and knows all your needs before you ask Him, is there any point in making private prayers?
- Do private prayers in fact suggest a *lack* of faith in God? Give reasons for your answer.

Tasbih

Sometimes Muslims hold a little string of ninety-nine beads, each representing one of the ninety-nine names of God. This is called a **subha** or **tasbih**.

After the rak'ahs, Muslims may remain to praise God using the beads as an aid. They say 'Subhan-Allah' (Glory be to Allah), 'Alhamdu lillah' (Thanks be to Allah), and 'Allahu Akbar' (God is great) thirty-three times each, as they pass the beads.

Muslims often make God their first thought on waking, and the last before sleeping. They often think of Him throughout the day. This is also du'a.

Any prayer for yourself, for your family, for the solution to some problem, or for protection, is du'a.

But Muslims always remind themselves that God knows everything – all their sufferings and problems, and that they are always for a reason.

The best du'a prayer is not a cry to God for help, but to ask for strength and faith to endure the tests.

Bismillah – In the name of Allah, the most Merciful, the most Kind

*'O Allah, I have been unjust to myself
and no one grants pardon for sins except You.
Forgive me, therefore, in Your compassion,
for surely You are the Forgiver, the Merciful.'*
(du'a prayer)

*'In the name of Allah, the Most Merciful, the Most Kind.
I seek refuge in the Lord of the Daybreak
from the evil of what He has created;
from the evil of the intense darkness;
from the evil of those who provoke it;
from the evil of the envious one.'*
(surah 113)

Tasbih

FOR YOUR FOLDERS

▶ Is it better to worship God alone, in the secrecy of your heart, or shoulder to shoulder with companions? Are both necessary? Give reasons for your answer.

▶ Copy out the words of one of the Muslim prayers.

▶ Du'a prayers are personal requests. Salah prayers are disciplined training in shutting out the world and its distractions. Which do you feel to be the most important sort of prayer, or do you think they are both equal? Give reasons for your answer.

Zakah

Giving

All Muslims are expected to be charitable, which means 'generous and kind'. To a Muslim, the word 'charity' implies any good deed that is done purely for the sake of God – and not out of any selfish hope of getting some reward for it. Any act of giving done out of compassion, love or generosity (e.g. famine appeals) is called **sadaqah**.

Zakah, on the other hand, is a duty performed on a regular basis, and not regarded as a charity. The word 'zakah' means to purify or cleanse. It is a contribution paid once a year on savings at the rate of 2½% or one-fortieth in order to 'cleanse' your money and possessions from excessive desire for them, or greed. This rate applies to cash, bank savings and jewellery. There is a different rate for agricultural produce and livestock.

'Be steadfast in prayer, and regular in giving. Whatever good you send forth from your souls, you will find it again with God; for God sees well all that you do.'

(surah 2:110, 270, and other passages)

Aims

The aims of paying zakah are to keep your wealth free of greed and selfishness. It is also a test of Muslim honesty and expenditure.

It tries to clean the heart of love of money and the desire to cling to it. Money is for the service of humanity, and for promoting good and justice in the world.

Zakah money may only be used for certain set purposes:
- to help the poor
- to release from debt
- to help needy travellers
- to free captives
- to win people over to the cause of Allah
- to pay those who collect it.

It is one of the basic principles of Muslim economy, based on social welfare and fair distribution of wealth. Making interest on money (called usury) is absolutely forbidden (see surah 2:275, 278, and other passages.)

'He is not a believer who eats his fill while his neighbour remains hungry by his side.'

(Hadith)

Zakah is usually paid in secret so that rich people receive no false praise or admiration, since they are doing no more than their duty; and poor people are not made ashamed in receiving. Giving openly is only encouraged when it is necessary to influence others to give (see surah 2:271).

What is given must not simply be things that are not wanted or needed, or are second rate. When you give for God's sake, it must be nobly done – for He sees all.

'Don't cancel your charity by reminders of your generosity, or by holding it against them – like those who give their wealth only to be seen by others . . . . They are like hard, barren rock on which is little soil. Heavy rain falls on it and leaves it just a bare stone.'

(surah 2:264)

Rates of Zakah

(The table below is a simplified version.)

Wealth	Amount	Rate
Cash in hand or bank	Over value of 595 g silver	2.5%
Gold and silver	85 g gold, 595 g silver	2.5%
Trading goods	Value of 595 g silver	2.5%
Cows and buffaloes	30	1
Goats and sheep	40	1
Mining produce	Any	20%
Agricultural	Per harvest	10% from rain–watered land, 5% from irrigated land
Camels	Per 5	1 sheep or goat

God is the owner

Muslims may not pick and choose; they are obliged to help those who are poor and those who cannot earn a living, or earn such a low wage it does not cover basic needs. Muslims must remember they are all one family, and the poor have a claim upon the rich.

Muslims believe that:

- People do not own anything, but are loaned things in trust by God. So if anything is sacrificed for God, it is only being given back to its rightful owner.
- God chooses who to make rich or poor. The wealthy are obliged to give to the poor.
- Naked you came into the world and naked you leave it – so there is no point in clinging foolishly to possessions, or even worse, letting them become your masters.
- Only by giving something away for the sake of God will you receive its true value; this is not its earthly value, but is increased beyond measure.

TALKING POINTS

- **The person who gives money away is richer than the person who keeps it.**
- **The most valuable possessions in life cannot be bought with money.**
- **Helping the poor should be left to the government.**

THINGS TO DO

- ► Copy out the saying from the Qur'an at the beginning of this unit about giving.
- ► Find a newspaper picture to illustrate the world's poverty. Use it to make a poster stating that we are all one family, and should look after each other.
- ► Make a list of things which are more valuable than money.

FOR YOUR FOLDERS

- ► In what ways does the practice of zakah help a person to become detached from love of self and love of possessions?
- ► Do you think zakah is a reasonable amount of a person's wealth to devote to God? Should more be demanded, or none at all? Give reasons for your answer.

QUICK QUIZ

- ► What is the difference between zakah and sadaqah?
- ► What does the word zakah actually mean?
- ► Who is the true owner of all wealth?
- ► What is the zakah rate for cash savings?
- ► What is the zakah rate for cows, sheep and camels?
- ► What is the zakah rate for coal or oil?

*'O believers, you must fast so that
you may learn self-restraint.
Fasting is prescribed for you during
a fixed number of days, so that you
may safeguard yourselves against
moral and spiritual ills.'*

(surah 2:183–4)

Saum, or fasting, is the deliberate control of the body by an act of will. During the 29 to 30 days of the month of **Ramadan** healthy adult Muslims will go without all the pleasures of the body during all the hours when it is possible to distinguish a black thread from a white one. Hunger, comfort and sex are the three things which have to be brought under control.

Nothing must pass the lips (not even chewing-gum, a cigarette, or the smoke of someone else's cigarette!), and a real conscious effort must be made to make sure no evil deed or thought is committed. If the emotions of the heart or mind or the behaviour of the Muslim are wrong, then the fast will lose its real significance.

*'If you do not give up telling lies
God will have no need of your giving up
food and drink.'*

*'There are many who fast during the day and
pray all night, but they gain nothing but
hunger and sleeplessness.'*

(Hadith)

Aims of saum

- to develop self-control and overcome selfishness, greed and laziness
- to restrain passion and appetite
- to prepare for any real sufferings that may be faced later
- to experience hunger, and thus develop sympathy for the poor
- to gain spiritual strength
- to experience brotherhood through shared 'ordeals'.

After a couple of hours the body is sure to feel uncomfortable, and starts complaining like a spoilt child for its usual supplies of food and drink. But Muslims allow the mind to take control. The body will not get its way. The path of obedience gradually becomes easier, and so does resisting temptation.

It is possible to cheat, but Muslims believe that God sees everything. Human beings might be deceived, but you can never deceive God. Therefore there is no point in fasting in order to show off – the fast is a matter between the individual and God alone.

Those excused fasting

Muslims are excused if they would suffer real hardship. The following people do not have to fast:

- children under twelve
- pregnant and nursing mothers
- the aged
- those sick or on a journey, if it would cause real pain or suffering.

It is obvious that a ten-mile journey on foot carrying baggage would be much harder than 1000 miles by aeroplane.

Whenever possible, the days of fasting missed should be made up later. Those excused fasting could provide food for needy people.

Ramadan

Ramadan is the ninth month of the Muslim year, and it is regarded as a very special month, because it was during this time that Muhammad received his first message from God.

Since Muslim months are based on the moon, Ramadan falls eleven days earlier each year. When it falls in the blistering summer heat it is a real challenge to faith and devotion.

There is enormous excitement at the start of the fast, as Muslims await the announcement that the new moon has been sighted. Some make telephone calls to Makkah. In some countries the start of Ramadan is announced on the radio. Sometimes a cannon is fired, or there is some other public signal.

Breakfast

Even more exciting is the end of the fast. There is a wonderful feeling of joy and achievement after each day's successful discipline.

The food that breaks the fast after sunset is called **iftar**. It is sensible not to eat too much (Muhammad himself had only a couple of dates or a drink) otherwise you can feel sick.

More substantial meals follow, for at night feasting is allowed. Often there are many friends and relatives to visit. The object is not a slimming exercise, and sometimes the night-time festivities are so liberal that Muslims actually put on weight.

If the day's fast starts very early – (in 1988 it began at 3.15 a.m. and ended after 8.15 p.m.!) – an extra meal called **suhur** can be squeezed in before first light.

Ramadan ends with the great feast of **Eid ul Fitr** (see p. 92).

Interview with a new Muslim (a first time faster)

Interviewer: How did you get on with your fast, Ruqaiyya?

Ruqaiyya: Not too well, I'm afraid. I only managed the first seven days, then I went away on business and gave up. My friends were disgusted – they said it was only for 30 days out of 365!

Interviewer: Seven days sounds a lot. Did you really go without food and liquid all day?

Ruqaiyya: I tried. In fact, the hardest part for me was giving up my 11 a.m. coffee and cigarette! By 3 p.m. I was in agony, but by 6 p.m., when I had to feed my non-Muslim family, I was really past eating. I felt a bit sick. A couple of times I felt really bad and ate a few grapes. So I failed, really.

Interviewer: Did you lose any weight?

Ruqaiyya: Yes, I lost five pounds! And yet each night I had an enormous meal with my Muslim friends. We couldn't move for half an hour afterwards! Another failing, I'm afraid – over-indulgence.

Interviewer: Did you feel all right?

Ruqaiyya: Yes and no. I got a bit bad-tempered, and twice I had to lie down in the afternoon. I wanted help with my jobs, and became very slow and sluggish – but this did pass after two days. It made me realize how hard it is for Muslims who are out at work – no allowances are made! Actually, it was rather nice to go on the streets and see other Muslims, and know that we had a kind of secret, that passers-by had no idea what we were up to.

THINGS TO DO

► Imagine you are a Muslim. Write a letter to a friend explaining how you keep Ramadan, and how it might affect your behaviour at work or at school.

► Try to fast for one day – but don't be silly about this. Drink a glass of milk if you feel faint. Keep a log book of your feelings and experiences as you go through the day. (Perhaps your class could do this together, or even make it a sponsored event.)

QUICK QUIZ

► What is meant by fasting?
► Which is the special Muslim month for fasting?
► Why is Ramadan harder if it comes in the summer?
► Which people are excused from fasting?
► What is the name of the 'breakfast'?
► What is the name of the feast that ends Ramadan?

MINUTE DETAILS

● Nothing must enter the body through the nose or mouth. This includes sniffing any substance, e.g. scent or chemicals.
● Intravenous nutritional injections are not allowed.
● Cleaning the teeth and putting drops in the eyes are allowed.
● Water swallowed in showers is excused.

The fact that both hijackers and hostages started keeping Ramadan together helped to end the 1988 hijack of a Kuwaiti airliner.

FOR YOUR FOLDERS

► In what ways do you think the experience of the Ramadan fast draws Muslims together in a special feeling of brotherhood?
► In what circumstances would a person's fast be of no value whatsoever?
► How does the practice of discipline and self-control build up a defence against moral and spiritual weakness?

Pilgrims in Ihram catching the bus to Makkah

The dearest wish of any devout Muslim is to be able to perform the **Hajj**, or pilgrimage to Makkah. 'Hajj' means to 'set out with a definite purpose', and it is the duty of every Muslim who can afford it, and who is physically fit, to visit the Ka'ba and stand before God at **Mount Arafat**, once in their lifetime.

For Muslims who live near Makkah the journey can be made many times, but many live so far away and are so poor that it is virtually impossible. Some people save for a lifetime in order to be able to go. Sometimes a family or community will club together in order to be able to send one representative.

The true Hajj has to be made between 8 and 13 Dhu'l Hijjah (the twelfth month). If a Muslim goes at any other time it is known as **Umrah**, or the lesser pilgrimage, and the significance is not the same.

All the pillars of Islam require a breaking-off of normal everyday life, but Hajj demands much more. It is a complete suspension of all worldly activities for a few days, when the pilgrim becomes just a naked soul, living and moving for God alone.

Conditions

There are certain rules for pilgrims. They must be:

- Muslim. It is not a side-show for tourists, so non-Muslims are not allowed
- of sound mind, and able to understand the significance of the experience
- physically fit and able to take the strain and rigours of the journey
- in a position to provide for any loved ones left behind
- able to pay for the Hajj without recourse to dishonest ways of raising the money.

Before modern transport it sometimes took many months, perhaps years, of hard travel to get to Makkah and back. Nowadays many pilgrims fly in to the Hajj Terminal at Jiddah airport.

Pilgrims of every race and social class meet in equality before God. It is the climax of a Muslim's life. Rich, poor, employer or servant, all are united before Him who made them.

Niyyah

If a Muslim cannot go on Hajj because of
- ill health
- lack of funds
- unavoidable circumstances

then it is the **niyyah**, or intention (see p. 55), that counts.

Muslims can join the pilgrims in spirit and in prayer. They can, if they wish,

- pay for a substitute (who has already done his or her own Hajj) to go on their behalf
- give their Hajj savings to charity.

Any Muslim who does not offer a sacrificial animal should fast (see surah 2:196).

Nowadays over a million people gather on Hajj, and the Saudi Arabian Government allocates around 300 million dollars a year to the Ministry of Pilgrimage. The new King Abdul Aziz Airport at Jiddah is the largest in the world, and the Hajj Terminal takes ten jumbo jets at a time.

Pilgrims are organized into groups under the leadership of people who know what to do and where to take them. Fitting so many into a mosque that only holds 75000, and putting them in tents in a valley less than 2 kilometres wide, is no easy task!

People get split up, lost, or overcome with heat – yet despite every obstacle there is a wonderful feeling of being one great family. Inconveniences and difficulties are brushed aside by the emotion, joy and triumph of being a pilgrim.

FOR YOUR FOLDERS

▶ Why is the niyyah, or intention, to do Hajj as important as the pilgrimage itself? How could Muslims take part in Hajj, even if they could not go?

▶ In what ways is Hajj different from all other pillars?

▶ Explain why a Muslim might be forgiven for taking the title 'Hajji' (a Muslim who has completed Hajj) with some pride.

THINGS TO DO

▶ Make a list of the conditions necessary for pilgrims on Hajj.

▶ Copy and complete the word square using the clues below.

Clues:

1 Hajj is a _____
2 The number of times Hajj must be done in a lifetime
3 The name of the lesser pilgrimage
4 These people are not allowed to go on Hajj
5 and 6   You can be excused Hajj on the grounds of _____ and _____ _____
7 The arabic word for 'intention'
8 The month in which Hajj takes place
9 The place where Muslims 'stand before God'
10 The largest airport in the world

1				G		I				
2			C		■	■	■	■	■	■
3	U					■	■	■	■	■
4	N		N	M	U			I		S
5	P	O					Y		■	■
6			L	■		E				
7	N			Y			■	■	■	■
8		H			H		J			
9			A			T		■	■	■
10	A					■		Z		

The Ka'ba in the mosque at Makkah

Adam and Eve

The symbolism of Hajj goes way back to the beginnings of the human story, to Adam, the first man, and after him to Ibrahim, the friend of God.

The story begins with a small mountain in the Plain of Arafat which is known as Jabal ar-Rahman, or the Mount of Mercy. It was here, according to tradition, that Adam and Eve were forgiven by God for their sins, and were brought back to His love and protection.

After they had given in to the devil's temptation they were banished from their lovely paradise and lost each other. They wandered the earth in confusion and terrible unhappiness.

God watched over them, waiting for them to turn back to Him and exchange their defiance for a desire for forgiveness. When at last they understood what separation from God was, they prayed to be restored to grace, and the Lord of Compassion was able to forgive them. Their dramatic reunion took place at the little mountain of Arafat. In gratitude, they built a simple shrine nearby, the first building on earth constructed for the worship of God.

For Muslims, to be on that mountain on 9 Dhu'l Hijjah is the main part of the Hajj ritual. As for Adam and Eve, this 'meeting' between themselves and God, if done with spiritual awareness, brings total forgiveness of all past sins and gains the promise of paradise.

Ibrahim

The second important moment celebrated by Hajj is the occasion when the loyalty of Ibrahim was put to the test.

Ibrahim had vowed to sacrifice everything in his life to God. He was a most humble and devout man, even though he was the wealthy owner of vast herds of sheep and goats.

He lived peacefully with his childless wife Sarah, and a second wife – an Egyptian woman called **Hagar (Hajara)** – who had given birth to his son **Isma'il**.

One day God decided to test Ibrahim's faith and loyalty. Ibrahim had a vivid dream in which he was asked to sacrifice that which he loved most, his only son Isma'il. When he awoke, in fearful agony of mind, he told his son the dream.

The test

Isma'il was terrified, but replied bravely – 'O my father, do what you are commanded to do, and do not worry about me.'

Such was their obedience, that even though they did not know *why* God had ordered this, they accepted that if it was His will, it had to be done.

They set out for **Mina**, the place of sacrifice. On the way the devil appeared in human form using various arguments to make Ibrahim change his mind and doubt whether the dream was genuine. Each argument was so reasonable that it made the sacrifice much harder to bear:

- Only the devil would ask Ibrahim to do such a wicked thing, not God. Ibrahim was being tricked by the evil power.
- Didn't Hagar love her son? Didn't Ibrahim love her, and wouldn't he do anything she asked? How could she allow him to take the foolish dream so seriously, and kill their only boy?
- Didn't Isma'il realize his father was mad? He was being cruel and unloving. Where were his feelings? Isma'il should run away and not get himself killed like a fool!

All three of them resisted these temptations. According to tradition, they picked up stones and flung them at this stranger to drive him away.

The sacrifice

They reached the appointed place. 'Put me face downwards,' begged Isma'il, not out of fear, but so that his father would not hesitate when he saw his face. Ibrahim lay him on the altar, and such was the boy's acceptance and courage that he did not need to be tied. Both had consented to the sacrifice.

But at the last moment God stopped Ibrahim, and the reward for his obedience was that his barren wife Sarah gave birth at last to a son of her own – Isaac.

Isma'il was the founder of the Arab tribes, and Isaac the founder of the Jews (see surah 37:100–113).

Hagar's thirst

Because of Sarah's jealousy on behalf of her son, Ibrahim was told by God that he should separate from Hagar and Isma'il, and leave them to God's care beside the remains of the ancient shrine associated with Adam.

In this barren, waterless desert Hagar and Isma'il were tested again, for God seemed to have abandoned them, and they were dying of thirst. Hagar ran frantically between the tops of two hills,

Safa and **Marwa**, to see if she could spot a passing camel train that would be carrying water – but there was none to be seen.

At last, when all hope had gone save her hope in God, the angel Jibra'il appeared and showed her a spring at the feet of her suffering child. This is the spring now known as the **Zamzam** well.

Makkah

Later the family was reunited, and Ibrahim and Isma'il built, out of rough stone laid dry, a square-walled sanctuary with no roof, the walls a little higher than a man. To lay the top layers, Ibrahim stood on a large rock, the **Maqam Ibrahim**. The building became known as the Ka'ba, or Cube, a very holy place quite unlike the grandiose ziggurats (temples) and pyramids of the surrounding nations.

For around 4000 years the Ka'ba has been reconstructed on that same foundation, and the faithful have gone there on pilgrimage.

> '*O our Lord, receive this from us . . . make us submissive to You, and of our seed a nation submissive to You . . . and our Lord, send among them a messenger, one who will tell them Your signs and teach them the Book and the Wisdom, and purify them.*'
> (surah 2:127–9, see also surah 14:35–8)

A village of tents swiftly grew up around the water-supply in the desert, and eventually the town of Makkah grew up.

Prayer at the Ka'ba

TALKING POINTS

- Should believers always have the right to know the reasons why God wants them to do certain things, or should they act out of trust? Why do they feel they can trust God?
- Is it possible for a believer to live a life of submission to God without facing the tests and temptations of the devil?

FOR YOUR FOLDERS

▶ What do you think are the most important lessons to be drawn from the stories of:
  a Adam and Eve
  b the testing of Ibrahim and his family
  c the sacrifice of Isma'il
  d the testing of Hagar in the desert?
▶ In what ways does the Ka'ba symbolize for the Muslim the idea of complete submission to God?

THINGS TO DO

▶ Using the characters in this unit, write a short play script about the testing of Ibrahim and his family, and their refusal to disobey or lose trust in God. (You could form several small groups, and act out your play in front of the class.)
▶ Write a poem to express the feelings of either Adam or Eve, who thought they would never see each other again, but were forgiven and reunited by God; or Hagar, at the moment when all hopes of survival had failed, discovering that she was safe and that God was with her all the time.

Ihram

On arriving at certain points outside Makkah, pilgrims must enter the sacred state known as **ihram**. They have to make a conscious effort to attain purity, as the pilgrims dedicate themselves to worship, prayer and denial of vanity.

All normal clothing must be put away. Male pilgrims put on just two sheets of unsewn white cloth, one wrapped round the waist, the other over the left shoulder. Women wear a plain undecorated ankle-length long-sleeved garment, and a veil covering the head. For once, women from countries that normally keep **purdah** (see p. 106) must *uncover* their faces.

These clothes symbolize three things: equality, single-mindedness and self-sacrifice. All pilgrims give up their personalities, so often expressed in dress, and are equal with their neighbours.

Ihram also reminds Muslims of death, when all 'disguises' of rank, wealth and appearance are left behind.

Other rules are:
- Do not do anything dishonest or arrogant, but behave like servants of Allah.
- Flirtatious thoughts of the opposite sex are forbidden; one may not get engaged to marry on Hajj; normal marital relations are set aside (any sexual act on Hajj would nullify it).
- Men must not wear jewellery or rings, and women may wear wedding rings only.
- No one may use perfume or scented soap – unscented soap is on sale for pilgrims.
- To express humility, men must not cover their heads (an ordeal in fierce heat – but they may carry an umbrella).
- To express confidence in the atmosphere of purity and that all lustful thoughts have been put aside, women may not cover their faces.
- To express non-interference with nature, no one must cut hair or finger nails.
- To express simplicity, everyone must go barefoot or in sandals that leave the toes and heels bare.
- To curb aggression and feel unity with God's creatures, no blood must be shed by killing animals except fleas, bedbugs, snakes and scorpions.
- To develop mercy, no hunting is allowed.
- To feel love for nature, no plants may be uprooted or trees cut down.
- Muslims must strive to keep their minds at peace, and not lose their tempers, quarrel or get exasperated by difficulties.

Pilgrim in state of ihram

> 'Here I am, O God, here I am!
> I am here, O Thou without equal,
> here I am!
> Thine is the kingdom,
> the praise and the glory,
> O Thou without equal, God Alone!'

This is the prayer called the talbiyah which the pilgrims utter over and over again as they arrive in Makkah – the answer to the divine call to come. Some shout it joyfully, others are overcome with emotion and weep.

To stand in the midst of hundreds of thousands of people and feel that *you* are important to God, that God has seen *you* arrive, is a humbling experience, and can be quite shattering. It is no wonder that so many pilgrims shed tears.

'O God,
this sanctuary is Your sacred place,
and this city is Your city,
and this slave is Your slave.
I have come to You from a distant land,
carrying all my sins and misdeeds
as an afflicted person seeking Your help
and dreading Your punishment.
I beg You to accept me,
and grant me Your complete forgiveness,
and give me permission to enter
Your vast garden of delight.'

This is the prayer said as pilgrims enter Makkah.

The women unveil for Hajj

Steep and stony path to Allah's holy city

THE pilgrimage to Makkah this year was not simply a matter of seeking forgiveness of sins from God; it was as much about convincing the Saudis that pilgrims were not intent on fomenting revolution in Arabia.

For most pilgrims, the Hajj began with a five-hour grilling at a Saudi airport before access was granted to Islam's holy land. My own uncomfortable interrogation went on for two days.

Iran's fundamentalism has cast a long shadow across the Gulf, and the Saudis, who were shaken when 402 people died in rioting at Makkah last year, were determined to prevent a repetition.

At every stage of the annual pilgrimage – which for most Muslims is the highlight of their life – security was oppressive. Even at the climax of the pilgrimage, when 1.5m pilgrims converged on the desert of Arafat to look to the sky for forgiveness, all they could see were police helicopters hovering above.

Makkah, the holiest city of Islam, was turned into an armed camp, with thousands of soldiers, many of them from other Muslim states, stationed outside holy places and patrolling the streets.

Even the mosque which houses the *Ka'ba*, Islam's holiest shrine, was guarded by soldiers carrying machineguns who searched pilgrims at random as they entered the building.

Tunnels had been bored into mountains over the last 12 months, and roads and bridges built to divert vehicles from the city, where they could have been turned into barricades.

In the end there was no trouble, but the security angered many pilgrims. "We feel like pawns in a war game rather than pilgrims," said one Muslim from London. "It's sacrilege. When we kneel down in prayer to God, we have to kneel before soldiers."

The Saudis, however, felt that they had good cause to protect Makkah from Iranians and their Shi'ite sympathisers, who seem intent on causing trouble for a Saudi regime which they regard as hopelessly corrupt.

Sunday Times, 31 July 1988

THINGS TO DO

▶ Write out the talbiyah prayer or the prayer of the pilgrims entering Makkah. You could do this as a decorated scroll or poster.

FOR YOUR FOLDERS

▶ Imagine you are a Muslim. Write a letter to a friend describing the things you must do or must not do while in the state of ihram. Explain what the experience of entering this state means to you.

▶ Read the newspaper article. Check the ihram rules. Can you explain why so many pilgrims would feel outraged by the atmosphere of the 1988 Hajj?

▶ Why do you think it is significant that Muslim women do not cover their faces during Hajj?

THINKING POINTS

● Why do you think pilgrims on Hajj – who must be very tired, uncomfortable, hot and hungry – are normally so happy and excited?

● Why do you think the ihram cloths later become treasured possessions?

A The Holy Mosque, Makkah

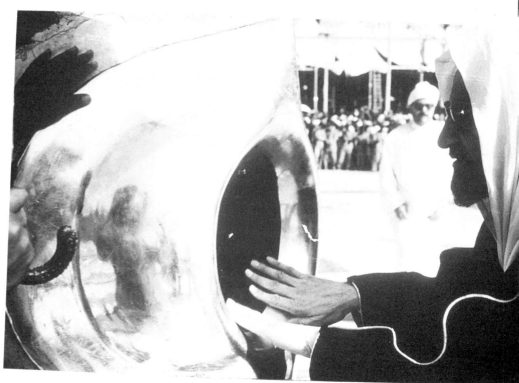

B The Black Stone (see page 82)

C Pilgrims pray before commencing say (see page 86)

D The say (see page 86)

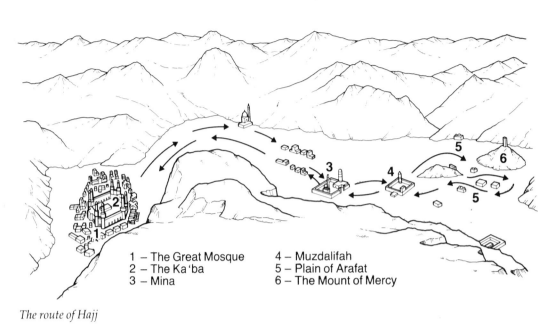

1 – The Great Mosque
2 – The Ka'ba
3 – Mina
4 – Muzdalifah
5 – Plain of Arafat
6 – The Mount of Mercy

The route of Hajj

Baitullah

The Ka'ba is known as **Baitullah**, the House of Allah. It is a plain cube-shaped building made of concrete blocks, not very pretty or striking to look at. Yet Muslims claim it is on the site of the oldest shrine to God on earth, built originally by the first man Adam. Later it was abandoned and broken down, but Ibrahim and Isma'il were shown the foundations and rebuilt it.

The plain dull exterior guarding a brilliant and exciting treasure within symbolizes the plain dull wrappings of the body hiding from the world the shining brilliance of the soul; and the fact that the most splendid being of all – God Himself – is invisible, and yet glorious to those who have 'eyes to see'.

When Muhammad captured Makkah he broke up the idols of 360 other 'gods' that had been placed there.

Nowadays only very rare visitors are allowed inside the Ka'ba to stand at the very centre and pray in all four directions, a unique experience. Inside is simply a room decorated with texts from the Qur'an.

Al-Kiswah

The Ka'ba is covered by a huge jet-black cloth known as the **kiswah**. There is a different one every year, because at the end of Hajj it is cut up into pieces and sold to the pilgrims as mementoes of the greatest moment of their lives. The rim of gold lettering round the cloth is usually sewn by specially chosen men, traditionally from Egypt.

The Black Stone

This is an oval boulder about 18 cm in diameter, set in the south-east corner of the Ka'ba that marks the start of the walk encircling the shrine. It is encased in a silver frame. The pilgrims try to touch it or kiss it. Traditions suggest:
- It was dug out of the earth by Isma'il at a place indicated by the angel Jibra'il.
- Jibra'il brought it from paradise and gave it to Adam.
- It was given to Noah's descendants after the flood.

It certainly existed long before Muhammad's time, and was mentioned by the writer Maximus of Tyre in 2 CE. See photograph B on page 80.

It is probably a meteorite, and therefore a symbol of that which comes to earth from heaven.

Marwa and Safa

These are two small hills, now enclosed under domes and joined by a walkway – the two hills between which Hagar frantically dashed in her search for water. See photographs C and D on page 81. You can see the long covered walkway in the photograph on page 74.

This search symbolizes the soul's desperate search for that which gives true life.

Zamzam

The angel showed Hagar a spring of water near the place where she had laid the dying Isma'il. A tradition suggests the water issued from the place where his feet had scoured the sand as he suffered his fever. Hagar called the well Zamzam, from the sound made by rushing water in the Babylonian language. It symbolizes the truth that when all seems lost, God is still present, with healing and life for the soul.

The Zamzam well is in the courtyard of the Great Mosque in Makkah. Pilgrims buy water from it to drink and take home. Many dip their white garments in it, and keep them to be used one day as the shrouds for their burial.

Arafat

This is the plain where the pilgrims erect a vast camp site. During Hajj the plain is dotted with little tents in neat rows and squares as far as the eye can see (see p. 84). About two million people camp here.

Mount Arafat

This is the Mount of Mercy where God reunited Adam and Eve. The prayer during the Night of Standing here is one of the most important parts of Hajj. See photograph on p. 86.

Muzdalifah

Pilgrims camp overnight at **Muzdalifah** on their journey between Makkah and Arafat. Here they pick up pebbles to hurl at the pillars of Mina (see p. 87).

Mina

Here are the pillars, or **Jamras**, which represent the places where Ibrahim and his family resisted the temptations and stoned the devil. The Saudi Arabian Ministry of Pilgrimage has recently built a huge walkway to Mina. See the photograph below.

THINGS TO DO

► Copy the diagram of the pilgrimage route. Explain what is significant, or what is done, at the following places:

Ka'ba shrine   Black Stone
Safa and Marwa   Zamzam
Mount Arafat   Muzdalifah   Mina

The walkway to Mina

The stand on Mount Arafat

The first thing the pilgrims do on arrival in Makkah, no matter what time of day or night, is to hurry to the Ka'ba and encircle it seven times at a fast pace, running if possible, to symbolize love for God. This is called the **tawaf**.

As they arrive they call out *'Labbaika, Allahumma, Labbaika!'* which means 'At Your command, our Lord, at Your command!' – the cry of response to the call to come and dedicate their lives to God.

If the pilgrims can get near the Black Stone they will kiss it or touch it, but if it is impossible because of the vast numbers, they shout and raise their arms in salute each time they go past. An example of the prayers used is this one, used on the fourth round:

> *'O God
> who knows the innermost secrets of our hearts,
> lead us out of the darkness
> into the light.'*

The next event is the **say** (or **saai**), the procession seven times between Safa and Marwa in memory of Hagar's search. It symbolizes patience and perseverance, and can be quite an ordeal in the summer heat. Special provisions are made for people in wheelchairs or on stretchers.

Next comes a rest, and a visit to the Zamzam well.

On 8 Dhu'l Hijjah the pilgrims set off for Mina, and camp there for the rest of that day and night. On 9 Dhu'l Hijjah they head for Mount Arafat – a good day's journey on foot. Many pilgrims nowadays take modern transport straight to Arafat and miss out Mina, because of the sheer numbers involved.

The Stand

On the plain of Arafat, at the Mount of Mercy, the pilgrims make their stand before God, the **wuquf**. They stand from noon to sunset in the blistering heat, meditating and praying, and concentrating on God alone.

Latecomers rush to be in time, for if the stand is missed, the Hajj is not valid.

It is a time of great mystical and emotional power. To be there with a repentant heart wipes out all the sins of the past, and enables life to begin anew. There is a tremendous sense of release – being totally wrapped in love, totally 'washed', totally cleansed.

Stone steps lead to the top of Arafat, and from

there a sermon is delivered to the people. Then they all spend the night in the open, in thankfulness and prayer.

After this, Muslims may go home from the Hajj 'released', as sinless as the day they were born, and full of inner peace.

Muslims return to Mina via Muzdalifah, where they hold the night prayer and gather pebbles to stone the Devil. The night of 10 Dhu'l Hijjah is spent at Muzdalifah. As dawn approaches there is another mass standing before God, and the pilgrims depart for Mina just before dawn breaks.

'What can we do to make God's light shine forth in the darkness around us? We must first let it shine in our own true selves, and with that light in the niche of our innermost hearts we can walk with steps both firm and sure, we can humbly visit the comfortless and guide their steps. Not we, but the Light will guide! But oh! The joy of being found worthy to bear the Torch, and to say to our brethren: "I, too, was in darkness, comfortless, and behold, I have found comfort and joy in the Grace Divine."'

(poem by A. Yusuf Ali, Islamic Propagation Centre, 1946, in chapter 299 of his commentary on the Qur'an)

FOR YOUR FOLDERS

▶ Pilgrims slip into Hajj like drops being merged into a vast ocean. In such a mass of people, can you explain why Hajj is such an intensely personal experience?

THINGS TO DO

▶ Explain what is meant by tawaf, say and wuquf.
▶ Copy out the Ka'ba stone prayer.
▶ Imagine you have been all night in the vast crowd at wuquf. The dawn is breaking. Write a paragraph describing what you might feel.

Pilgrims stoning a **jamra***, which represents the devil (see p. 83)*

43 THE UNFURLING

The remainder of the pilgrimage is called the unfurling.

- When the pilgrims arrive at Mina, they hurl pebbles at the pillars to symbolize their rejection of the Devil and all his works.
- Next, on 10 Dhu'l Hijjah, the Feast of Sacrifice (Eid ul-Adha, see p. 94) begins. The pilgrims all camp at Mina for the three days of the feast. Every man must sacrifice an animal.
- The Saudi authorities organize the disposal of the carcases. Nowadays, with about two million pilgrims, it is impossible for all the meat to be eaten, even if it is shared among the poor.
- After the sacrifice, the men have their heads shaved and the women cut off at least 2.5 cm of their hair.
- The pilgrims then return to Makkah for another encircling of the Ka'ba. At this point ihram is over, and the final events are enjoyed in the holiday spirit. Many go back to Mina for a period of rest and recovery.
- Finally they return to Makkah for the farewell. They buy water from Zamzam, and dip their white cloths in it to be used later as shrouds. They drink as much water as possible, believing it cures diseases, and they take as much as they can carry home to their families. They buy pieces of the Black Cloth as souvenirs.
- They are at last entitled to take the name Hajji or al-Hajj.

Muslim tourism

After the Hajj, most pilgrims go to visit Madinah, to pay their respects at the Prophet's tomb. At Madinah there is the mosque that was Muhammad's home, and behind it the **hujurah** or chamber which was the room of his youngest and beloved wife Aisha. Here Muslims may see the graves of Muhammad himself, his friends Abu Bakr and Umar, and, according to some traditions, a place reserved for Jesus after his second coming.

The energetic can visit Mount Nur, where Muhammad first saw the angel, and Mount Thawr where he sheltered from the Quraish. Other places of interest are the battle sites, and the Masjid at-Taqwa – the mosque built when Muhammad entered Madinah. This one is notable for having two mihrabs, one facing Jerusalem.

The cemetery of al-Baqee contains the graves of Uthman, Aisha and Hasan (Ali's son, see p. 136), plus other celebrities. It is notable for the extreme simplicity of the tombs, which are simply mounds of small stones. There had been grander mausoleums in the past, but these were destroyed by the strict Islamic sect of Wahhabis during the reign of King Abd al-Aziz al-Saud, who wished to discourage hero-worship cults.

Pilgrims on a bus to Makkah. Notice that women are not expected to ride on top

Head shaving

Murals on the houses of Hajj pilgrims

FOR YOUR FOLDERS

▶ Explain how Hajj:
  a brings 'release' and inner peace
  b builds up courage and trust in God
  c draws all Muslims together whether on Hajj or not
  d unites Muslims not only with each other but with their beloved prophets of the past.

▶ Imagine you are one of the pilgrims. Write a letter home to a friend describing what you have seen that impressed you most. Which memories do you think would particularly influence and stay with you for the rest of your life?

Comment

'To have stood before God at Arafat is like having a baby. You have either had the experience or you have not. No one can truly explain how it feels – but those who know it, know. Perhaps those whose hearts God has seized can understand.'

(a woman pilgrim's comment)

THINGS TO DO

▶ Look at the picture above showing the house of a Hajj pilgrim. Explain how this particular pilgrim travelled to Makkah and what event is shown on their house walls.

44 FESTIVALS AND SPECIAL DAYS

Festivals

The Muslim word for a festival is 'id' or 'eid', taken from an Arabic word meaning 'returning at regular intervals'.

Muslim festivals are happy occasions when families and friends get together:
- to praise and thank God
- to enjoy themselves and His blessings
- to remember loved ones (including those in distant parts of the world, and those who have died)
- to remember all the members of the family of Islam, whether rich or poor, known or unknown.

The fact that festivals occur in regular cycles is important, for this gives a repeated opportunity to:
- forgive enemies
- put right quarrels
- get into contact with people not seen for a long time
- make up for things you have forgotten to do.

The festivals are times for reducing tensions and establishing new and renewed relationships.

Atmosphere

The atmosphere of a festival is one of devotion and prayer, happiness and family spirit.
- The poor must be remembered.
- The rich must share.
- The lonely and the stranger must be made to feel at home.
- The orphan must feel loved and cared for.
- The lazy and forgetful must make an effort.
- The quarrelsome must make peace.

Dates

Months in the Islamic calendar are calculated according to the moon. Therefore each month has 29–30 days, and the Islamic year is shorter than the solar year by eleven days. For this reason, feasts are not like the Christian festival Christmas, which is always on 25 December. Instead Muslim festivals come eleven days earlier each year and thus move round the solar calendar.

Islam has only two chief festivals, **Eid ul Adha** – the feast of sacrifice during Hajj, and **Eid ul Fitr** the breaking of the month-long fast of Ramadan (see p. 70).

Muslims also keep six days as special occasions.

Maulid an Nabi

Maulid an Nabi is the birthday of the Prophet, probably originally 20 August, 570 CE. The day is celebrated with joyful processions and accounts of Muhammad's life, mission, character, sufferings and successes.

Months	Festivals
Muharram	Muharram (New Year), one day Ashura (10 Muharram), voluntary fast, two days
Safar	
Rabi al-Awwal	Maulid an Nabi (12 Rabi al-Awwal), one day
Rabi al-Akhir	
Jumada al-Ula	
Jumada al-Akhrah	
Rajab	Lailat ul Miraj (27 Rajab), one night
Shabaan	Lailat ul Bara'at (14 Shabaan), one night
Ramadan	One lunar month of fasting; Lailat ul Qadr (27 Ramadan), one night
Shawwal	Eid ul Fitr (1 Shawwal), one day
Dhu'l Qidah	
Dhu'l Hijjah	Hajj, five days and nights; Eid ul Adha (10 Dhu'l Hijjah), one day; sacrifice (11 and 12 Dhu'l Hijjah), two days

In some parts of the world the whole of the following month is marked by gatherings in remembrance of his life.

Lailat ul Qadr

This is the Night of Power, when Muhammad received his first revelation of the Qur'an. Because the date is not certain, it can be remembered on any night during the last ten days of the Ramadan feast. It is often held on 27 Ramadan.

Many Muslims stay up all night in prayer, or reciting the Qur'an. Some spend all of the last ten nights of Ramadan in this way, remembering God's mercy and forgiveness (not so difficult when the dawn is around 3 a.m.!) A quick meal precedes the first prayer, then they snatch some sleep.

Lailat ul Miraj

This commemorates the night Muhammad made the miraculous journey to Jerusalem and ascended through the heavens to the presence of God.

Muslims gather in remembrance that it was at the height of his persecution that Muhammad was given this special moment, one feature of which was the institution of the five daily prayers.

Lailat ul Bara'at

This is the night of the full moon before the start of Ramadan. It was at this time that Muhammad used to begin his preparations for Ramadan by passing nights in prayer. Many Muslims celebrate this night by staying awake and reading the Qur'an.

Muharram

Muharram was declared the first month of the Muslim calendar by caliph Umar, the New Year's Day being celebrated after the sighting of the new moon. It commemorates the Hijrah, the departure of Muhammad to Madinah, the moment that marked the beginning of his successes and led to the spread of Islam. Muslims date their years from this event, so the year after the Hijrah is year 1 AH. The intention is for Muslims to 'migrate' from their past to their future, put old sins and failings behind them and make a fresh start with new year resolutions.

10 Muharram or Ashura

This was a traditional day of fasting before the time of Muhammad. In the Jewish tradition it was the Day of Atonement when sacrifices were made for the sins of the people. In Muslim tradition it was also the day when Noah left the Ark after the flood, and the day on which God saved Moses from Pharaoh. Fasting is not obligatory, but many Muslims fast anyway, and enjoy special meals at night.

It is a particularly important day for Shi'ite Muslims, those who have separated from the mainstream of Islam in support of the family of Ali (see p. 136). For them, it is a day of great sorrow and mourning, as it marks the day when Muhammad's grandson **Husain** was martyred. Public grief is expressed dramatically with processions, plays and religious gatherings at which emotions are stirred until the tears flow. Sometimes the more fervent men even beat themselves with chains and cut their heads with swords – to share in some small way the sufferings of Husain.

THINGS TO DO

▶ Calculate the date: to find the Muslim year (AH) you must take 622 (the year of Hijrah) from the year in the calendar we use and multiply it by $\frac{33}{32}$, e.g.

$$1902 = \frac{33}{32} \times 1902 - 622$$
$$= \frac{33}{32} \times 1280$$
$$= 1320 \text{ AH}$$

What is the Muslim year for 1990?

FOR YOUR FOLDERS

▶ List the six special days, and state briefly what each one commemorates.
▶ In keeping the special days connected with the life of Muhammad, are Muslims really remembering Muhammad or God? Give reasons for your answer.

TALKING POINT

● **Would Muhammad have approved of too much celebration of these days? How do you think he would have liked people to honour his memory?**

45 EID UL FITR

The preparation

Eid ul Fitr is the feast that marks the end of the month-long Ramadan fast. It begins with great excitement. On the last evening of the fast, as the time draws near, most Muslims go out into the open to catch the moment the new moon appears in the sky when there is an outburst of rejoicing and goodwill.

Preparations for the feast begin well in advance.
- Food is bought and carefully prepared beforehand (sometimes Muslim shops are so busy they stay open all night the few days before).
- Decorations may be bought and hung up.
- Cards are bought or made, and sent to relatives and friends.
- Gifts and sweets are prepared for the children.
- Houses may be painted or generally smartened up.
- Money is collected for the poor.

The Eid day is the last day for sending zakah (see p. 68), and post offices are often busy as people fulfill this part of their duty.

Muslim girls in Eid clothes

The announcement

Originally Eid ul Fitr was announced by the eagerly awaited call to prayer from the mosque, which appeared more moving and significant than normal. Nowadays the time is announced on radio and television. In the West (where skies are often too cloudy to see the moon!) mosques receive the news by radio, telex and telephone.

As soon as the signal comes, everyone rushes to congratulate and greet each other. There is much hugging and handshaking, and wishing of 'Eid Mubarak' or 'Happy Eid'. There is great holiday spirit – people are out on the streets in happy mood. Visitors call round on friends and congratulate each other on completing a successful fast.

In memory of Muhammad, and because it is sensible, the fast is usually broken with something very simple, like dates or a drink. One popular drink is 'qamar al-din' (moon of religion) which is made from apricots.

After this the family leaves the table to pray together, and then comes back to enjoy what is probably the most appreciated meal of the month!

Eid day

On this day there is no work or school. In non-Muslim countries understanding employers make allowances for absence; in Muslim countries it is a three-day holiday.

The routine

- a bath or shower
- putting on best clothes or new clothes
- quick breakfast
- huge special gathering in the largest mosque, or maybe a park or playing field, or even a car park – this congregation can consist of thousands of people!
- women and children are encouraged to come, but many mothers stay at home getting things ready
- everyone prays together, as one huge family. The sermon is usually about the importance of giving
- more greetings and embraces, then round to the houses of friends and family. The children are very excited because they know they will receive presents and pocket money. Whole convoys of cars may go back to one house. People come and go all day
- a splendid dinner – the first meal eaten at midday for over a month! It may be in many sittings,

according to the number who arrive. Everyone pitches in and helps with supplies and cooking
- a visit to the cemetery, to remember the loved ones who are divided from their families by death
- it is a day of joy and tears, forgiveness and love. The day ends with more visits to friends, as people are anxious to leave no one out, and the celebrations often go on late into the night.

THINGS TO DO

▶ Design and draw your own Eid card.
▶ Make a diary or list of the preparations you would have to make in order to celebrate Eid in your own house.

QUICK QUIZ

▶ What is the Muslim word for festival?
▶ Eid ul Fitr comes at the end of which month?
▶ What must be seen before Eid can begin?
▶ What are sent to friends and relations?
▶ What money is paid now?
▶ How does the Eid congregation differ from the usual ones?

FOR YOUR FOLDERS

▶ In what ways does Eid ul Fitr bring Muslims close together as
  a individual families, and
  b one complete family, the ummah (see p. 45)?
▶ Why is Eid ul Fitr especially enjoyed by children?
▶ Why is the fact that festivals must occur in a regular cycle important? What might the consequences be if the festival did not keep coming around each year?

The end of Ramadan at the Regent's Park Mosque

Animal sacrifice

The feast of **Eid ul Adha** is not only the climax of the Hajj pilgrimage (see p. 88), but is the major festival in the Islamic year and takes place in the Hajj month, two months after the close of Ramadan. It commemorates the triumph of Ibrahim's faith over the temptations of the devil, and his complete submission to the will of God.

For those taking part, it symbolizes the submission of each individual Muslim, and renewal of total commitment to God.

Every Muslim takes part in this feast, not just those on Hajj. It is a family occasion, bearing in mind the whole family of Islam and not just your own relations.

It is a serious occasion, and concentrates the mind on self-sacrifice, symbolized by the sacrificing of an animal.

In Muslim countries schools, businesses and shops are closed for three days. Town streets are deserted and family homes packed with visitors.

Everyone thinks about the pilgrims making their Hajj and joins with them in spirit, particularly any who have gone from their own family or community. In Muslim countries Hajj events are now followed on television.

On the day commemorating the story of Ibrahim's testing (see p. 76) there is a sense of emotional release, and real sharing in the experiences of the pilgrims, many Muslims remembering their own journey, and others wishing they could have gone too.

The feast represents Muslims' readiness to sacrifice all feelings, personal wants and needs, even life itself if necessary, to the service of God.

> *'Neither the flesh of the animals of your sacrifice nor their blood reaches Allah – it is your righteousness that reaches Him.'*
>
> (surah 22:37)

Preparations

These begin well in advance. Gifts are bought, new clothing is prepared, food supplies are organized for the big day and an animal must be selected for the sacrifice and kept apart. These include sheep, goats, cows and camels, and they are usually purchased two or three weeks before the feast day.

The sacrifice

When possible, the animals are cared for at home. Muslims are not hard-hearted, and they often become fond of these animals, especially the children.

Facing the responsibility of slaughter for yourself, instead of leaving it to a butcher, makes you realize in a small way how hard it must have been for

Ibrahim to pass his test when he thought he was going to have to sacrifice his own son. A mixture of tenderness, love, grief and above all duty is what the sacrifice is all about.

It is the duty of a Muslim man to know how to kill an animal quickly and kindly, and take this responsibility for himself.

Nowadays many families have their feast animals slaughtered at an abattoir, by a specially trained person. This is compulsory in Britain.

The atmosphere should be such that the animal is not frightened, and its throat must be cut with a very sharp knife across the jugular vein, so that it loses consciousness immediately. Prayers are said throughout the proceedings. Killing the animal in this way causes very little distress or pain, and the blood drains away easily.

In the West, a special licence is needed to kill an animal, and licence holders go to the slaughterhouse to sacrifice there on behalf of the community. There have been isolated incidents of Muslims killing goats at home (to the horror of their non-Muslim neighbours), but these are usually caused by newcomers unaware of the facilities provided.

Meat killed in the correct way is called **halal**, or permitted. Other meat is **haram** or forbidden. (See also p. 116.)

The meat is divided up for the poor, for friends and relatives, and for the family use. In the East, Eid ul Adha is sometimes the only time in the year that the poor get meat to eat.

Instead of meat, money can be donated to the poor.

FOR YOUR FOLDERS

▶ Explain how the feast of Eid ul Adha is an integral part of the Hajj, and how it binds together all Muslims, whether on Hajj or not. Explain what it celebrates, and the significance of the sacrifice.

▶ You might never have to take a life, or be called upon to sacrifice your own life. How could you show your readiness to love and serve God in your normal daily life? What other kinds of sacrifice have to be made for God?

▶ Some people never stop and consider how they would react if they were called upon to face the final challenge. You may not be particularly religious. Are there any things or people you would be prepared to lay down your life for?

FOR DISCUSSION

▶ Having to sacrifice an animal teaches compassion and responsibility.
▶ Eid ul Adha is wasteful and cruel.
▶ You can't learn about duty and obedience unless faced with the hardships of performing them.

Eid cards

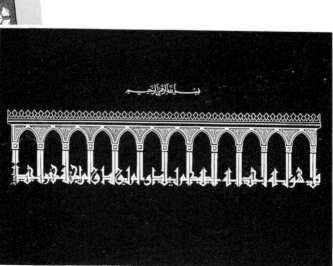

'This is my straight path, so follow it, and do not follow other paths which will separate you from this path.'

(surah 6:153)

'God does not accept belief if it is not expressed in deeds; and He does not accept your deeds unless they conform to your beliefs.'

(Hadith)

Taqwa

The moment a Muslim 'opens the eyes' and becomes conscious of God, the most important questions become 'What shall I do now? How shall I live?' Awareness of God, or consciousness of Him in your everyday life, is known as **taqwa** (see p. 40).

Being in a state of taqwa is quite different from ordinary living. It alters Muslims' entire motivation for doing things, and stops them doing many things that would give a great deal of selfish pleasure. Being aware of the 'eyes of God' alters even the way they think.

Justice

Muslims believe that societies have made many attempts to establish justice and fair living without making their laws dependent on God's will, and without His divine help – and that none of these attempts have worked.

They believe that people must start by living the right sort of life themselves as individuals, but that true justice can never come about until the whole society follows the will of God.

Believers attempting to live holy lives should not shut themselves off from the world – that is seen almost as a form of selfishness. They are to live within the community, with all its problems, and try to make it a better place They must find the **Shari'ah** which means the 'path', and follow it.

This Shari'ah is the code of behaviour for a Muslim, the law that determines the rightness (halal) or wrongness (haram) of any particular action.

It gives a criterion for judging all behaviour and conduct, and relationships with other individuals, with society as a whole, and with your own self.

The principles behind Shari'ah

- God *does* exist, and so does life after death.
- There *will* come a time of judgement.
- God *is* aware of everything you do and think.
- The world is full of hardships and evils that should be put right, and not just ignored.
- All humans belong to the family of God, the **ummah**, and are equal whatever their colour, class, or national background. Their *worth* comes from the quality of their lives.

'The basis of Shari'ah is wisdom, and the welfare of people in this world as well as the Hereafter. This welfare lies in complete justice, mercy, care and wisdom. Anything that departs from justice to oppression, from mercy to harshness, from caring to misery, and from wisdom to folly, has nothing to do with the Shari'ah.'

(Ibn Qayyim, a famous Muslim teacher)

To follow Shari'ah means living a morally responsible life.

All humans are to

'hold tight to the rope of God, and never let it go again. Remember that God showed mercy to you and blessed you while you were still enemies. Remember how He united your hearts together in love, so that by His grace you became brothers.'

(surah 3:103)

If humans live in this way, recognizing all people as one family, aware of their rights and defending them, grieving when they get hurt, being determined to bring about their good and not their harm, then they have already started living according to Shari'ah.

'We created Man, and We know what his soul whispers to him. We are nearer to him than the vein in his neck.'

(surah 50:16)

'Muslims who live in the midst of society and bear with patience the afflictions that come to them, are better than those who shun society and cannot bear any wrong done to them.'

'Believers are like parts of a building; each part supports the others.'

'If any single part of the body aches, the whole body feels the effects and rushes to its relief.'

'Every one of you is a shepherd, and will be questioned about the well-being of his flock.'

(Hadith)

Muslims have no time for people who talk as if they are religious and make a show of it, but in their lives remain heartless, selfish, lazy or mean.

Morality is seen as the basis of self-confidence and strength. The ideals to be aimed at are:
- love of God
- humility
- modesty
- naturalness
- unselfishness.

Pride and arrogance are not acceptable, for no individual is superior to another except in amount of faith and performance of good deeds.

The essentials are kindness, gentleness, consideration for others, and the general promotion of the happiness and welfare of society.

Basic rules

In fact, the basic rules of Shari'ah are laid out clearly in many surahs of the Qur'an. Here are examples:
- Do not associate anything with God.
- Show kindness to your parents.
- Do not kill children because of poverty – God will provide (this applies nowadays to abortions).
- Do not indulge in shameful acts, either openly or in secret.
- Do not take human life, except through process of law.
- Do not touch an orphan's wealth, except to improve it.
- Give full measure and weigh fairly.
- Whenever you speak, be just.

(Surah 6)

THINKING POINTS

- Why do you think Muslims disapprove of men and women living religious lives separated from ordinary society?
- Why do you think that Muslims believe modesty and unselfishness to be qualities that God particularly requires?
- Do Muslims regard equality as the same thing as worth? Does being 'equal in the sight of God' mean something different from 'being equal'?

FOR YOUR FOLDERS

▶ What is meant by taqwa, and what do you think might be the effects of taqwa on a person's life?

▶ Why do Muslims believe that it is not possible to create a truly just society in purely human terms, with no reference to belief in Divine Justice?

▶ Explain what is meant by the ummah. Read carefully the passages from the Qur'an and Hadith given here, and show how they reinforce the idea of ummah. (See also pp. 40 and 112.)

▶ Explain what is meant by 'haram' and 'halal'.

THINGS TO DO

▶ Conduct an interview, if you can, with a practising Muslim, to discover what it is like living according to Shari'ah in your community.

▶ Look at the quotation of Ibn Qayyim given in this unit. What are the main aims of the Shari'ah according to this teacher?

▶ Copy out the rules of Shari'ah as given in surah 6. Make a decorative border round them.

The Qur'an is the basis of Shari'ah, and gives all the principles and commands to be accepted by Muslims without question.

Further guidance comes from the **Sunnah**, the example of Muhammad, who spent his entire life after the Night of Power in guiding and directing the people. Whatever he said, did or approved provided an example. His teachings are preserved in the Hadith. (See p. 46 and questions throughout this book.)

Problems

How can a law laid down fourteen centuries ago in the Middle East meet all the complex demands and pressures of modern technological civilization? How can a person know whether it is right or wrong to drink whisky, play transistors, go to discos, and so on? Why should any human being in this day and age bother to look for a source of guidance outside the human level? And why should God, if there is one, condescend to bother with such trivial matters? The Muslim thinks in a different way. No Muslim can accept the idea of a society without God; the Compassionate One *cannot* be unconcerned, uncaring, or unable to help humans in the task of living their lives.

Working out the rules

Working out Muslim principles is called **ijtihad**. This means using reason and judgement to decide on a course of action most in keeping with the spirit of the Qur'an and Hadith. Decisions made in this manner are called **ijma**, but they are not regarded as totally binding since they are based on human opinions. The only ones accepted as binding are those made by the very first caliphs (see p. 130) who had been Muhammad's close companions.

Later decisions can be accepted as guidelines, but it is possible to replace them by others. Therefore fresh thinking can always be offered on past decisions, and so keep pace with the ever-changing world.

Principles

In making a decision, account must always be taken of:
- the opinions of respected people
- previous decisions
- justice and concern for the public good

- the acceptance of the masses.

The technique of working out Shari'at law is called **fiqh**, from the word for 'intelligence' or 'knowledge'.

Limits

The principles behind the Shari'ah deter various pressure groups (even highly religious ones) from imposing on people burdens and duties which go beyond the spirit of Islam, and keep the opportunities for solving problems as wide as possible. Fanaticism is not encouraged. An over-zealous religious leader may not force anyone to do a sixth prayer during the day, or charge more than the usual amount of zakah. If he tried this, any Muslim would have the right to demand to see the basis for it in the Qur'an or Hadith. The dictates of a narrow-minded tyrant would never be acceptable.

The job of the Shari'ah is to provide the rules of divine guidance in any new or changed situation, so that God's will may be done on earth as it is in heaven.

Freedom

Muslims must *submit* to God, and that means they must not pick or choose which of the revealed laws they will or will not keep. How can they judge which ones are more important than others? Only God knows the full reasoning behind them.

Yet submission to God is the highest freedom, for it implies that a person can choose to *disobey* God, and many do.

However, in submitting to God alone, all slavery to other things is broken – a person is no longer a servant of any other person, set of ideas, or artificial objects or institutions. In submitting to God, a person becomes God's **khalifa**, or vice-regent, on earth.

Rules of behaviour

These are divided into five categories:
- **fard** or **wajib** – things which *must* be done, e.g. prayer
- **haram** – things *never* to be done, e.g. worshipping another besides God
- **mandub** – recommended actions, e.g. unselfish hospitality
- **makruh** – actions not forbidden, but disapproved of, e.g. divorce

- **mubah** – actions to be decided by conscience, because there is no clear guidance, e.g. smoking. Most of modern life falls in the mubah section. Whatever is not actually forbidden is permitted, under the guidance of your conscience. If an action is harmful to yourself or anyone else, it cannot be recommended by a Muslim.

Difficulties

When you realize the full extent of true Muslim commitment, you can see how sometimes venturing out into life in a non-Muslim environment can be full of difficulties and embarrassing situations, and a real obstacle course, for a Muslim.

Some Muslims who come to the West are from very poor backgrounds, and find themselves surrounded by all sorts of luxuries unavailable back home. Others come from very wealthy backgrounds and can buy anything they want, including corrupt practices.

Muslims tend not to mix very much with non-Muslim society, but keep themselves to themselves. The reasons are largely
- food problems
- presence of alcohol
- unaccustomed freedoms.

Some areas that cause quite severe difficulties are:
- schools (especially for girls)
- enforced non-Muslim communal life (e.g. hospitals, prisons)
- burial customs
- aggression, hostility and racism
- sexual freedom
- finding lodgings.

THINGS TO DO

► Imagine you are a Muslim who has recently arrived in Britain. You may not be able to speak the language, and your skin is probably not white. Find out what is meant by 'racism' and see if you can collect any press cuttings illustrating this problem. How might racism affect an immigrant's chances of feeling 'at home'?

THINKING POINTS

- **What do you think Muslims consider to be the chief qualities that set the tone of a civilized society? Explain why the quiet acceptance of tyranny is not acceptable to a Muslim.**
- **Why do Muslims regard the details of seemingly small laws to be as important as the seemingly more serious laws?**
- **Why do you think acceptance of ijtihad is so important for ordinary Muslims in countries where governments (even Muslim 'extremist' ones) have come to power through military coups?**

QUICK QUIZ

► What is meant by the Sunnah?
► What is meant by ijtihad?
► Whose 'ijma' are regarded as binding?
► What is meant by fiqh?
► Give an example of something mandub.
► Give an example of something mubah.

FOR YOUR FOLDERS

► What are the main aims of Shari'ah?
► Explain what the five categories of behaviour are. Which ones are ordered in the Qur'an? Which is the largest area? How are the rules worked out to deal with that area?
► Why is submission to God seen by the Muslims as the greatest of freedoms?

A Muslim family

'The family provides the environment within which human values and morals develop and grow in the new generation. The family system and the relationships between the sexes determine the whole character of society and whether it is backward or civilized.'

(Sayyid Qutb, a modern Muslim reformer, in *Milestones*, Dar-al-Qur'an, Beirut 1978)

The basis of society

Muslims regard the family as the basis for the human race, culture, society and civilization. They accept it as an institution founded by God (see surah 4:1) and intended to give a secure atmosphere for the growth and progress of all its members.

Anything which weakens or disrupts it is therefore regarded as a serious matter. The home is considered to be far more important, sacred, creative and rewarding than any place 'outside'.

The complex unit

The family is a complex interwoven unit consisting of many people. It is not just a husband and wife plus their parents and children. It includes brothers and sisters, uncles and aunts, cousins. In the atmosphere of a loving, outgoing unit, it also includes friends and neighbours, and anyone who falls within the sphere of that love and who needs help (see surah 2:83).

'Those who show the most perfect faith are those who possess the best disposition and are kindest to their families.'

(Hadith)

Mother

A household in which there is love, peace and security is considered to be valuable beyond price, and it does not come about by accident. It has to be worked for by all members, and requires a strong commitment to patience, forgiveness, tolerance, sense of duty and love.

All these things are regarded as vital, and the key person in the household who sets the tone and does most of the work is undoubtedly the mother.

To be a good mother is so important in Islam that she is considered to be the most precious treasure in the world. Her role is the decisive factor in the family.

When a woman becomes a mother, she takes on an enormous responsibility. In allowing her body to produce a new living being she should bear in mind the inalienable rights of every child:
- the right to life, and equal chances in life
- the right to legitimacy – which means that every child should have a legal father
- the right to a good and loving upbringing.

Muslim society places kindness to all children as a very high priority. Whether a child's parents are alive or dead, present or absent, the child must be provided for with the best possible care, either by relatives or by the state if need be.

Children, for their part, are expected to respect and love their parents with kindness, patience and good manners. Parents always believe they are more experienced, wise and right than their children, even if they are wrong. They feel that they are still the child's guardians (even if the child is fifty years old!) – so they should be treated with great understanding, compassion and respect.

'Show kindness to your parents and near relatives, orphans, the needy, and the neighbour.'

(surah 4:36)

Recommended rules of conduct towards parents

- Listen when parents speak. Never interrupt or argue with them.
- Do not walk in front of them.
- Do not sit down before they do.

Part 5   SHARI'AH

- Do not speak ill of them, or anyone else's parents.
- However much you disagree, do not say things to hurt them.
- When they get old, be aware of their increased physical weakness and possible mental weakness. This may be accompanied by impatience, lack of energy, increased sensitivity and misjudgement. Be aware, and increase your patience and kindness.
- Help them without being asked.
- Avoid anything that irritates them.

'Serve them with tenderness and humility, and say 'My Lord have mercy on them, just as they cared for me as a little child.'

(surah 17:23–4)

Recommended rules of conduct towards children

- Avoid over-confidence and false pride arising from your love for them, and be on your guard against misdeeds.
- Give them the best possible education, not just to be clever but also so that they may be able to earn a living.
- Help them to make happy marriages.
- Always deal with them justly and with love. Never be unfair.
- Don't be overprotective, or negligent.
- Don't put heavy burdens on them by trying to force them to do things beyond their capability, or by being disappointed with their achievements.
- Accept their gifts with appreciation.
- Train them in Muslim worship. They should begin learning prayer and fasting by the age of seven.

'He who has no compassion for our little ones, and does not acknowledge the honour due to our elders, is not one of us.'

(Hadith)

Old age

As far as Muslims are concerned, the family is the only place for the care of its old people. The idea of sending them away from those they have given life to, cared for, and brought up to adulthood, is shocking to a Muslim.

Muslim women sometimes wonder why women in the West go on making sacrifices for children who are not going to keep them in return. It makes no sense to them, and they cannot see how it can possibly be justified morally.

Grandparents are the head of the whole family.

'May his nose be rubbed in dust who found his parents approaching old age and did not enter Paradise by serving them.'

(Hadith)

FOR YOUR FOLDERS

- ▶ Read this unit carefully, and also the first part of the next unit. Explain why the mother's job is so vital in the Muslim home.
- ▶ How are children in a Muslim home expected to show their love and respect for their parents?
- ▶ How do you think living in an 'extended' family would be different from the parents and children situation common in Britain? In what ways might it be an advantage in helping people to grow together in loyalty and love?

THINGS TO DO

- ▶ Make a list of the various things that happen to old people in the West when they can no longer fend for themselves, and explain why Muslims are so shocked by Western practice.
- ▶ Make a list of the sorts of things or behaviour that you think spoil happy home life.

THINKING POINT

- Can Muslims sometimes cope better with their old people because of their stronger, bigger families? Is the strain of lack of privacy due to possible overcrowding less than the strain of loneliness and depression?

101

Father

A Muslim mother is expected to take responsibility for
- food for the hungry
- refuge for the weary
- hospitality for the guest
- comfort for the distressed
- peace for the troubled
- hope for the insecure
- encouragement for the weak.

The father is expected to *provide* the means whereby all this can actually be achieved, to *protect* the home, and generally to make the mother's role possible.

The father is responsible for bringing in money, and therefore it is his duty, as far as possible, to be strong, respected and honourable. Just as the mother's role involves far more than just cooking and cleaning, the father's involves leadership, responsibility and duty, and an involvement in the world of economics, business, trade and commerce.

The economic principles of Islam aim at building up a just society in which people behave responsibly and honestly, and are not just out to grab all they can for themselves.

Muslims bear in mind that whatever they do, it is known to God, and they will be held to account for it on the Day of Judgement.

Therefore they may not make earnings from
- falsehood, deceit or fraud
- robbery or burglary
- hoarding of foodstuffs and basic necessities in order to take advantage of hardship situations
- exploitation or artificial creation of shortages
- immoral practices
- production, sale and distribution of alcohol
- gambling or lotteries.

(See surahs 5:90–92, 2:275, 2:188, 4:2, 6:152, 7:85, 3:180, 9:34–35.)

Muslims should be honest, decent, truthful, trustworthy and responsible. They should not waste money irresponsibly, or use it for any dishonest purpose. Extravagance and waste are strongly discouraged. Employed people have a duty to their employers, and also to the families they are supporting.

*'Little but sufficient
is better than the abundant and alluring.'*

*'It is not poverty which I fear for you,
but that you might begin to desire the world
as others before you desired it, and it might
destroy you as it destroyed them!'*

A Muslim father is expected to provide for his family

*'Riches are sweet, and a source of blessing
for him who acquires them by the way;
but they are not blessed for
him who seeks them out of greed. He
is like one who eats but is not filled.'*

*'No-one has eaten better food
than what he earns with the toil of his own hands.'*
(Hadith)

Interest

Making interest on loaned money and in banking is
the basis of modern capitalism, but it is totally
forbidden by the Qur'an. (See surahs 2:278–9, 30:39,
3:130, etc.)
Apart from these basic principles, Islam lays down
other guidelines.

- All productive resources should be brought into
  use as far as possible, including unemployed
  people, unused land, water resources and
  mineral resources.
- Corrupt and harmful pursuits should be rooted
  out, even if they are highly profitable.
- Individual freedom may have to be sacrificed if it
  interferes with the good of the community, which
  must come first.

*'The parable of those who spend their wealth in the
way of God is that of a grain of corn; it grows
seven ears, and each year has 100 grains. God
gives enormous increase to whom He will; He
cares for all and He knows all.'*
(surah 2:261)

*'If the debtor is in difficulty, grant him time
until it is easy for him to repay. If only you knew
it, your repayment would actually be greater if
you cancelled the debt!'*
(surah 2:280)

Women

Women are not subservient to men in Muslim
societies. It is basic in Muslim society that the man is
responsible for the family's welfare and business
outside the home, but the woman has virtually
absolute rights within it so long as her behaviour
does not shame her provider.

No institution works well without a clear leader,
and therefore there should be one in every family
unit. Most Muslim women are quite happy for this

leader to be the man they love. If the man is not
worth respecting, divorce is a straightforward
matter, and the woman may look for a better one.
Sometimes the woman in a household is more
intelligent or organized or practical than the man, so
he will quite sensibly leave most matters to her – but
in Islam he is still responsible for her.

FOR YOUR FOLDERS

▶ Explain the role of a Muslim father
  towards his family. Do you think it is a
  good thing for the man to take
  responsibility for his household?
▶ Muslims value greatly the quality of
  'manhood'. What do you think this implies
  a in the home
  b at work
  c in society?

THINKING POINTS

- **Should a woman be obedient to her
  husband? Give reasons for your answer. In
  what circumstances do you think a Muslim
  woman should *not* be obedient to her
  husband?**
- **What kind of results might you expect in a
  household where the wife does not respect
  the husband? How should a husband earn
  his wife's respect?**

THINGS TO DO

▶ Make a list of a dozen jobs traditionally
  done by **a** men and **b** women. Put a
  tick against those jobs which you think
  would be acceptable to Muslims. Explain
  why certain jobs would *not* be
  acceptable.
▶ Copy out two of the sayings from the
  Qur'an or Hadith and explain what they
  teach about income.

A South Yemen woman doctor wears a veil in public

It is possible for Muslim women to go out to work, but in practice not many, as yet, do so. It is worth noting that women are well educated in Muslim countries and about 25 per cent of university students are women – so more employment for women will undoubtedly come about.

However, the idea of ending the difference between the roles of men and women is unthinkable to Muslims. They have observed how the West has tried to do away with traditional roles, with catastrophic consequences for sexual morality and child rearing and the break down of families, leading to stress, depression, crime and suicide.

It often comes as a shock for non-Muslims to discover what Muslims think of their societies. Europeans, for example, have become used to regarding themselves and their opinions as superior, although the need for a re-examination of morals and standards is becoming increasingly obvious.

In everyday life there are six things which are expressly forbidden to Muslims:

- premarital sex
- adultery (sex with someone who is married to someone else)
- drinking alcohol
- gambling
- making interest on loaned money
- eating forbidden meat.

The object of these rules is to prevent Muslims becoming slaves to cravings and selfish instincts, and damaging society by breaking up the family unit.

In Muslim eyes, the permissive society of the West has become so tolerant of sex outside marriage, illegitimacy, exploitation and greed, plus the behavioural patterns associated with drinking, drugs and gambling, as to be actually guilty of encouraging them.

All these things, according to Muslims, have contributed strongly to the pyschological and emotional stress in society, and have particularly damaged the family unit.

Muslims are appalled by the influence of Western television – the blatant advertising of alcohol, the portrayal of sex (both normal and perverted), the acceptance of so many things they regard as socially evil. There is no check on materialism, selfishness or greed. The young seem to be condoned when they live dangerously or selfishly, and the old are abandoned to end their days with strangers.

Many Muslims see only the bad, and regard the West as being corrupt and callous, with weak men who do not do anything to protect their women, children and old people.

Muslim women expect to be treated with respect. They certainly regard themselves as equal to the men – this was made quite clear in the Qur'an – but because of their biology they expect consideration. Men do not have to put up with menstruation, pregnancy, childbirth and suckling children. Men are not usually harassed because of their attractiveness, or forced to accept sex in order to 'get on' or not lose a job.

The powerful urges of nature are not denied in Islam – it is considered every woman's right to be a protected virgin, a beloved wife, a respected mother and a cherished grandmother – and therefore Muslim society does not like to see a woman obliged against her inclination to live alone or without protection, help, or a natural sexual relationship.

Islam tries to create a society in which belief in God is basic, and a person's honour is vital.

No one pretends, of course, that there are no weak people or criminals in Muslim society – of course there are. Not every citizen is a believer, and not every believer is perfect. Many give in to the increasing temptations of the modern world.

However, many Muslims would still rather live with a law that cut the hand off a thief than in a society whose youngsters had sexual freedom without marriage, resulting in the killing of millions of unborn babies and appalling unhappiness; or where people wander drunk in the streets, behave abusively, noisily and violently, and abandon their widowed, divorced and old people to loneliness.

TALKING POINTS

- Why do Muslims think it better for the family if mothers stay at home?
- Is the permissive society more cruel than the harsh extremes of Islamic law?

FOR YOUR FOLDERS

▶ Why are Muslim women often sorry for the women of the West? Are there any ways in which you think they might perhaps envy them? In what ways would they think that sexual permissiveness harmed
  a the individual
  b parents
  c unwanted children?

▶ Discuss the possibilities that a drop in moral standards is inevitably caused by
  a people no longer believing in God
  b permissive use of television, films, magazines, etc.

Muslim women scientists at al-Azhar university, Cairo

THE GUARDIAN
Thursday, January 5 1989

WE MUSLIM women can expect little sympathy from Christian feminists like Catherine Matheson (Gone to hell and back, December 22). But I do hope in the interests of a balanced argument that you will allow me to point out the bias against Islam in her article.

Muslim women were the first to have rights of property and inheritance 1,400 years ago (Qur'an 4:7–9) and there is nothing against women working when necessary. Some women are mistreated in every society and a group equally tragic as the one in Ms Matheson's article could be found at any battered women's hostel in this country. Real women's liberation is to be found in Islam. Why else would millions of modern women choose to be Muslims?
Zahara Barry
UK Islamic Propagation Centre International, Birmingham

The Shari'ah tries to maintain values in societies that are becoming increasingly corrupt. Millions of Muslim women do not go round wearing black tent-like veils, but simply dress modestly according to the customs of their particular country.

Some traditional costumes are not acceptable as Muslim because they are not modest – they are too attention-seeking, by being either too revealing or too colourful. Muslim dress is always modest.

Muslim women are no more nor less ugly than other women, but they do not flaunt their attractions. They certainly should not wear clothes that are revealing, low-cut, short, transparent or tight. To dress in such a way is to be regarded as 'naked', and the only object in dressing like that must be to stir up the passions of men, which is not fair, kind or sensible.

Passions, if not under control, cause endless hurt and disturbance, therefore a woman who deliberately causes temptation is badly thought of. Muslims regard sex as healthy and wholesome, but not to be indulged in when it causes hurt to others or to self. They believe that sexual freedom harms individuals, parents, unwanted children, and the security of other families. Therefore behaviour and dress should be studied carefully.

Muslim women expect to be appreciated for their minds and characters, not just for their bodies. Modest dress does not degrade women, but it discourages lust in men.

In practical terms, many women prefer the traditional long dress and head-veil (**hejab**) because

- it is easy and practical
- it removes the burden of having to look beautiful
- it covers up the less-than-perfect and disguises the results of increasing age, comfortable diets, etc.

Purdah

Dressing in such a way that the body and face are not 'visible' is called **purdah**.

This is much misunderstood in the West. Covering the face is a matter of local tradition in certain countries, and is not actually part of Islam. In certain parts of the world women hide their faces from strangers, yet are not devout Muslims. Elsewhere very devout Muslim women do not veil because this would be regarded as odd, or attention-seeking, which defeats the object.

However, where Muslim women are reluctant to talk to strangers, wearing a veil or **chador** gives complete privacy. They can get on with their business without being disturbed, flirted with, or made the object of unwanted attention. Since they cannot be recognized, they can ignore people they do not wish to meet or spend time with on the streets.

Wearing a veil shows a woman to be virtuous and modest, and not the type to welcome attention from male strangers who are not her business. Amongst family and friends, and in female company, the veil comes off.

In recent years, some women who had previously been unveiled have started wearing the chador for political reasons. The anonymity and 'disguise' it offers can sometimes be abused – the chador has been used to disguise terrorists or escaping criminals.

Sadly, in this modern world, in some places veiled women are no longer 'untouchable' but are subjected to cat-calls and abuse from people who regard them as old-fashioned and stupid, or who are actively anti-religious.

Wearing the black chador

Women modestly dressed

*'Indecency disfigures everything,
modesty adds to the charm.'*

(Hadith)

Protection

In the West, people often consider Muslims make too much fuss when they demand separate education for teenage boys and girls, ask girls to wear trousers for PE, cover their legs even when swimming, and insist on them covering their arms and legs in the street.

But Muslims consider themselves to be realistic and unhypocritical. Sexual attraction starts in the young, and young girls need

- protection from exploitation
- providing with a husband as soon as they show interest in and readiness for sex. This is regarded as being much more sensible and honourable than allowing sex before marriage.

Naked arms and legs are regarded as sexually provocative to a normal male, and outrageous in an older woman. A Muslim grandmother would be horrified at the thought of revealing half her body to the gaze of all and sundry, uncovering her hair – which might be going thin or grey – and perhaps dying it blue, or applying obvious make-up to her face.

Muslim women expect to be allowed to consult female doctors and not have male strangers examining their bodies, and men expect to be examined by male doctors. Men are not allowed to wash the bodies of deceased women, unless they are close relatives.

FOR DISCUSSION

▶ Has a female western tourist the right to walk through Muslim streets in shorts and a sun-top, or a transparent blouse? What sort of reaction might she expect if she does so?

'Modesty and faith are joined closely together; if either of them is lost, the other goes also.'

'Every religion has a special character; the characteristic of Islam is modesty.'

(Hadith)

THINGS TO DO

▶ Make a list of the kind of garments often worn by women in various countries of the world that would be unacceptable to a strict Muslim woman.

FOR YOUR FOLDERS

▶ People often think that veiled women are treated as inferior to the men. What are the real aims of Muslim clothing?
▶ Should Muslims who come to live in the West accept the West's standards and customs and give up their own?
▶ Make a list of what Muslim women regard as the advantages of purdah. Why would dressing like this not appeal to all women?

Muslim bridal couple

Bringing a new husband or wife into the family is a very serious business, and never to be taken lightly. Two completely separate family units will be joined by the marriage, with all its implications, unless the new partner happens to have been chosen from the same family.

It is quite normal in Islam for relatives outside the immediate family to marry, and thought preferable that the new husband or wife is someone whose character and background is well known and understood.

Muslims are urged to choose their partners very carefully, and to remain loyal to them for the rest of their lives, for the girl will become a mother, in due course, and the youth a father.

Arranged marriages

For this reason, Muslim marriages are often arranged for young couples by their parents. In the West, most young people think it is natural to fall in love, get engaged, and then married. Muslims sometimes regard 'being under the influence of love' as a dangerous and intoxicating state of mind that could easily cloud the judgement.

Parents will always seek to find good, compatible partners for their children, and they may not approve of an unwise romance.

However, marriages should always be with the consent of both partners, and they have the right to disagree with the parent's choice. A forced marriage is usually doomed to failure.

The wedding

The actual ceremony is a simple affair, and the bride does not even have to go, so long as she sends two witnesses of her agreement.

If the wedding is to take place at a mosque she may wear a white wedding dress. If she is from Pakistan she will put on scarlet shalwar trousers and tunic, and all the gold jewellery she owns. She may paint a pattern in red henna on the palms of her hands and the soles of her feet.

The wedding takes only a few moments, and consists of readings from the Qur'an, the exchange of vows in front of witnesses, and prayers. No special religious official is necessary – any two adult male witnesses will do; but often the **imam** (teacher) is present for the happy occasion.

Walima

The **walima** is a party given for all friends and family. It usually consists of a sumptuous meal, and lots of presents are given, sometimes money. It takes place within three days of the wedding.

As this is a religious occasion, the women celebrate separately from the men. It is considered very wrong for an invited person not to attend.

Money matters

Muslim women have the right to be paid for being a housewife, and for breast-feeding their own children. A woman's salary, if she goes out to work, is regarded as her own and not her husband's. Any property she may own before marriage remains hers, and she does not have to give it to her husband unless she wishes.

Even if he is poor, the husband is expected to provide for her. A woman does not have to take her husband's name, but keeps her own.

Mixed marriages

Muslim boys may marry Christians and Jews, but Muslim girls are not permitted to marry non-Muslims because in Islam the children have to take the religion of the father, and so would become non-Muslims. If a youth wishes to marry a Hindu, Sikh or Buddhist girl, it is only permitted if she converts to Islam.

'A woman is sought in marriage
on account of four things:
her property,
her family,
her beauty,
her piety.
Seek to win one for
the sake of her piety.'

(Hadith)

'Do not marry only for the sake of beauty; the beauty may become the cause of moral decline. Do not marry for the sake of wealth, for this may become the cause of disobedience. Marry rather on the grounds of religious devotion.'

(Hadith)

'The best of treasures is a good wife. She is pleasing to her husband's eyes, obedient to his word, and watchful over his possessions in his absence; and the best of you are those who treat their wives best.'

(Hadith)

FOR YOUR FOLDERS

► Why do Muslims consider marrying 'under the influence of love' to be a dangerous practice?
► What kind of qualities does a Muslim look for in a bride?

TEENAGE BRIDE AND THE LAW

SINCE Mr Tariq Raja has lived in this country for at least 14 years, I assume he is, by now, well acquainted with our laws.

How, then, can he confidently assert (Herald Express March 5) that his daughter's "husband" will live with her as "man and wife" while she is still under 16? He must know that sex with an under-age teenager is a criminal offence!

Or is he fully confident that this law will join a long list of our laws (ritual slaughter of animals, crash helmets, to name but two) conveniently adjusted to suit those people of a different religion and culture?

The laws governing under-age sex were made to protect our young from exploitation and abuse, and the fact that Mr Raja's religion permits what we have outlawed matters not a jot.

If his religion and customs mean so much to Mr Raja, then why does he not return to live where such things are in keeping?

I have one word of advice for him. Study the phrase "when in Rome do as the Romans do." It is very pertinent when wishing to live among the Romans!

Source: Torquay Herald Express

TALKING POINTS

● This letter concerns a Muslim girl who was married at the age of fourteen. Why might a Muslim family consider it a sensible thing for a girl to marry at that age? Why might Western law be regarded in Muslim eyes as hypocritical?
● Is it better for a girl to choose her own husband, or does the arranged marriage system have any advantages for the young couple?
● How important do you think it is for a person to marry someone who shares the same religious beliefs?

Polygamy

Sometimes a man may marry more than one woman. The Prophet Muhammad had thirteen wives after the death of his beloved Khadijah; other Muslim men are allowed four wives, but only on certain conditions:

- The first wife should give permission.
- Later wives must not be a cause of distress.
- All wives must must be treated equally, i.e. equal homes, gifts, and nights spent with each in turn unless permission is given by the wife involved.
- Making love equally is not required (or possible!), but sharing time equally is.

Some elderly wives are quite pleased for the husband to take on a younger wife, especially if she is a good worker and may have had modern training, for example as a nurse.

Reasons

Sometimes the reasons for polygamy are based on the needs of the community, particularly if there is a surplus of women as, for example, after a war. It is considered unkind for women to be condemned to spinsterhood without the chance to become cherished mothers in a household.

The idea of unmarried mothers appals Muslims, neither do they think much of ageing wives being cast out the moment a man allows himself to fall for a younger woman.

The spirit of Islam is to protect the weak and vulnerable, and not leave women to fend for themselves if they do not wish to do so.

Polygamy may also be allowed if a wife is barren and the husband wants children, or if a wife is unable to cope with the household through chronic sickness.

*'The rights of a woman are sacred;
ensure that women are maintained in
the rights assigned to them.'*

*'The lowest person in the sight of God
will be the man who is intimate with his wife
and then broadcasts her secrets.'*

(Hadith)

Adultery

Muslims regard the stealing of another man's wife as the most dishonourable and shameful thing a man can do. It is taken for granted that an unscrupulous man knows how to arouse a woman and seduce her, and could easily take advantage of her.

Adultery, giving in to having a sexual relationship with someone other than husband or wife, is the most dangerous threat of all to a family, and most people find it almost impossible to forgive because the hurt and betrayal is too great. Once discovered, trust has gone.

Therefore Muslim men are forbidden to tempt married women, and a wife should never willingly betray her husband's trust. A good wife should prefer death to dishonour.

When adultery is discovered it is despised, and the penalty according to the Qur'an should be a flogging of 100 lashes. Sometimes adulterers are even put to death, but this is a local custom and goes beyond the statement in the Qur'an, although some Muslims justify it from Hadith.

Non-Muslims may disagree with such severe punishment for adultery, but Muslims cannot understand why other cultures make divorce laws so difficult and traumatic. For them divorce (although disapproved of) is quick, dignified and simple, and adultery therefore shows lack of self-control and a breaking of the family honour.

*'Either keep your wife honestly,
or put her away from you with kindness.
Do not force a woman to stay with you who wishes
to leave. The man who does that only injures
himself.'*

(surah 2:231)

Divorce

Not all Muslim marriages are perfect, of course, and some unfortunately do break down – though nowhere near so many as in the West. A man or woman could be disappointed and dissatisfied with their spouse for good reason, and be so unhappy that they seek love elsewhere.

If this happens, divorce is the only honourable course of action.

In Shari'at law this is the 'allowed' practice most disapproved of, and marriages should only be terminated as a last resort, after every effort has been made to put the problem right. The entire family of both parties gets involved, since the ending of a marriage is almost like a death, splitting up the close unit.

If the differences cannot be resolved, Muslims do not consider it right for a person to be forced to live with someone who no longer loves them. Divorce is quick and easy, and the woman is to be provided for fairly. Children are to be paid for, and usually go to the custody of the father after breast-feeding.

This seems hard to Westerners who are used to custody going to the mother, but Muslims disapprove of young women being stranded with babies and infants, unable to find another man to take them on, and being condemned to a lonely struggle supported by the state. In Islam it is expected that a girl will remarry – indeed her friends and relatives will all push forward suitors – and will soon bear more children.

This is considered far more natural and kinder than the fate of 'emancipated' women, who may end up exhausted, bitter and resentful, desperately lonely, and unable to control the growing wildness of their fatherless offspring.

The procedure of stating 'I divorce you' three times (**ta'alaq**) is not as simple as Westerners think. One month must pass between the first two statements. Meanwhile the couple must live in the same house without physical contact; if the physical relationship is resumed, the marriage continues unbroken. Relatives and friends do all they can to reconcile the couple. Only after three months with no reconciliation is the divorce complete.

Remarriage cannot happen for four months, to be sure that the woman is not pregnant, so that there will be no doubt as to the fatherhood of a child. If she is pregnant, she may not remarry until after the child is born. Couples who regret divorce may easily remarry, but if they divorce and wish to remarry a third time, they should marry a different person in between.

FOR YOUR FOLDERS

▶ How do Islamic principles of marriage and divorce compare with those in the West, in your opinion? Give reasons for your answer.

▶ Do you think it can be possible for a Muslim woman to accept that her husband has taken another wife? Give reasons for your answer.

TALKING POINTS

● **The Qur'an states that all wives should be treated equally. In practical terms, this is impossible so does it really mean that no man should have more than one wife?**

● **Is it better for a married couple to stick together 'for better, for worse', no matter how bad the 'worse' part happens to be? What unfortunate results can come about, particularly for women, after a divorce?**

THINKING POINTS

● **Why is it a serious matter for a woman to be divorced by her husband in a Muslim society? Why would most women not want to be divorced unless they had already found another man to marry?**

● **Why are the penalties for adultery so severe in Islam?**

THINGS TO DO

▶ Make a list of the conditions under which a Muslim man might take more than one wife into his household.

▶ Read the press cuttings on p. 120. State the reasons given in the letters why some people might think polygamy was kinder than forcing women to live alone if they do not want to.

The head of the family whispers the Adhan and Iqamah

The birth of every new baby should be an eagerly awaited event, and in Muslim families virtually no babies are born illegitimate or unwanted. Babies are not regarded as 'accidents' or 'mistakes', but as 'gifts from God'. A large number of children is regarded as a great blessing.

The new baby is welcomed into the **ummah** – the one big family of Islam – as soon as it is born. The head of the family takes the baby into his arms and whispers the call to prayer (the **adhan**) in the right ear and the command to rise and worship (the **iqamah**) in the left ear. Sometimes the words are whispered down a hollow reed or tube. Thus, the first word a baby ever hears is 'God'.

Next comes the tahnik, when a tiny piece of sugar, date or honey is placed in the baby's mouth by the oldest or most respected relative, perhaps the grandfather or a much-loved elderly aunt. This is to symbolize making the child 'sweet' – obedient and kind. Prayers for the baby and the family follow.

Seven days after birth comes aqiqah, when relatives and friends come to a feast and the baby is named.

The baby's head is shaved, and by tradition the same weight as the hair in gold or silver is set aside for the poor. Even if the baby is bald, a money donation is still given, and usually the amount is well above the weight of the hair.

Next comes a sacrifice, the ancient practice of thanksgiving – two animals are offered for a boy and one for a girl. The meat is cooked and shared with the visitors and the poor.

The choice of name is important, and it is usually a family name or one of the names from the Prophet's family. Names declaring that the baby possesses certain excellent moral qualities are avoided, and names suggesting slavery to anyone other than God are forbidden. Some of the best names start with '**Abd**' which means 'slave', added to one of the names of God, e.g. Abdullah, Abdul Rahman, Abdul Karim (Servant of God, Slave of the Merciful, Slave of the Generous One).

The parent of a first-born child may then drop their own name and become known by the name of the child. So, if the child is called Husain ibn (son of) Dawud, the parents become Abu Husain (father of Husain) and Umm Husain (mother of Husain).

If the baby is a boy, he must then be circumcised. **Khitan**, or circumcision, is the practice of cutting the foreskin from the penis – the sign and practice of all the prophets of Allah. This is sometimes done at the same time as aqiqah if the baby is well and there is no need for delay.

If the baby is not healthy circumcision can be left for a few months. In some places, however, it has become a kind of initiation into manhood, and takes place when the boy is between seven and ten years old. In Turkey, the boy is dressed up like a little prince, and the circumcision takes place at a family party.

If the ceremony was left until after the age of ten, it would subject the boy to a form of shamefulness in Muslim eyes, and the parents would be considered cruel and neglectful.

Circumcision is not cruel. It is a healthy practice, particularly in hot areas of the world, and avoids discomfort and disease. It in no way prevents the boy from enjoying a sexual relationship later on.

On the fourth birthday comes **bismillah**, the occasion when the child learns the first lesson from the Qur'an by heart – 'In the name of God, the Compassionate, the Merciful'. The child has to repeat each word carefully and is taught how to pray. The education as a Muslim has begun.

Little Turkish boy dressed ready for circumcision

FOR DISCUSSION

▶ Why do you think Muslims regard it as important to start training children in the faith early?
▶ Why would a Muslim not want to have the name Abdul Muhammad or Abdul Hussein, but would be pleased to be called Abdullah or Abdul Rahman?

THINGS TO DO

▶ Look at the picture of a Turkish boy. Explain why he is dressed like this, what will soon happen to him, and why.
▶ Explain why most Muslims have their boys circumcised shortly after birth.
▶ See if you can find out the figures for the number of abortions carried out on babies in Britain over the last few years. Make a chart to show the numbers.

QUICK QUIZ

▶ What is meant by ummah?
▶ What are the first words a Muslim baby should hear?
▶ What is the tahnik?
▶ What happens at aqiqah?
▶ What sort of name should not be given to a baby?
▶ What happens on a Muslim's fourth birthday?

THINKING POINT

● Whatever *your* views on the right to abort babies, why do you think a Muslim would find these figures very shocking and sad, and conclude that British men were weak and lacking in responsibility?

FOR YOUR FOLDERS

▶ Imagine that you are a guest in a Muslim home where a baby has just been born. Write to a friend describing what celebrations and customs took place for the first week of the baby's life.

'God fixes the time-span for all things. It is He who causes both laughter and grief; it is He who causes people to die and to be born; it is He who caused male and female; it is He who will re-create us anew.'

(surah 53:42–7)

'When a person dies his deeds come to an end except in respect of three matters which are left behind: a continuing charity, knowledge which still brings benefit, and righteous offspring to pray for him.'

(Hadith)

Saying goodbye to a beloved member of the family causes deep sorrow and pain, and a terrible sensation of loss. It is natural for those left behind to wonder how on earth they will be able to continue without the loved one.

Yet Muslims, if they have lived their lives constantly according to Shari'ah, have been preparing for this day from the moment of birth, and hope to face the passing with calmness and acceptance.

Some people do not care whether there is life after death or not. Others do not believe in it at all. But Muslims are certain that all humans belong to God and will return to Him. They do not see death as the end of life, but the time when a person withdraws from the earthly family before going to be close to God.

The separation may seem long to those left behind, but a consoling feeling of closeness is renewed during prayer and at each family festival.

Not to care about life after death is unreasonable, since we are certain that all humans die.

Muslim funeral

*'Does Man think that We shall not assemble his bones?
Yes, surely, yes – We are able to restore even his finger-prints.'*

(surah 75:3–4)

The last word

When a Muslim knows death is approaching, friends and relatives are sent for and gather around the bed. The dying one asks for forgiveness and blessing from the loved ones and from God. Just as the first word heard by a Muslim is 'God', so it should also be the last word uttered or heard, if possible.

The waiting

Muslims believe that the soul waits in **barzakh** until the Day of Judgement (see p. 52). Judgement Day, or the Day of Resurrection, may not come for centuries, but unlike earth time this will pass in a flash – for those in barzakh are outside time.

At the Judgement Day God will deal with everyone, living and dead. Since the dead will have their bodies restored, cremation is forbidden, and all Muslims are buried in the earth.

The final salah

Grief is normal and expected, but shrieking and other excesses are regarded as lack of faith.

As soon as possible after death the body is given the final ritual washing and prayers. Hospitals may be alarmed if relatives come and ask for the corpse of a newly-deceased, but Muslims believe it is not fitting to leave this last service to strangers.

The washing, which is a complete one, or **ghusl** (see p. 58), can either take place at the mosque, in a community facility, or at home. Afterwards, the corpse is anointed with scents or spices and wrapped in a shroud made of unsewn sheets of white cloth, three for a man and five for a woman.

Martyrs are buried unwashed, with their blood, preferably at the place where they fell.

No difference is made whether a person is rich or poor, of great importance or very humble. Death has levelled them, they are the same. The shroud cloths may be the precious ones dipped in Zamzam water on Hajj.

The prayers are called **Salat ul Janaza** – the usual salah words but with no prostrations to earth. Some special words are added, including:

'O Allah, forgive us all, the living and the dead; those near at hand and those far away; keep those of us who remain here always true to Your will; keep those who are experiencing death steadfast in strong faith.'

The funeral

Funerals should be simple and inexpensive. Extravagance is forbidden, and since there is no class system for the dead, there are no special cemeteries for leaders.

Muslims prefer that coffins should not be used, except to comply with special regulations for health reasons. The body should be buried simply in the earth, not wasting precious wood, and should be carried to the cemetery rather than taken in a vehicle. Walking is considered more respectful than riding comfortably.

Muslims request burial with the face turned to the right, facing Makkah. It is therefore preferable if they can have their own cemeteries, or their own special plot, because if cemeteries are organized according to garden design or the customs of another religion, Muslims may not be able to have their graves facing in the right direction. Also, Muslims only allow one body per grave, and this sometimes causes a problem for local authorities.

As the body is lowered, they say:

'In the name of God we commit you to the earth, according to the Way of the Prophet of God.'

A little earth is then thrown down with the words:

'We created you from it, and return you into it, and from it We will raise you a second time.'
(surah 20:55)

Money should not be spent on tombstones or memorials, but donations given to the poor. The only writing on the grave should be the person's name.

Mourning should not last for more than three days, except for widows who may mourn for four months and ten days, and should not remarry during that period.

Shi'ites (see p. 136) hold memorial gatherings known as rawdahs on the fortieth day, but these are disapproved of by Sunni Muslims (see p. 91).

Any outstanding debts are paid off by the relatives, and the bereaved family is visited by countless well-wishers who help them over their grief by not abandoning them to loneliness. They often fill the house of the deceased for weeks,

bringing their own cooked food so as not to be a burden, and do not withdraw until they are sure the bereaved person is ready to cope again.

'To God we belong and to Him we return.'
(surah 96:8, 2:156, 28:70)

FOR YOUR FOLDERS

▶ Give reasons why it is not thought to be a good thing for Muslims to show too much grief at a funeral, or to pay for an expensive tombstone. How are dead Muslims best honoured and remembered?
▶ Why do Muslims prefer to have their own cemeteries if possible?

THINGS TO DO

▶ Imagine you are invited to the funeral of a Muslim boy. Give a brief outline of what happens from the moment of his death to his burial.
▶ Construct a diagram for a cemetery with a special area set aside for Muslim graves. Indicate on it the directions of the East and of Makkah.
▶ Copy out one of the prayers or passages from the Qur'an or Hadith. What does this passage reveal about the belief of Muslims about the afterlife?

TALKING POINTS

● In 1975 only 51 local authorities in Britain gave special burial plots to Muslims. Should Muslims accept local customs, and give up their own?
● Bereaved people should be left alone to get over it. Too many visitors are just a burden. You cannot make rules to control personal grief.
● Muslim burial practices shouldn't be allowed to shock and upset the neighbours.

Muslim laws about food and drink are not a matter of likes and dislikes, but of discipline. Since Muslims believe that every thought and action must be dedicated to God, and His will accepted, so the basic need to eat must also be under discipline.

The Qur'an ordered certain foods to be 'haram' or 'forbidden'. Any food not declared haram is quite lawful for the Muslim to eat, or 'halal'.
The unlawful foods include:

- any product made from a pig
- meat containing blood
- meat from an animal which 'dies of itself' due to disease or other natural causes
- any flesh-eating animal
- any animal which has been strangled, beaten to death, killed by a fall, gored by another animal, or partially eaten by another animal.
- any animal sacrificed to idols.

(see surah 5:3–4.)
Muslims consider that eating certain things, such as blood or dead meat with congealed blood in it, would disgust any refined person. If an animal dies by one of the methods outlined above, it is presumed that its blood will have congealed, and its flesh will have become carrion. Muslims should not eat anything of that nature, or anything dedicated to superstition. A similar rule applied to Jews and to the early Christians (see Acts 15:29).

Halal killing

Animals which do not eat other animals are lawful food, but they must be killed according to the halal (permitted) method. This means that they must have the jugular severed by a sharp knife, while the name of God is invoked.

Sometimes non-Muslims not used to animal slaughter think this method is barbaric and cruel (though they may not know how their own meat is killed!). Muslims regard their method as being the kindest there is, and refuse to eat meat killed any other way.

Muslims do not eat animals which have been killed by electrocution or shooting, which they regard as very cruel methods. (They also disapprove of factory farming and animal experimentation.)

Pronouncing the name of God is a rite to call attention to the fact that Muslims are not taking life thoughtlessly, but solemnly for food, with the permission of God, to whom the life is being returned.

The principle is of kindness to the animal. If one creature has to die to provide food for another, it should be killed as swiftly and painlessly as possible. It should not have to die in the terror of a slaughterhouse atmosphere, but be gently led away, not knowing its fate, and killed with compassion.

Most people do not like the thought of killing animals at all, and would not wish to have to do it themselves. Some argue that the halal method is cruel, and that it is kinder to stun the animal with an electric shock first. Muslims insist that when this is done it is not kinder at all. If a human patient had to be stunned like this, an anaesthetic would be given first! Passing a high-voltage electric current through an animal's brain so that it is unable to feel the knife is illogical.

Permitted foods

Muslims are allowed to eat fish, poultry, all the meat of sheep, goats and camels, and game caught by hunting animals which are trained not to kill out of savagery or their own appetite, but for their trainer's needs. In this case, the name of God can be pronounced when the hawk or dog releases the quarry.

Chicken is one of the meats most frequently eaten. All fruit, grains and vegetables are permitted. In an emergency, if nothing else is available, anything edible becomes permitted.

'O ye who believe!
Eat of the good things that We have provided for you, and be grateful to God if it is Him you worship. He has only forbidden you meat of an animal that dies of itself, and blood, and the flesh of pigs, and that on which any other name has been invoked besides that of God. But if one is forced because there is no other choice, then one can eat other food without being guilty.'
(surah 2:173, see also surahs 5:4 and 6:145)

'Why should you not eat of meats on which God's name has been pronounced, since He has explained in detail what is forbidden to you – except under compulsion of necessity?'
(surah 6:119)

Social consequences in non-Muslim society

These laws greatly affect the Muslim's ability to mix socially with non-Muslim neighbours, since nearly all meat in the West has been killed by electrocution or firing a bolt into an animal's brain, and is therefore forbidden to Muslims. They should not buy meat from a market unless it is known to be halal.

If they cannot get access to halal meat, they are obliged to follow a vegetarian diet, although they may not wish to be vegetarians.

Non-vegetarians may not realize that if Muslims are carrying out the ban on pork products and non-halal meat, it not only means that they cannot eat bacon, pork sausages, ham, tinned luncheon meat, or salami, but a whole range of other products is forbidden – certain bread, biscuits, soups, chocolate, ice-cream, fried breakfasts – in fact anything that contains animal fat as opposed to vegetable fat. You have to examine every packet!

Many Muslims actually fear eating pork by accident, thinking it will make them ill. Non-Muslims might scoff at this, but it is becoming increasingly known that pork products are responsible for many allergy conditions.

The ban against pork products is shared by Jews, and Muslims think it should also be shared by Christians, who have apparently ignored completely the example of Jesus, who never ate pork himself and left instructions that the laws of God were not to be broken.

Many Muslim children do not eat school dinners because of the food restrictions.

Alcohol

Muslims should not only refuse alcohol, they should really not even be in a place where alcohol is served. If they do go, to be sociable to a non-Muslim friend, they would be embarrassed if the conversation turned to the subject of religion – for a Muslim should not discuss God or the Qur'an in the presence of alcohol.

FOR YOUR FOLDERS

▶ It is the duty of a Muslim wife to safeguard the purity of the home, and make sure all the food eaten is halal. Explain what is meant by halal. What laws regarding food and drink do Muslims have?

▶ What difficulties do you think a Muslim family might have in keeping the food laws?

THINKING POINTS

● **Why do Muslims pronounce the name of God when slaughtering an animal?**

● **What is the intention behind halal killing? Why would a Muslim not be shocked by the thought of slaughtering a sheep in his or her own garden? Discuss the reasons why such an action gives offence in the West.**

THINGS TO DO

▶ Make a collection of lists of ingredients on food packets. Underline the words 'animal fat' each time.

▶ Read the letter about halal killing on p. 120. On what grounds do Muslims argue that halal killing is not cruel?

FOR DISCUSSION

▶ People shouldn't eat meat if they are not prepared to be responsible for the animal's slaughter in the kindest way.

58 DIFFICULTIES IN NON-MUSLIM COMMUNITIES 1

School

School problems fall into four main areas:
- immodest dress, especially in compulsory PE lessons
- not separating boys and girls after the age of ten
- sexual instruction in the classroom
- religious instruction that is either Christian or Jewish (i.e. Bible based), or Islam presented in an incorrect manner.

Muslims consider that:
- girls and boys should be educated separately as soon as their sexual urges begin, to protect them, and make them concentrate on lessons
- girls should not be forced to wear short skirts – the uniform should allow trousers for girls
- PE should be carried out in track suits
- communal showers are immodest and should not be forced on girls or boys
- sex should not be discussed in class, especially in a mixed-sex class.

Religious education

This can be a problem if it is concerned with Bible material only (since the Muslim interpretation of many passages is different, e.g. the sacrifice of Isma'il rather than Isaac), or if it teaches Islam with prejudice, or inaccurately.

Muslims do not mind knowing about other religions, but cannot agree with teachers who:
- believe nothing themselves
- regard Muslims as non-believers, and try to convert them to Christianity
- think all religions are equal.

Muslims are also expected to withdraw from school worship because they will not pray to Jesus or 'in Jesus' name'; they must also be left out of preparations for Christmas and Easter.

FOR YOUR FOLDERS
▶ How does Shari'ah make life complicated for Muslim girls in a Western school? Do you think Muslim girls should give up their customs and adopt the Western ways, or should they have allowances made for them? Give reasons for your answer.

THINGS TO DO
▶ Imagine you are a Muslim parent. Write a letter to the head teacher of your daughter's school explaining the problems she is facing, and why you take your point of view so seriously.

Prayer

Some employers are not sympathetic if workers want to break off for a few moments to pray. Often there is no private place for them to go, or facilities to wash first.

Non-Muslims are surprised to see people washing their feet in a high sink, and some even think it is dirty – although the opposite is obviously the case.

Prayer times are flexible, and tend to follow the normal breaks of the day, so timing should not really be a problem, but it is not always easy to find somewhere quiet where you will not be laughed at. In Muslim countries, of course, people can set aside an area and pray anywhere, while life goes on around them, and no one thinks anything of it.

Friday prayers

Muslim men require time off to go to the mosque for an hour or so during Friday lunchtime, the time taken depending on the distance from the mosque.

It is expected that young boys should go too, so they often miss some lessons before or after lunch.

Ramadan

Non-Muslims who have not experienced fasting can have no idea of the effects it sometimes has on people. Some get bad-tempered, impatient, or light-headed and giggly; many feel sick or faint at certain times; most feel very tired and drained of energy in the afternoons until their bodies get used to the regime of no food or drink until evening. Some find it hard to eat at night, even when allowed, and become quite weak by the end of the thirty days (see p. 70).

It becomes very difficult to do hard physical work. Teachers might tell pupils off for being sleepy or lazy, without realizing that a pupil is probably very hungry and may have been up until 3 a.m. with the family the previous night.

In a Muslim country, the whole system is sympathetic, and people might be able to take it easy, or sleep, during the day.

Medical treatment

It is not thought proper for a Muslim woman or girl to be examined by a male doctor, or vice versa. This is not usually a problem in a group practice, where you can choose a doctor.

The only major problem comes when there is no choice of doctor in hospital, and when a Muslim dies in hospital.

Muslims find the 'red tape' difficult to put up with, and expect to be with their relatives when they die, and to take them away immediately for washing, prayers and burial.

Dogs

Many non-Muslims keep dogs in their houses, and are pleased if they paw or snuffle at guests as a sign of affection. Muslims do not dislike dogs, but they are regarded as ritually unclean animals, so if a dog touches them before prayers they have to change their clothes as well as doing the ritual wash. If a person walking a dog meets a Muslim friend, they should not be surprised if the Muslim backs away!

Airports now send Alsation dogs on board to sniff out drugs and explosives. This presents a problem when the plane is bound for the Middle East, especially planes for Hajj, since on any long journey many Muslims will want to pray at the correct times. Officials might suspect any fuss made to be due to terrorists' fearing detection, when really it is only that the plane was prepared for prayer, and was then made unclean again.

Prison

The two main problems here are attitudes to crime and prison visitors. Non-Muslims are allowed the visit of a priest – but there are no priests in Islam, and an imam (teacher) has no official capacity. Any adult male could be an imam; this could include relatives of the inmate, and hence arouse charges of unfair privilege.

Muslims do not automatically understand the Western attitude to crime. Theft is regarded as particularly shameful to a Muslim, and would bring dishonour on the criminal's entire family.

On the other hand, to kill in defence of your honour is understood, if not legally condoned.

FOR YOUR FOLDERS

▶ How far do you think it is true that living according to Shari'ah makes it impossible for Muslims to mix socially with a non-Muslim community?

▶ How does the fact that imams are not paid priests affect the visitors allowed for Muslims in prison or hospital?

FOR DISCUSSION

▶ Why might non-Muslim prisoners or patients think Muslims were getting an unfair advantage? *Are* they getting an advantage, or are they really being deprived?

▶ Muslims who live in the West ought to accept the West's standards and customs and give up their own.

THINGS TO DO

▶ Imagine you are a Muslim who has recently arrived in Britain. You are finding things difficult and strange – the weather, food, shops, the people on the streets, the mosque in a converted house. Write a letter back home describing some of your experiences and problems.

Islam versus dancing

SIR — Your article on Islam in Egypt ("Two legs bad, if they wriggle", May 21st) refers to the permissibility of dancing.

In Islamic law, there are graduations between Halal (lawful) and Haram (unlawful). Some acts do not come within either category and are therefore permissible.

Hymns, carols, patriotic songs, national anthems and dancing and singing by children are allowed in Islam. But there is a big difference between these and the ballet, belly-dancing, rock music and sensuous songs of our time.

Ballet dancing is doubly Haram, so to speak. First, because any public dancing by females is Haram. Second, because wearing short skirts by females in public, except in the presence of their husbands, excites passion and is thus Haram as well. It also violates Islamic injunctions regarding decent covering of the body.

Dhaka,   A.B. Sarker
Bangladesh

(*The Economist*, 25 June 1988)

Cultural [...] has it[...]

MRS S. Cornish suggests t[...] Mr Tariq Raja, whose yo[...] daughter has recently marri[...] should cast off his own cult[...] and customs in favour of ou[...] since he chooses to live in [...] country.

We hear a lot of this, usu[...] from those who would pre[...] to see no Asian or black peo[...] in our streets, but pretend th[...] objection is not to colour [...] skin, but to foreigners w[...] "won't fit in with us."

This may not apply to [...] Cornish. I hope it does not.

But really, the phrase "wl[...] in Rome, do as the Rom[...] do" should stick in the thr[...] of anyone English.

Over several hundred ye[...] very many from these isla[...] have emigrated to far-fl[...] parts of the world, to In[...] Africa and Australia, and t[...]

The advantages of polygamy

Dear Sir,
Now that the Lambeth Conference says that polygamy is OK, perhaps, from now on, Muslims will be spared the customary derisory remarks about the "four wives". There is nothing wrong with polygamy – if it is for the right reasons, especially when the choice for some women is not between polygamy and monogamy but between polygamy and divorce.

Contrary to popular belief, the purpose of polygamy in Islam has never been to satisfy the lustful needs of some men, but, rather, to satisfy the needs of certain women, such as orphans or widows who are poor, and God knows there are many of those in post-drought Africa, for whom marriage is the only way to have a normal share in life. The near impossible condition attached is that the husband should give each of his wives exactly the same as the others: an horrendous task which a one-wifed man such as myself would not even contemplate. In fact polygamy in Muslim societies is, believe it or not, quite uncommon.

But having accepted polygamy after 14 centuries, of criticizing Islam for it, perhaps the established church may allow us to point out, in the interest of the women involved, that polygamy should not be swallowed whole but rather with the Islamic condition of justice, that is attached to it.

It is perhaps worth noting that Islam was not the only religion that allowed polygamy but is in fact the only religion that puts limits and conditions to it. A Muslim may have four wives, yes, which is the same as the prophet Jacob had, but not 99 wives like the prophet David or 700 like the prophet Solomon. Had polygamy been wrong from the biblical point of view, none of these great prophets would have practised it. In communities where there are many more women than men, polygamy becomes much more merciful than monogamy, and to that end one would understand and support the decision by the Lambeth Conference.
Yours sincerely,
HESHAM EL ESSAWY
Chairman
The Islamic Society for the Promotion of Religious Tolerance in the UK
London, W5
16 August

Dear Sir,
Polygamy in the Islamic World (Letters, 11 and 15 August) is surely only a reflection of its warlike history. In the early years of Islam the Muslim world was in a constant state of *jihad.* When you start from a low population base, you cannot afford monogamy and war. A marriage system that permits a 75 per cent mortality rate among fighting men while maintaining population levels is a formidable advantage.

Males are more expendable in the West too – women and children get first crack at the lifeboats. When one considers the number of Soviet women who remained alone after the war because 13,000,000 men were dead, one wonders whether polygamy might have eased their loneliness. There again, polygamy is a sad alternative to peace.
WILLIAM BRANDON
London, WC1
15 August

LETTERS TO THE EDITO[...]
RITUAL SLAUGHTER CO[...]

THE CASE FOR

Fact not my[...]

Sir, — How disgusting it was [...] letters last week concerning ani[...] could not perceive any reaso[...] bigotry.

I think it's about time we sorted ou[...] the facts. Firstly, during shaving it i[...] ledge that we do not perceive the p[...] until the wound starts bleeding. This[...] the cut because the bleeding is not s[...]

(left column, cut off)

sity
efits

rdly notable for the
hich they observed the
l adopted the cultures
ligenous peoples.
e contrary, British law
osed, along with Brit-
re and religion. British
lived in tight knit en-
communities, where
customs were rigidly
ed.
urn to the present day,
e those who live here
bserve the law. But we
ever demand of others
y abandon their cul-

time we started to see
ty of cultures as en-
ur national life, rather
eatening it?

IAN WELLENS
l Express, Torquay, 29
April 1988)

Pakistani girls in Britain

December 5.

Sir, — In her article (November 28), "Pinning hope on Benazir's blow for womanhood," Deedee Cuddihy has written sympathetically about Pakistani girls in Great Britain who have expressed their feelings on Benazir Bhutto's recent triumph. However, may I set the record straight on one or two misconceptions?

One of the reasons orthodox Muslims are strict with their offspring is that they fear for their daughters becoming imitation Western women with all that it implies and they fear for their sons' spiritual well-being. Indeed Muslim parents have the hardest of tasks trying to instil moral values that the West have largely lost.

Yes, Muslims do believe a wife's main job is that of carer and comforter and generally the main source of income is that of the husbands. Contrary to popular belief Islam is not against educating females, a Muslim woman may work (particularly in the caring spheres), provided she has adequate domestic help in the home and that the family do not suffer.

Deedee Cuddihy mentions particular customs such as preference of a male child to that of a female. This is tradition only and not a tenet of Islam. The Holy Qur'an, from which Muslims derive their law, exhorts males to cherish and guard females, indeed they are held in great esteem.

Regarding arranged marriages, again, yes, they may be arranged but certainly not imposed. Both parties should give their honest consent without being psychologically blackmailed as so often happens.

Let us hope that young Muslims, both male and female growing up in Great Britain, learn about their God-given rights and in doing so re-educate their well-meaning parents.

Zarina Choudry (Mrs),
Secretary,
Islamic Society for the Promotion of
Religious Tolerance in the UK,
20–22 Creefield Road,
London.

(*Glasgow Herald*, 13 December 1988)

(lower left)

AL
SY

render us unconscious. The animals, likewise, do not feel the pain on the cutting of the skin of the neck by a very sharp instrument.

Secondly, during the cutting of the neck, the four large blood vessels are opened and as a result so much blood is lost instantaneously that the animal becomes unconscious. Unconsciousness deepens as bleeding proceeds and thus the animal cannot feel pain.

Thirdly, blood flowing from the wound by the Halal method gives an impression of cruelty to those who are ignorant of the physiology of pain. The process of bleeding is pain free and this can be confirmed by any blood donor.

And finally, convulsions occurring in the animal with an open neck wound and with blood around also impart an impression of pain and suffering. This again is untrue. Convulsions are due to the lack of oxygen in the brain cells. Indeed, their occurrence confirms that the animal is unconscious.

Those who have seen epileptics undergoing convulsions, falling and hurting themselves, will bear witness that the patients do not feel pain from the injuries they suffer during convulsions. They, in fact, do not even remember when they get hurt.

So I hope this clears the air and I also hope that one day we can all eat Halal meat! — Yours, etc.,

K. AHMED

(*Nelson Leader*, 29 July 1989)

QUICK QUIZ – RECAP ON SHARI'AH

- ▶ Which animal is banned as food by both Muslims and Jews?
- ▶ What is the halal method of killing?
- ▶ Why is talking about religion in pubs frowned on?
- ▶ Why don't Muslims touch dogs?
- ▶ Why do Muslims at work need a private place?
- ▶ Why is a water supply at work necessary?
- ▶ How is a Muslim girl expected to dress for PE?
- ▶ What food problems are faced in school or factory canteens?
- ▶ What might happen when an imam tries to visit a prisoner?
- ▶ Why do Muslims lack energy in Ramadan?
- ▶ Why are Muslim women sometimes embarrassed by hospital treatment?

The Blue Mosque, Istanbul

A **mosque** is a building set aside for worship. Its name in Arabic is **masjid**, which means 'a place where people prostrate themselves', in other words, where they bow and touch their heads to the earth before God.

Some mosques are very special buildings, like those at Makkah, Madinah, Jerusalem, Damascus, Cairo, Instanbul, Isfahan, Qom and even at Regent's Park in London.

At the other extreme are little rectangular areas marked out by road-side tea-shops, or in fields, or at railway stations, where you might find just a basic mat and something to indicate the direction of Makkah. (See p. 60.)

In Muslim countries, there are often arrows at railways stations, so that travellers know at once in which direction to pray.

In Britain, Muslims have taken over all sorts of buildings to use as mosques – old churches, houses, even a fire station. Anywhere will do, as long as it is clean.

As Muhammad said:

> *'Wherever the hour of prayer overtakes you,*
> *you shall perform it. That place*
> *is a mosque.*
>
> (Hadith)

The place does not matter. The Qur'an states:

> *'God knows everything in the heavens and on earth.*

> *Three men cannot talk together in secret,*
> *but He is the fourth . . . . Neither fewer than that*
> *or more, but He is with them,*
> *wherever they may be.'*
>
> (surah 58:7)

However, out of respect for God and for practical convenience, many Muslims set aside a certain place in their houses, perhaps in a spare room, or part of a bedroom, so that there is always somewhere ready to set aside the thoughts and cares of the world and come before God in prayer.

The first mosque in Madinah was built around Muhammad's family house. This was a typical desert dwelling, consisting of several huts for Muhammad and his wives set around a square courtyard, surrounded by a mud-brick wall. Houses built like this can be seen all over the Middle East where there is mud available, hot sun to dry it, and no rain. The northern side had palm trees supporting a thatched roof to provide some shade. The first Muslims met together for prayer in the courtyard.

FOR YOUR FOLDERS

▶ Is it important for a group of believers to have a special place where they can meet? What do you see as the advantages or disadvantages of such a place?

▶ Copy out surah 58:7. What does this teach about the presence of God?

A peasant mud-brick house, Egypt

Uses

Muhammad did not separate religious life from his normal daily activities. In the open courtyard he entertained visitors, conducted business, and guided the day-to-day affairs of the community. It was the place where believers gathered for communal prayer and to hear his sermons, and it was also used for giving shelter to the poor, homeless and wayfarers, and for caring for the sick.

In the courtyard was a well, not only for washing before prayers, but for ordinary refreshment. Travellers could arrive there and have a cool drink and food. Visitors were allowed to rest in the corners, or even stay overnight.

It is important to realize that mosques today, no matter how grand the buildings, are still used to fulfil all these other functions.

The community function is particularly important in places where Muslims are in the minority – they need a place to meet and discuss their problems.

Mosques are also used:

- as schools – for learning Arabic and studying the Qur'an
- as law courts – for matters of Islamic law
- for functions such as birth, marriage and burial celebrations
- for parties, welcome home meetings, lectures, as a games room or reading room, for fund-raising activities.

Behaviour

People are expected to behave quietly and respectfully at all times, even if prayers are not taking place.

Shoes are taken off and left outside or carried in a bag, and the feet carefully washed.

But people can relax there, and you can often see adult students (sometimes white-haired old men) reading and studying, or taking a peaceful nap, or maybe even playing table-tennis in a modern 'community room'.

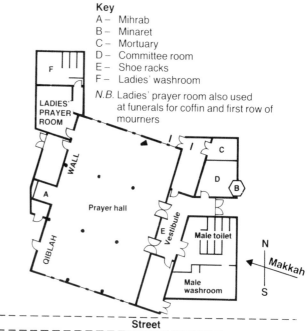

Key
A – Mihrab
B – Minaret
C – Mortuary
D – Committee room
E – Shoe racks
F – Ladies' washroom

N.B. Ladies' prayer room also used at funerals for coffin and first row of mourners

Note how the prayer hall is angled in relation to the street so that prayers are directed to Makkah

Interior plan of the Jamia Mosque

THINGS TO DO

▶ Copy the diagram above carefully into your folder.

▶ Write a few sentences to answer the following questions:

a Why do Muslims set aside a room (or part of one) in their homes to be used as a place of worship?

b What do you see as the advantages or disadvantages for them in this?

c What does having such a place in a Muslim's house say about that family's attitude to religion?

FOR YOUR FOLDERS

▶ Look at the picture of the Blue Mosque in Istanbul and the simple mud-brick building. Which is closer to the mosque built by Muhammad, and in what ways?

▶ What are the main uses of mosques?

FOR DISCUSSION

▶ God can be worshipped anywhere, and the most important place of worship is the heart.

▶ Splendid buildings should be disapproved of as a waste of money and effort.

East London Mosque

Interior of Regents Park Mosque, London

Before entering a mosque Muslims take off their shoes and perform the ritual washing. There will be a well, fountain or tap in the courtyard, or a special washroom in a modern building. It is normal for modern mosques to have separate facilities for women.

Shoes are left outside the prayer area on a rack. When there is a huge congregation they are carried in a bag to avoid a frantic scramble after the service.

Inside, visitors immediately feel a sense of peace, air and space. This is because the interior is not cluttered up with furniture. There are no seats to sit on, and no pictures or statues to decorate the building. Everyone is expected to sit or kneel on the floor, which is generally covered with carpets.

No one has a special place, as all are equal in God's sight. There is often a design on the carpet, or lines marked out, to help the believers form neat rows. Often, little individual mats are used, with designs showing Makkah or the mosque at Madinah. All are placed pointing in the direction of Makkah.

In the roof there may be a dome. This gives a feeling of open space and represents the universe. It also permits the voice of the imam to be heard clearly by the worshippers. It encourages a powerful, calm atmosphere.

Mihrabs

The prayer leader usually stands in front of the **mihrab**, a special niche set in the wall that faces Makkah. Mihrabs are usually beautifully decorated with coloured tiles and texts from the Qur'an, and are sometimes known as the 'niche of lights', the symbol for divine presence in the heart.

Many are shell shaped, from the tradition that shells house a pearl formed when they rise to the surface of water at night and open to receive a dewdrop. The shell symbolizes the 'ear of the heart' which absorbs the 'dewdrop of the divine word'. It is characteristic that the most sumptuous decoration is used to frame and venerate something which is not itself visible.

Mimbar and Mihrab, Cairo Mosque, Egypt

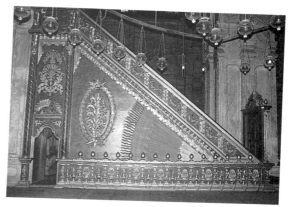

Mimbar, Muhammed Ali Mosque, Cairo

No pictures

There are no statues or pictures in case simple people begin to treat them as idols. Representations of God or spiritual beings are regarded as blasphemous and, in any case, misleading. Pictures of Muhammad could only be guesswork and would give a false impression.

Mosques are not dull places, however, as they can have rich carpets, often scarlet or green, brightly-patterned tiles, marble pillars, huge chandeliers, and intricate stonework and stained glass windows.

To one side is the pulpit or **mimbar**, from which sermons are given. It may be very ornate, or just a little platform at the top of a few stairs.

In modern mosques, men and women enter by separate doors and have separate rooms for worship.

At the men's entrance there is usually a notice-board for general business and a set of clocks giving the prayer times for the day. These will vary according to the seasons, or the country, depending on the times of dawn and dusk.

There is sometimes a room used as a mortuary, the place where bodies of dead Muslims are carefully washed and wrapped in shrouds before burial.

Outside the courtyard, dome and **minaret** are visible. In the East most courtyards are uncovered, because it seldom rains. The minaret is a tall tower from which the call to prayer is given. Some mosques have more than one minaret. The Blue Mosque in Istanbul is the only one in the world that has six. The **qiblah wall**, which marks the direction of Makkah, is often higher, or has a huge archway.

Qiblah wall, Delhi Mosque, India

Decorative tiles at Attarine Mosque, Morocco

THINGS TO DO

▶ Imagine that you are interviewing Mr Qasim at the mosque. These are the questions to put to him. Can you work out what his answers will be? (If you can speak to a Muslim you could conduct a real interview.)

a What does the word qiblah mean, and what does it show?
b What is a minaret used for?
c Why do mosques need a water supply?
d What do Muslims do when they enter a mosque?
e Why are pictures or statues regarded as undesirable?
f What do clocks in a mosque entrance show?
g Why are there no chairs for worshippers?
h Why are there lines on the carpet, or a pattern?

FOR YOUR FOLDERS

▶ Write to a friend giving a full description of the main features found at a mosque
a outside, and
b inside.
▶ How far do you think that the design of a mosque fulfils the practical purposes of Muslim worship?

School

Every mosque has its **madrasah** or school, where young Muslims do their 'Islamiat' or Islamic studies. In Britain this usually takes place between 4 and 6 p.m., five nights a week, and some schools even demand weekend work.

Children in Muslim countries do not have to work so hard, because they can do Islamiat during the day as part of their normal lessons. Indeed, it is usually considered to be the most important part of their education.

Boys and girls usually start Islamic studies at the age of five. Girls generally finish at the age of twelve, and boys continue until they are fifteen. Good students can spend the rest of their lives continuing to learn, and become teachers themselves.

Schools turn down Asian lessons plea

ASIAN youngsters who are having to crowd into a private house for religious instruction have been told they cannot use local primary schools.

Community leader Mr Mohammed Shafi Bhatti has searched in vain for alternative premises for the religious lessons which he has been holding at his home in Fountain Street, Accrington.

Mr Bhatti was recently given a 12-month conditional discharge by magistrates after admitting crowding up to 70 children into his home. He was in breach of planning regulations and is now having to limit the numbers to no more than 20 children at any one time.

The Islamic lessons are given by trained teachers from Accrington mosques.

But although the numbers have been cut back, the situation is still far from satisfactory.

And the governors of nearby Hannah Street Primary School, Accrington and Spring Hill Primary School, Accrington, have spurned Mr Bhatti's request to let him use their premises after school hours.

The governors of Hannah Street said there would be a difficulty in cleaning the school before and after the lessons. The cleaner in charge works only a small number of hours and may not wish to do overtime, they said.

However, Mr Bhatti replied, "We can assure all concerned that their fears are unfounded and we will keep the premises clean and tidy."

Mr Bhatti added that he had made an offer to the governors, saying that if the youngsters did not leave the place tidy they could be thrown out.

An application to hold the lessons in Spring Hill primary School was rejected for similar reasons.

The governors said they had no objection to letting the school out for the purpose of Islamic religious instruction but again were worried about cleaning and tidying-up before and after.

Now Mr Bhatti has written to Lancashire Education Committee's chairman Councillor Mrs Josie Farrington to appeal for help. He says the children are in a "desperate situation."
(Accrington Observer, 24 June 1988)

Madrasah

It is important to realize that most Muslims are *not* Arabs, and therefore Arabic, the language of Islam, is not their native language. If Muslims want to study the Qur'an properly they should attempt to learn Arabic.

Good students learn a great deal of the Qur'an by heart. Some learn it all.

There is an exam every year, and few children fail it. They all change classes after Ramadan. Most teachers are not specially trained, but are willing volunteers. They are allowed to use the cane, but almost never do in normal circumstances because the children learn from an early age to respect their elders and behave politely.

Khutbah

Before the Friday prayer, the teacher or **imam** will give a short talk called the **khutbah**. This is a sermon, usually based on verses from the Qur'an, or traditions about Muhammad, or some subject of immediate interest to the people. Sometimes the sermons can be highly political, especially in times of persecution or suffering from tyranny.

There are no priests or paid religious leaders in Islam. The imam can be any Muslim of decent character who:

- has good knowledge of the faith
- is respected by his fellow Muslims
- has studied the Qur'an and Hadith
- is known for his piety and common sense.

Some mosques do not have full-time imams, and their chosen leaders have full-time jobs outside the mosque.

Some imams are great scholars and have become very famous, especially those who train students at the Muslim universities such as those of al-Azhar in Cairo and Qom in Iran. The head of al-Azhar, Ali Gad al-Haq, is the leading authority for all Sunni Muslims. Shi'ite Muslims were led from 1978–88 by the Ayatollah Khomeini who became famous for his fiery political sermons which led to the downfall of the previous ruler of Iran.

There has been no supreme caliph (see p. 153) since 1924, when a Turkish socialist movement overthrew the last Ottoman (see p. 147).

THINGS TO DO

- Explain why it is important for a Muslim to
  a learn Arabic, and
  b learn as much of the Qur'an as possible by heart.
- Read the press cutting. Explain what Mr Bhatti wanted to use the local school for, and why he was so sure the authorities were worrying about nothing.

FOR YOUR FOLDERS

- Explain the purpose of the madrasah. Why is studying Islamiat particularly hard for youngsters in
  a non-Arabic countries?
  b non-Muslim countries
- What advantages or disadvantages do you think there could be in a community choosing its own religious leader or imam?

QUICK QUIZ

What is:

- the age Muslims start studying?
- the time of the communal prayer?
- the meaning of khutbah?
- the chief Sunni university?

FOR DISCUSSION

- Many young people in the West find it strange that Muslim women pray at home instead of going to the mosque, as women hugely outnumber men in Christian churches. Muslim women who go to the mosque too often are sometimes thought to be show-offs, or self-seeking and immodest, or too interested in the men. But the women are certainly no less religious – many of them are extremely pious indeed, and do not find the rules about modest clothing, the forbidding of make-up or scent at prayer time, or the removal of tights for foot-washing, a burden.

  What effects do you think their habit of praying at home have:
  a on the atmosphere within the home, and
  b on the behaviour and attitude of a Muslim housewife during her normal working day?

Dome of the Rock, Jerusalem

Madinah-Quba Mosque, Saudia Arabia

'The East and the West are God's, therefore whichever way you turn, there is the Presence of God. Truly God is everywhere and knows all.'

(surah 2:115)

Blue Mosque, Isfahan

Abu-Darwish Mosque, Amman (Jordan)

Regents Park mosque, London

The successors

During the first thirty years after Muhammad's death the Muslims were governed by four **caliphs** who were outstanding men chosen by the community for their closeness to Muhammad and their good characters. They were unselfish, tolerant and well-versed in the Qur'an, and had been Muhammad's dearest friends. They had learned from him all his ways and attitudes.

The word caliph or **khalif** means 'successor'. These first four caliphs were known as the 'rashidin' or 'rightly-guided' or 'orthodox'.

Way of life

Instead of living like princes (as you might expect, for they had access to enormous wealth), they lived very simple lives as Muhammad had done, in close touch with the people.

They ate little and were famous for the ragged state of their hand-patched garments, and their refusal to take any luxuries for themselves. (Their definition of a 'luxury' was anything that they did not actually need.)

They were just and kind, and totally dedicated to serving their people. They were the most important people in the Muslim state, but were horrified if anyone started to think of them as kings – they were simply servants. Only God was King.

Duties

- No caliph was to make a law against the law of God, and if he did, he was not to be obeyed.
- Justice was to be done and oppression put down.
- No one was to live in hunger, or without shelter, education or someone to care for them.
- Good was to prosper and evil to be weakened.

Abu Bakr

Abu Bakr was the first male adult to have believed in the message delivered through Muhammad. He was the father of Muhammad's youngest wife Aisha.

Outwardly, he was not an impressive man to look at, but he was highly respected for his gentleness, wisdom, piety and humility.

Although many Muslims favoured the election of Muhammad's adopted son Ali, Abu Bakr was the senior male Muslim and his supporters won the day. Ali, a man of exceptional piety and humility, stood aside, although his wife Fatimah, the Prophet's daughter, felt deeply hurt.

When Abu Bakr became caliph, he was already about sixty years old, and in fact he ruled for only two years, 632–4 CE. He was known as As-Siddiq (the witness to the truth) and Amirul Muminim (ruler of the believers).

On his deathbed, he did not give the community the chance to elect the next caliph, but nominated Umar. Ali and his supporters considered this to be wrong, but Ali refused to bear a grudge and accepted the authority of the Prophet's friend.

Aisha

Abu Bakr's daughter Aisha married the Prophet when she was only a small child, between seven and nine years old, but she did not go to live with him until she was twelve. She had known Muhammad from the time she was a baby, for he went almost daily to visit Abu Bakr's house. Like her father, she learnt all the surahs of the Qur'an by heart.

Aisha became famous for her intelligence and sharp judgement, and her training made her one of the most notable Muslim women in history. It was she who kept Muhammad company on the many occasions when he stayed awake all night in prayer. She later became a leading authority in Islamic law, especially on matters concerning women. She is said to have passed on 2210 sayings of Muhammad to the collection of Hadith.

However, she was a humble person who enjoyed loving and serving her husband. She used to do all the housework, including grinding flour and baking bread. It was she who did all the washing for the family, and set aside water for Muhammad's wash before prayer.

Once she disappeared in mysterious circumstances when she was on an expedition with the Prophet. She had been left behind when his camel train moved on, and was rescued by a young tribesman. For this, she was accused of adultery. However, Muhammad was granted a special revelation that declared her innocence, and that henceforth four witnesses would be required in such a case. False witnesses should be sentenced to forty lashes.

Wages

Early one morning, after Abu Bakr's election, he appeared in the market place carrying heavy bales of cloth. All his life he had been a cloth merchant. The Muslims were puzzled.

'What are you doing, Abu Bakr'?

'I am going to the bazaar.'

'But now you must guide the affairs of our whole community. How can you find the time to carry on in trade?'

'I must earn my livelihood, otherwise, how shall I feed my family?'

It was decided that Abu Bakr must be paid a salary from the treasury to take care of his needs. He reluctantly agreed to accept as wages two sheets of cloth in summer and two in winter plus the food for his family every day. In return, he handed over everything he owned to the treasury, saying that it was not honest to keep it while the treasury took care of his needs.

'O People. I have been chosen by you as your leader, although I am no better than any of you. If I do well, give me your support. If I do wrong, set me right!'

(Abu Bakr)

Sayings of Abu Bakr

- *Always fear Allah; He knows what is in men's hearts.*
- *Be kind to those who are under your care and treat them well.*
- *Give brief orders; speeches that are too long are likely to be forgotten.*
- *Improve your own conduct before asking others to improve theirs.*
- *Honour the envoy of the enemy.*
- *Always speak the truth, so that you get the right advice.*
- *Be sincere to all with whom you deal.*

The sweets

Abu Bakr's wife wanted to buy a little sugar to treat him to some sweets. She scrimped and saved from their very meagre allowance, but when she surprised him with them, he was not pleased.

'How did you manage this?' he demanded.

When she told him what she had done, he replied 'I am amazed. This shows we have been taking more than we really need.' And he instantly reduced their grant.

Aisha's death

Aisha died in 678 CE, the last survivor of Muhammad's close family.

She had hoped to be buried next to her beloved father, but when Umar asked for this favour Aisha modestly agreed, saying he was more fit to be buried there than herself.

FOR YOUR FOLDERS

▶ What were the qualities expected of a person chosen to be caliph? Look at the stories given about Abu Bakr and show how they revealed him to be a worthy successor to Muhammad.

▶ Make a list of the duties expected of a caliph. Explain what the Muslims had a right to expect for themselves.

THINGS TO DO

▶ Choose three of the sayings of Abu Bakr and write them out as a scroll or a poster. What do these three sayings tell you about the character of Muhammad's successor.

▶ Aisha was known as one of the 'mothers of the faithful'. Give a brief account of her life, showing how she was specially fit for her role as wife of the Prophet, and how she was able to help and support him.

QUICK QUIZ

▶ What does the word caliph mean?

▶ What is meant by rashidin?

▶ Who was the first caliph?

▶ What did Abu Bakr do for a living?

▶ How old was he when he became caliph?

▶ For how long did he rule the Muslims?

▶ How was he related to the Prophet Muhammad?

Sayings of Umar

- *Do not be misled by a person's reputation.*
- *Don't judge a person by his outward actions but by his truthfulness and wisdom.*
- *Don't leave your task until tomorrow.*
- *He who has no idea of evil can easily fall into its trap.*
- *Judge a man's intelligence by the questions he asks.*
- *It is easier not to commit sins than to be sorry for them afterwards.*
- *Be grateful when you are shown your faults.*

Conversion of Umar

Umar ibn al-Khattab was converted to Islam by his sister Fatimah. He was completely opposed to Muhammad at first. He had actually set out to kill him, when someone told him that his sister and her husband had become Muslims. He rushed to their home in a fury. She tried to hide the section of the Qur'an they had been reading. Umar burst into the house and wounded his sister as she tried to protect her husband. When he saw her blood-stained face he calmed down, took the text away from her and read it. It so moved him that he was instantly converted, and asked to be taken to Muhammad as a convert.

Conquests

Umar was a bald giant of a man, who became one of Muhammad's chief advisers. He was caliph from 634–44 CE.

During his reign the Muslim warriors (under Khalid Saifullah – the Sword of God) captured Syria and Palestine.

In Jerusalem, the Christian ruler Sophronius declared that he would surrender to none other than Umar himself. So in 637 the caliph, wearing his famous shabby patched cloak, set out for the city with one servant and a camel, which he and the servant took turns to ride. His lack of pride and grandeur was legendary, and he found himself welcomed into the Holy City.

He discovered that the site of the old Jewish temple was a delapidated ruin, and had been used as a rubbish dump for centuries. He began to clear the debris with his own hands, and the people joined in and laboured until the 'holy rock' was uncovered.

The Holy Rock in Jerusalem

A simple wooden mosque was constructed nearby, on the site of King Solomon's palace, which was said to have been the spot from which Muhammad ascended to heaven on his Night Journey.

The most important Christian shrine in Jerusalem was the burial place of Jesus. Umar happened to be there one day when the call to prayer sounded. He immediately hurried to say his prayers elsewhere, so that the Christians could keep their shrine. Had he not done so, it would automatically have become a mosque.

This is the contract Umar made with the Christians of Jerusalem:

'This is the protection which the servant of God, Umar, has granted to the people of Jerusalem . . . . Their churches shall not be taken away, nor shall they be pulled down, nor shall any damage be done to them . . . . They shall not be forced to give up their beliefs, nor shall they be persecuted for them. Whatever is written here is under the covenant of God, and the responsibility of His messenger, of the caliphs and of the believers; it shall hold good so long as they pay the tax for their defence that has been imposed upon them.'

(Halid M. Halid *Bayon Yaden Omar*, Da al Ma'arif, Egypt, 1983)

Khalid and Amr

Umar, who lived all his life without luxuries, became worried that **Khalid**, a Muslim warrior, would grow too rich and powerful. He feared that the people might forget it was God who granted the victories. So Khalid had to prove his humility by serving under another commander.

In order to protect the newly-won Syrian territories from Byzantine raids from the south, another military leader, **Amr**, led 3500 cavalry into Egypt in 640 CE. There, they were welcomed as liberators, and the Byzantine soldiers and sailors were allowed to return home.

Hafsa's story

Umar's daughter Hafsa was one of the Prophet's wives. One day she and Aisha tried to make Umar live in a little more comfort. Umar would have none of it. He protested: 'O Aisha, was the Prophet's stomach ever full, or his bedcover anything other than the cloak he wore by day?' She could not deny it. Then he asked Hafsa: 'And when he slept, did he not just lie on a rush mat on the bare earth?'

Hafsa told him how the Prophet always slept very badly because he was so uncomfortable. One day, unable to bear his sufferings any longer, she had folded the reed mat over double without telling him, to try to make it a little softer for him. That night he slept peacefully, but he overslept and missed the pre-dawn prayer. He was so distressed when he found out that he never slept like that again.

'So,' said Umar, 'when the Prophet lived like this, caring so little for his own comfort, how can his followers live in luxury?'

Death of Umar

In 644 CE Umar listened to the complaint of Firoz, a Persian Christian, but gave judgement against his case. Firoz took revenge; he waited until the dawn prayer, and when Umar was kneeling he stabbed him six times. Umar died three days later, having appointed a six-man committee to elect his successor.

FOR YOUR FOLDERS

▶ *'Every religion has a special character, and the characteristic of Islam is modesty.'*
'Modesty and faith are joined closely together. If either of them is lost, the other goes also.'

(Hadith)

Copy out one these sayings of Muhammad and show how Umar was a good representative of Islam.

▶ What did Umar's activities in Jerusalem reveal about
  a his character and leadership
  b the Muslim attitude to the Christians?

▶ How was Umar's modesty and simplicity revealed by
  a his mode of dress
  b the way he treated his servants
  c his sayings?

QUICK QUIZ

▶ Who converted Umar to Islam?
▶ Which warrior was known as the Sword of God?
▶ How did Umar show consideration for the Christians of Jerusalem?
▶ For what garment was Umar famous?
▶ Why was Khalid removed from office?
▶ Which of Muhammad's wives was Umar's daughter?

Uthman

The six-man committee appointed by Umar to choose the next caliph included Ali and Uthman.

Uthman was a rich merchant from the powerful **Ummayyad** family of the Quraish, the only member of the Ummayyads to become a Muslim during the time of Muhammad's persecution. He had been married to Muhammad's daughter Ruqaiyya, and after her death to her sister Umm Kulthum.

The caliphate was offered to Ali first, on the condition that he accepted not only the Qur'an and Sunnah, but also all the recorded judgements of the previous caliphs. Ali rejected the second part. He had publicly criticized some of their judgements, and being a man of integrity, he refused to compromise his principles at this stage.

The caliphate was then offered on the same conditions to Uthman, and he accepted them – and thus became the leader.

Uthman was a simple and kind-hearted man, but his administration was not so disciplined as that of Umar, and he tended to appoint his friends and relatives to key positions. Many of the faithful felt that the Ummayyads were trying to take over, and resented this.

When he was eighty years old, many Muslims – particularly the supporters of Ali, felt that he should abdicate, but he refused to do so. He had angered the Egyptians because he had replaced a perfectly capable governor there with his own cousin, who set harsher taxes.

A party of 500 Egyptians went to petition him and demanded his resignation but Uthman rejected all advice and preached a public sermon against them. Soon afterwards, while he was at prayer, a group of these Egyptians killed him – the second caliph to die in this manner. He had ruled from 644–56 CE.

His wife, Nailah, sent word (plus her fingers which were cut off as she tried to protect him) to his cousin Muawiya, whom he had made governor of Syria.

Ali and his family

At last, twenty-four years after the Prophet's death, the caliphate passed to Ali – the idealist who had previously let the opportunity go by because of one unacceptable condition. He ruled from 656–61. He had been the first male convert to Islam, and was famous for his extreme piety and faithful transmission of Muhammad's sayings. His supporters thought of him as the 'Conscience of Islam'.

Ali's conversion

Ali discovered the Prophet and his wife kneeling in prayer one day, and seeing no one, asked to whom they were prostrating themselves.

Muhammad explained about Allah and the revelations he had received. Ali was excited, but thought he ought to consult his father about it. However, the next morning he came rushing to Muhammad to declare his belief: 'Allah created me without consulting my father. Why then should I consult him in order to worship Allah?'

The dinner

When Muhammad first commenced his public ministry, he invited his kinsmen to a dinner, and tried to persuade them to believe. They were all embarrassed and would not support him. Only Ali, then aged ten years old, stood up and said: 'I am the youngest of you; I may be a boy and my feet may not be strong enough, but O Muhammad, I shall be your helper. Whoever opposes you, I shall fight him as my mortal enemy.'

The elders laughed at him, but Ali was to become known as Asadullah – the Lion of God.

The contest

Ali's appointment as caliph was opposed by Uthman's cousin Muawiya, who was supported by Muhammad's surviving wife Aisha.

Ali had condemned the murder of Uthman, but had understood the reasons for it and had not tried to track down or punish his killers. Muawiya and Aisha demanded that Uthman's murder be avenged.

The assassins claimed that since Uthman had not ruled according to Qur'an and Sunnah, he had ceased to be Islamic and should therefore be removed. (Throughout later centuries, including our own, Islamic revolutionaries have acted according to the same principle – for example in the murder of President Sadat of Egypt – or the overthrow of the Shah of Iran).

A battle was fought in 657 CE, known as the Battle of the Camel, in which Aisha was taken captive, but was treated with great respect and returned safely to her friends.

In the next encounter, the Battle of Siffin, Muawiya forced the end of the fighting by having pages of the Qur'an fixed to his troops' lances. Ali was obliged to accept arbitration. Representatives from both sides agreed to depose both of them and hold new elections, but somehow Muawiya's side tricked Ali's followers, and he was announced as caliph. Ali's supporters promptly declared allegiance to Ali again, and as a result, Ali was virtually recognized as caliph of the East, with Muawiya as caliph of the North and West. One group of Muslims (later known as Kharijites) were so outraged by the whole business that they decided to end the 'impurity' and conflict by killing both of them and starting again.

His marriage

Fatimah was the youngest daughter of the Prophet, and Ali loved her. He married her after the Battle of Badr. She herself took part in the Battle of Uhud, nursing the wounded soldiers (including her own father). She was said to have been very like her mother in looks, but like Muhammad in habits, manners and conversation. She used to sit beside him at meetings, and was highly respected for her kindness, politeness, grace and dignity.

She and Ali had three children. Sadly, she died a few months after her father, at the age of thirty. It was said she was the embodiment of perfect womanhood and her outstretched hand became a common symbol for good fortune and divine protection.

Sayings of Ali

- *One who knows himself knows his creator.*
- *If you love Allah, tear out your heart's love of the world.*
- *One who is proud of worldly possessions in this brief existence is ignorant.*
- *Learned men live after death; ignorant men are dead although alive.*
- *A sign of a stupid man is his frequent change of opinions.*
- *A hypocrite's tongue is clean, but there is sickness in his heart.*
- *Better alone than in bad company.*

The death of Ali

Ali was given many premonitions of his fate, including even the name of the man destined to kill

him. Despite this, he refused to hide or run away. The last two caliphs had been struck down while at prayer. Sure enough, Ali was also mortally wounded while in the mosque at Kufa. He did not die for three days, during which time he protected and fed his assassin, ordered that he should be spared if Ali should live, and killed with one stroke if Ali died. The man's family was not to be molested.

Ali's last words, before entering paradise, were 'O God, most fortunate am I!'

QUICK QUIZ

▶ Who was the third caliph?
▶ Which clan did he belong to?
▶ Who was his cousin, who later opposed Ali?
▶ What was Ali's nickname, and its meaning?
▶ Which woman sat next to Muhammad at meetings?
▶ How did Muawiya stop the Battle of Siffin?
▶ Which Muslim extremists killed Ali?

FOR YOUR FOLDERS

▶ Why did many Muslims feel uneasy about the appointment of Uthman as caliph? How did he come to be assassinated? Why did the Kharijites later oppose even Ali?
▶ What do the stories of Ali's conversion and defence of Muhammad, and the battles for succession, tell us about the character of Ali?
▶ How was the kindness and courage of Ali revealed even on his deathbed?

THINGS TO DO

▶ Choose four of the sayings of Ali and write them out carefully, explaining in your own words what each means.

The split

Some people felt right from the beginning that Ali should have been Muhammad's successor, and they were not content to see power going into the hands of the old chief family of Makkah which had so recently persecuted them. They claimed that Muhammad had always trained Ali to take over, and it was Ali who deputized for the Prophet in his lifetime. They claimed that those who had elected Abu Bakr had taken advantage of the fact Ali had been occupied in burying Muhammad. Those who supported Abu Bakr insisted *he* was the Prophet's choice, and was the senior male Muslim leader.

However, the supporters of Ali still felt the caliphate should have stayed in Muhammad's family, and now that Ali was dead, they insisted the next leader should be Ali's son Hasan.

Muawiya would not agree, and in the end Hasan came to an understanding that the caliphate would revert to his family only after Muawiya's death. However, when Hasan died (some claim he was poisoned) Muawiya made his own son **Yazid** the heir.

Those who supported Ali became known as the **Shiat Ali** or Party of Ali. They are now called **Shi'ites**. They refused to accept the first three caliphs and claimed Ali was really the first, followed by Muhammad's grandsons Hasan and Husain.

Sunnah is the Arabic word for 'custom' or 'authority', and **Sunni** Muslims regard themselves as the true followers of the Sunnah or Way of the Prophet. They insist that Muhammad had intended elections so that the best man would succeed, and not to start a family line of rulers, like kings.

Sunnis are the major branch of Islam. In fact, around 90 per cent of all Muslims are Sunni. They base the standards of their faith on the Qur'an plus the Hadith of Muhammad and the laws based upon them. They tend to regard the Shi'ite claim that leadership should be exclusive to the family of Muhammad and not a democratic election based on a majority vote with distaste and impatience.

The Shi'ites, on the other hand, are a smaller group – around 10 per cent of modern Muslims – but with a tendency to devotion that borders on fanaticism. Some accuse Sunni Muslims of being in need of drastic reform. The number of Shi'ite Muslims is increasing rapidly as people in many developing countries are reacting against the decadence of the modern world.

Shi'ism is the state religion of Iran, and is rapidly increasing strength in Pakistan, Iraq, India, the Yemen and the Lebanon.

The martyrdom of Husain

Hasan's brother Husain refused to acknowledge Yazid as caliph so warfare became inevitable. In 681 CE, Husain and about seventy supporters were surrounded by Yazid's army of 4000 warriors at Karbala. They were in sight of the river Euphrates, but Yazid's army tormented them by denying them any access to the water and watched them die of thirst.

For eight days they tried to negotiate Husain's unconditional surrender, but his belief in his right to be caliph was strong. He refused to give way, even when it meant his defeat and death. Husain had already foreseen his martyrdom in a vision.

On 10 Muharram, Husain put on the mantle of his grandfather the Prophet, and went out to die. Hopelessly outnumbered, his followers fell, one by one. When Husain held out his baby son Ali Ashgar for mercy, an arrow fired through the baby's neck pinned him to Husain's arm.

At the end, the body of Husain, riddled with arrows, was trampled in the mud. His head was hacked off and taken to Damascus, but Yazid did eventually return it for burial.

Yazid allowed safe passage to Madinah for the surviving women, plus Husain's son Ali Zain al Abidin whom the troops had left for dead on the battlefield. He was nursed back to health by Husain's sister Zainab, who led the Shi'ites until he recovered. Also saved was his four year old son Muhammad al Baqir. They became the next challengers for the leadership.

The shrine where Husain was buried, at Karbala, became a holy place that rivalled Makkah. Shi'ites hold a ten day festival there every year, in remembrance of his martyrdom. During the festival the people weep for the seeming triumph of tyranny and evil (symbolized by the corrupt, cynical Yazid) over the good (symbolized by the piety and refusal to compromise of Husain). They pledge themselves to keep up the fight to defend their faith and principles.

The main feature of the festival, which takes place in the month of Muharram, is a series of processions and passion plays commemorating the terrible deaths of Husain and his family. There are daily gatherings, or rawdahs, in which emotions are stirred up until everyone weeps and dedicates their lives anew. (See also p. 91.)

Sometimes the men in the processions gash themselves with knives and beat their backs with chains, in memory of the martyr's wounds.

Twelvers and Seveners

The title Imam, which generally means a leader in the act of worship, took on a new significance amongst the Shi'ites. They used this title in preference to caliph for the descendants of Muhammad who guided their movement.

The Shi'ites later divided into two major branches, according to whether they believed in twelve or seven imams. In each group, it is claimed that the last of their imams mysteriously disappeared without dying, and now follows the course of history in a mystical way. They believe that the Hidden Imam is forever present in the world, although unseen, appearing to the faithful in their times of need, and sending out his light to convert all mankind. He appears to people in prayer, and strengthens the faithful in times of persecution. He will eventually reappear to establish righteous rule and bring about the end of the world.

The Hidden Imam is also known as the Mahdi, and some Shi'ites believe that the final Imam will be Jesus returned to earth.

Extremism

The Shi'ite movement is marked by a sense of persecution and emotional devotion to its leaders, sometimes resulting in a fervour so extreme that many non-believers would describe it as a fanaticism. Shi'ism has tended to develop into secretive sects, which particularly attract rebellious or extremist young people who protest against any form of social injustice, and against those they regard as corrupt rulers.

They believe that they should challenge, with warfare if necessary, any form of government that has become unjust and oppressive, even if the chances of overturning it are slender. They feel it is better to fight and die in the cause of justice, rather than surrender and retreat.

Islamic government

In the absence of the Imam, no government is accepted as valid. Shi'ites, and many Sunnis also, are dedicated to creating pure Islamic states where the government is based on the laws of Islam and the ruler is God alone.

These ideas are no longer just dreams. In 1978, for example, the ruler of Iran was deposed by a religious leader, the Ayatollah Khomeini, and an Islamic state set up.

QUICK QUIZ

▶ What is a Sunni Muslim?
▶ What is a Shi'ite Muslim?
▶ What percentage of Muslims are Sunni?
▶ What are the two chief branches of Shia?
▶ What is meant by a Mahdi?
▶ Which countries have the most Shi'ites?
▶ Who was Husain?
▶ Where is Husain buried?
▶ Who is the Shi'ite ruler of Iran?

FOR YOUR FOLDERS

▶ Strict Sunni Muslims often accuse the Shi'ites of 'adding' to Islam, and paying too much reverence to the family of Muhammad. Give a brief outline of the beliefs that might be considered 'innovations'.

▶ Why do you think the Shi'ite movement has become so closely linked with martyrdom and fanatical behaviour?

Shi'ite procession

137

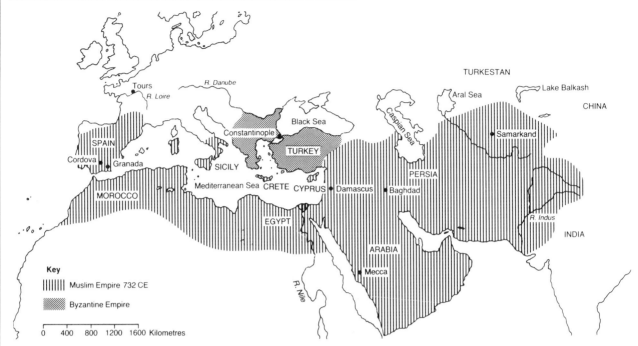

Muslim rule in 732 CE

Key

|||||| Muslim Empire 732 CE

▒▒▒ Byzantine Empire

0   400   800   1200   1600 Kilometres

The spread of the faith

The Muslim faith spread with the speed of a hurricane. When the Prophet died, virtually all Arabia was under his control, and in the next hundred years the Muslims set up a caliphate that stretched from Spain in the West to India in the East.

By 712 CE they had reached the frontiers of China, north of Tibet. In 732 CE Muslim rule reached its greatest expansion, and the Muslims were finally defeated only 250 miles from Dover. Under the leaders known as the Abbasids, Islam was the greatest force on earth and its capital, Baghdad, the foremost city in the world.

Reasons for the rapid spread

There were many reasons for this rapid and successful expansion.

- There was a white-hot enthusiasm amongst Muslim believers. Muhammad had inspired an almost unlimited devotion in his people.
- The new faith was vastly superior to the old idolatory of Arabia – any thinking person would acknowledge that.
- Many who knew Judaism and Christianity found Islam a more logical and reasonable belief. It insisted on loyalty, love and respect for such as Abraham, Moses and Jesus, but insisted that there was only one supreme God and that He was to be approached directly without a saviour,

for His compassion was without limit and could not be bought.

- Persia and Byzantium, which had been the most influential world powers, were both weak during this period after having fought each other for some 200 years. (For example, Persia had captured Jerusalem, and then been driven off again by the Byzantine Christians.)
- The ideal Muslim fought with courage, gallantry and compassion, and in most places Muslim warriors were regarded by the conquered people of the land as liberators from tyrannical oppression.

Belief or the sword

It is not true that people were forced to become Muslims at the point of a sword. The formula was 'Islam, tribute, or the sword', and that makes a difference! No one can be forced to believe any religion, and Muslims were actually tolerant to unbelievers so long as they did not threaten the rule of God as they interpreted it. Non-Muslims living under their regime had to pay taxes, but those who became Muslims lived tax-free. In fact, some rulers actively discouraged conversions in order to balance their budgets!

'Let there be no compulsion
in religion. Truth stands
out clear from error.'

(surah 2:256)

The Ummayyad collapse

The pure rule of Islam was not maintained. The Ummayyads, who ruled from 661 to 750 CE began to stray far from the example of Muhammad. The more powerful the caliphs became, the less Muslims were being led towards God.

- They stopped the practice of electing caliphs and handed the office down from father to son, thus creating a dynasty.
- They changed the capital from Madinah to Damascus, where most of their tribe lived.
- They did not live simple lives. Since they could have any goods they wanted from any part of the Empire, they began to enjoy all the wealth and luxury their rank brought them.
- They built lavish palaces and enjoyed exotic food, the best wines, beautiful women, etc.
- They stopped trying to make converts because they needed the tax money to balance their budget.

All this caused resentment and ill feeling. It was certainly not what Muhammad had intended. It was the very opposite of his simple, kindly life. There was much bitterness against these despots who were turning rotten.

The Abbasids

Anti-Ummayyad parties were formed among those who longed for the original purity of Islam, and among the Shi'ites who felt anyway that the Ummayyads had taken the caliphate away from the rightful heirs.

A new revolutionary force came into being, led by a descendant of Muhammad's uncle Abbas. These Abbasids were based mainly in Persia (Iran), and promised that they would bring back the pure rule of God alone – the kind of state called a theocracy.

In 747 CE revolt broke out, and the Abbasid armies overthrew Ummayyad armies wherever they went. By 749 CE their leader, Abdullah, was declared true caliph, and the Ummayyads were defeated. Only one escaped – Abd al-Rahman – who fled to Spain and founded a rival caliphate in Cordoba which lasted until 1031 CE.

Barbarossa Suleyman's Admiral (a caliph)

THINKING POINT

- **Can there be any value in conversion 'at the point of a sword'? Give reasons for your opinion.**

FOR YOUR FOLDERS

- ▶ Muslims did not use the word 'conquering' of their expansion, but 'opening'. Why do you think many conquered people regarded them as liberators?
- ▶ In what ways were the reasons for the rapid spread of Islam in the first 100 years
  - a military
  - b social
  - c religious?
- ▶ In what ways were the Ummayyad caliphs quite different from the first caliphs, the Rashidin? Give reasons for the collapse of the Ummayyad dynasty.

THINGS TO DO

- ▶ Copy the map of Muslim rule in 732 CE into your books, showing the extent of the territories to which Islam had spread by that time.

*'Go sweep the chamber of your heart.
Make it ready to be the dwelling-place
of the Beloved.
When you depart out, He will enter it.
In you, empty of yourself, He will
display all His beauty.'*

(Shabistari)

Sufism (tasawuf) means being particularly close to God and aware of His loving presence in an acute way that draws you away from normal life. More and more time is spent in prayer and contemplation, not always because the person wants to do this, but because the sensation of God's presence is so powerful and all-consuming that the person experiencing it can think of nothing else, and is sometimes even 'lost' in a trance-like state. This kind of experience is the beginning of **mysticism**.

Mysticism

Although it is not easy to speak in simple terms of what mysticism is about, basically the person who has been granted this kind of personal experience of God is so overcome by it, so thrilled and excited, that the rest of life becomes of little importance when compared to this moment of truth.
The mystic yearns to experience this closeness with God over again.

Sometimes people might only have one such experience in a lifetime, maybe only lasting a few seconds, or more rarely, several minutes or hours. Sometimes people develop techniques for making it happen again. Others seem to be specially blessed, and have mystical revelations occurring to them spontaneously, throughout their lives.

Wool

The name **Sufi** may come from the Arabic 'suf' meaning 'wool', in which case it refers to Sufi Muslims' simple garments of undyed wool. This basic robe was worn as a sign of giving up the luxuries of life – food, dress and shelter – and accepting simplicity and poverty. Another possible origin of the word is from the Greek 'sophos' which means 'wisdom'.

Aims and goals

Sufis wanted to:
- abandon the desire for worldly wealth and luxury

- search for an inner, spiritual life
- achieve union with God, with direct emotional experience
- become so close to God that human consciousness becomes totally lost and absorbed in consciousness of God
- overcome the appetites and desires of the human body with its concern for self.

Tolerance

Sufis are tolerant of other religions, since God can be 'seen' in so many ways. The truth is what counts, and inner peace and freedom. Particular religious rules and regulations are considered to be aids for the unenlightened. Enlightened people realize that all religious paths are attempts to find God – though all might not be of equal value.

This tendency to regard the rules which had been set for the masses as being of little importance inevitably led to suspicion on the part of the orthodox Muslim leaders.

The attitude of the saintly woman Rabia to the Ka'ba in Makkah reveals the typical Sufi attitude:

*'I see only bricks, and a house of stone.
It is only You, O God, that I desire.*

(Rabia)

The true 'Ka'ba' was felt to be the residence of God in your heart – a concept many orthodox Muslims would agree with.

One great teacher, al-Hallaj, was crucified for claiming that he had become one with God. This was regarded as blasphemy – whereas the true Sufi found such union and loss of self to be the greatest expression of humility.

Al-Ghazzali

What the orthodox most feared was that Sufis who practised union with God might be falling into the sin of shirk. Al-Ghazzali (1058–1111 CE), one of the greatest and most respected orthodox scholars of Islam, reassured them that this was not so, but that it was a continuation of the ancient stream of mystical understanding experienced by the prophets. His teachings revived Islam, and safeguarded Sufism from non-Islamic beliefs and practices.

Jalal ud-din Rumi

The most famous Sufi mystic was the Mevlana, Jalal ud-din Rumi (1207–73 CE), who founded the order of whirling dervishes (see p. 142). Son of an eminent theologian, he began experiencing visions at the age of six. His doctrines arose from three things – suffering, love and acceptance.

Acceptance of God's will, whatever it might be, was the highest form of sacrifice of self, the highest proof of love. He taught that you should be ashamed to ask for anything in prayer; you should be content. This was pure Islam, pure submission. Love was what mattered – not knowledge, greatness or striving. To achieve love meant understanding unity, God's light shining into all the dark places of the earth and making them one.

For a little while the Mevlana found another mystic who completely understood his teachings. They experienced great joy, but when they parted he knew the terrible pain of grief and loneliness. There is mystery over who his beloved guest really was, but the experience represented, for him, the awareness of the soul's separation from the Beloved, who is God.

Union with God was that sense of breathtaking joy, of coming home, of being released from fear, of being transported from loneliness to overwhelming love.

> 'O God, if I have worshipped You for fear of hell, burn me in hell.
> If I have worshipped you for hope of paradise, exclude me from it.
> But if I worship You for Your own sake then do not keep me from Your everlasting Beauty.'
>
> (Rabia)

> 'God speaks to everyone . . . . He speaks to the ears of the heart, but it is not every heart which hears Him. His voice is louder than the thunder, and His light is clearer than the sun – if only one could see and hear. In order to do that, one must remove this solid wall, this barrier – the Self.'
>
> (Rumi)

> 'Would that You might be sweet to me even if life is bitter, pleased with me, even if all else is angry. Would that what is between You and me might flourish even if what is between me and all else is desolate.
> If I secure Your love, then all else is insignificant and all on earth nought but earth.'
>
> (Rabia al-Adawiyya, a Sufi woman poet who died in Iraq, 801 CE)

> 'When you see with the eyes of your head you are no different from an animal. When you see with your heart's eyes all space opens up for you.'
>
> (Rumi)

> 'Sitting under a tree, clothed in rags you are wealthier than the richest – those who own the earth, and yet are in need.'
>
> (Rumi)

> 'There are many roads to the Ka'ba . . . but lovers know that the true Holy Mosque is Union with God.'
>
> (Rumi)

FOR YOUR FOLDERS

▶ Read carefully the mystical teachings in the sayings of the Sufis given here. Choose three of them, and see if you can explain what they mean.

▶ How is mysticism supposed to alter a person's life and consciousness? Why is it important for a mystic to be 'emptied of self'?

▶ Do you think it is true that union with God is the most valuable experience there is? Give reasons for your answer.

TALKING POINTS

● **'Mystical experience is no more than wishful thinking. It is all in the mind – and a peculiar mind at that!'**

● **If all religions are not ultimately the same, then how can God truly exist?**

QUICK QUIZ

▶ What is meant by the 'moment of truth'?

▶ What is meant by 'suf'?

▶ Name one famous female Sufi mystic.

▶ Who founded the whirling dervishes?

▶ Complete the sayings:
  'When you see with you heart's eyes . . .'
  'The true Holy Mosque is . . .'

70 DERVISHES, TARIQAS AND BROTHERHOODS

Whirling dervishes

Dervishes

The word 'dervish' or 'darwish' means the 'sill of the door'. It is a word much misunderstood in the West where it is usually thought to mean a mad, ragged savage. Some dervishes may well be ragged, for they renounce everything other than the clothes they stand up in, but they are in fact held in very high esteem. They are Sufi mystics who practise particular exercises (or **dhikrs**), which bring them to 'the sill of the door'. Beyond that door lies enlightenment.

Some live in communities, others as solitary hermits cared for by communities. The three leading types of dervish are:
- 'howling' dervishes who practise bodily control to gain freedom from physical sensations, such as pain
- 'wandering' dervishes who regard utter simplicity and homelessness as an obligation

- 'whirling' dervishes who seek a mystical frame of mind through sacred dance.

All dervishes believe that humanity is in a state of 'sleep', trapped by its own ignorance, dominated by what is called the 'lower soul'. The dervish seeks to be 'loosened from the earth's glue', to become one with God. Freed from all worldly cares and anxieties, they are to become channels for God's light.

They are not impressed by cleverness or academic learning. Personal experience is what counts, and the most simple of souls could be the richest in this respect. They are also critical of 'empty' learning, clever knowledge for its own sake that cannot be put to practical use.

'A donkey may be loaded with books,
but that does not make him intelligent.
How does he know whether he is
carrying books, or wood for the fire?

'You belong to the world of dimension, but you come from the world of non-dimension. Close the first shop and open the second.'

(Rumi)

Dhikr

Opening the second shop is not an easy task. It requires a devotion, an effort of will, and a certain frame of mind. The dhikrs are the various practices by which it might be achieved. These include:
- concentration on God in an intense way (fikr)
- chanting or repeating religious phrases, to wipe the mind clean of attachment to material things
- contemplation of certain symbols
- breathing exercises – these are also known as 'flying the magic carpet' or 'walking on water'
- the whirling dance, or **sema**, to bring about a feeling of loss of self and absorption into God
- the halt, or pause of time – when the teacher 'freezes' movement and projects his blessing on the disciples, who experience a sense of union.

The dance

The sema is sometimes ignorantly described as if it were a frenzied, mad whirling. This is not the case at all. The dance, which is offered as a prayer, is serene and dignified, and alters a dancer's state of consciousness so that he or she can experience direct knowledge of the eternal.

Every move in the dance is symbolic.
- The black cloaks symbolize the tomb, or worldly attachments.
- The tall hats symbolize the tombstone, or the self.
- The white robes symbolize the shrouds.
- Dropping the cloaks symbolizes readiness to leave the world of self and turn towards God.

As they turn, dancers murmur quietly to themselves 'Allah, Allah, Allah', emptying their hearts of all but the thought of God. They dance with the right hand raised to heaven and the left facing the earth, symbolizing their trance-like state – the point of intersection between the two worlds.

The movement is a serene gliding, the left foot never leaving the ground. After ten minutes or so the music stops, and they halt suddenly, turning to the leader, their skirts wrapping around their legs. This bow is called the selam.

The ritual ends with prayers and the chanting of the sound 'Hu', which represents all the names of God in one. They put on their cloaks and return to their 'tombs' in an altered state.

Tariqas

Tariqas or brotherhoods are now found all over the Muslim world, calling believers to a new state of spiritual awareness and vitality.

They also function as social clubs, give hospitality to travellers, and organize welfare such as schools, hospitals and relief work.

The Muslim brotherhood and sisterhood

This leading reform movement – functioning secretly in many countries where it is banned – was founded by Hassan al-Banna in Egypt in 1928. It demands total dedication to God from its members. Because of its extreme religious discipline, and unwillingness to compromise with lower standards, it is most feared in Muslim countries where, in the opinion of the Brotherhood, governments have become lax or 'over-Westernized'.

FOR YOUR FOLDERS

▶ Explain what is meant by a dervish, and make a list of their main beliefs.
▶ What is meant by 'the second shop'? By what ways and means could a person open it?

THINGS TO DO

▶ Imagine that you have been taken to see a sema. Write a letter to a friend describing what you saw, and explaining the meaning behind the dance.

FOR DISCUSSION

▶ Deliberate attempts to expand mystical consciousness are dangerous and might be misleading.

A young Palestinian soldier

Peace

One meaning of the word 'Islam' is 'peace'. The greeting used by all Muslims when they meet each other is 'salaam aleikum' – 'May peace be with you'.

Millions of people, both soldiers and civilians, have died as the result of wars. Whole generations have been wiped out, and billions of pounds spent on warfare.

Nobody in their right mind could possibly regard war as a good thing. No one could believe that it could be right to inflict suffering in order to take power, land, food or anything else, by force. When this is done, it is rightly regarded as tyranny.

When a tyrant is successful, even if there is no actual fighting, there is no peace, because:

- There is no security.
- People feel dishonoured and ashamed in allowing the situation to continue.
- People feel frustrated and helpless, and unable to do anything about it.
- People feel ashamed because they think they have acted in a cowardly manner.

'If anyone walks with an oppressor to strengthen him, knowing that he is an oppressor, he has gone forth from Islam.'

(Hadith)

Islam is intended to be a religion of peace, goodwill, mutual understanding and good faith. But it will not acquiesce in wrong doing, and warriors hold their lives cheap in defence of honour and justice.

The Muslim ideal is that of virtue combined with unselfish courage, obedience, discipline, duty and a constant striving by all the means in their power for the establishment of truth and righteousness.

They regard it as cowardice to ignore the challenge or to fail to root out the tyranny.

Muslims are commended to exercise as much self-restraint as possible. Force is a dangerous weapon. It may have to be used for self-defence or self-preservation – but it should always be for a principle and not out of passion.

'If God did not check certain people by using others, surely many monasteries, churches, synagogues and mosques would all have been pulled down. God will aid those who fight for Him.'

(surah 22:39–40)

In the spiritual sense, **jihad** really means the holy war against sin, a person's striving to be pure in spirit, and to resist evil.

War

Jihad does not mean every single battle fought by any Middle-Eastern soldier, who may be anything from a Marxist to a member of a private bodyguard, and not a martyr for God.

Many battles have nothing whatever to do with Islam. The Qur'an is quite clear on the limits that define jihad.

It should be declared only:

- in *defence* of the cause of Allah, not for conquest
- to restore peace and freedom of worship
- to gain freedom from tyranny
- if led by a spiritual leader and fought until the enemy lays down arms.

Women, children and the old and sick are not to be harmed, and trees and crops are not to be damaged.

Jihad does *not* include:

- wars of aggression or ambition

- border disputes or either national or tribal squabbles
- the intent to conquer and suppress, colonize, exploit, etc.
- forcing people into accepting a faith they do not believe.

Jihad on a national scale cannot be declared by anyone who feels like it, although individuals (in the sense that any devout and educated person could be an imam) might pursue their own personal campaign for righteousness. National jihad has to be commanded by a leader who is accepted as a spiritual guide and supreme judge, who can assess the need, the cause, and give the right guidance – someone not governed by personal ambition.

Sometimes after starting jihad in the correct spirit, a human leader then becomes ambitious (see the sin of Tughyan, p. 54). In this case, the qualification for leadership is lost and the community has the right to demand a change in his ways or his abdication, or even his death if he refuses to give way.

*'If the enemy incline towards peace,
do thou also incline towards peace.'*

(surah 8:61)

*'The reward for an injury is an equal injury back;
but if a person forgives instead, and makes
reconciliation, his reward will come from God.'*

(surah 42:40)

*'If two sides quarrel, make peace between them.
But if one trespasses beyond bounds against the
other, then fight against the one that transgresses
until it complies with the law of God; and if it
complies, then make peace between them with
justice, and be fair.'*

(surah 49:9)

Muslims are often accused of trying to convert people at the point of the sword, but this is untrue. It is totally against the principle of Islam, which defends individual liberties. (See also p. 138.)

The fact that various rulers claiming to be Muslim have acted incorrectly, some even to the extent of horrifying brutality, does not alter this fact – any more than one could judge Christianity by the atrocities of a ruler of a Christian country, such as Hitler.

Islamic jihad in fact insists that killing for the sake of religion is wrong. Religion should never become an oppressor. People should never be forced to accept things that they don't believe. The whole notion is impossible.

The principle of jihad is to fight against tyranny and oppression, to bring freedom and justice and a just peace.

*'And hold fast, all together, to the Rope which
Allah stretches out for you; be not divided
amongst yourselves; remember with gratitude
Allah's favour on you. For you were enemies, and
He joined your hearts in love, so that by His grace
you became brothers. You were on the brink of the
pit of fire, and He saved you from it.'*

(surah 3:103)

*'Goodness and Evil cannot be equal. Repay evil
with what is better, then he who was your enemy
will become your intimate friend.'*

(surah 41:34)

THINKING POINT

- **Why would Muslims regard pacifism in certain circumstances as being a weakness, and wrong? Do pacifists have the right to deny defence to others who do not share their opinions?**

FOR YOUR FOLDERS

▶ Make a list of the rules governing jihad.
▶ Read the passages of the Qur'an carefully and explain why Muhammad could not accept fighting for personal ambition or religious persecution.
▶ Just because there is no actual war does not mean that a country is 'at peace'. Explain what things are necessary in a country before it can feel peace.

THINGS TO DO

▶ Try to find out some facts about the war in Afghanistan and the Russian withdrawal in 1988. Why did the Muslims feel it was necessary to declare jihad against the Russians?

From 750 to 1258 CE the Muslims were ruled by Abbasids, ruthless warriors determined to wipe out all opposition. Under their rule, people who did not agree with them were persecuted.

The most famous Abbasid caliph was Harun al-Rashid (736–809 CE), whose reign was notable for progress in both sciences and arts – medicine, mathematics, astronomy, architecture, poetry and philosophy.

From 909 to 1171 CE there was a new dynasty in North Africa, Egypt and Syria. These were Shi'ite Muslims known as Fatimids because they claimed descent from Muhammad's daughter Fatimah, a claim that was hotly disputed by their enemies. They built a new capital in Egypt known as al-Qahira, the 'Victorious' – the city we now call Cairo. Fatimid rule was eventually overthrown by Saladin, who restored Sunni rule to Egypt.

The Ummayyad dynasty in Spain lasted from 736 to 1031 CE. Spanish Muslims were known as Moors.

The crusades

The eleventh and twelfth centuries were marked by battles between Christians and Muslims known as the crusades. Up until 1071 CE the Christians had been allowed to visit Jerusalem unmolested, but when the Seljuks (a fierce warrior race who only became Muslim after over-running Turkey) took Jerusalem, they closed the pilgrim routes. Later they even threatened the court of the Byzantine Christian Emperor in Constantinople, and the Emperor appealed to the Pope to send an army against them. So in 1095 CE the Pope declared holy war, promising that all who died in battle would have their sins wiped out and go to paradise.

After a great deal of bloodshed the Christians did recapture Jerusalem, and built a long chain of fortresses to protect it.

Richard the Lionheart was the best known crusader king; he and Saladin respected each other and acted honourably. Other knights and barons on the Christian side, however, behaved very cruelly and with less honour than the Muslims, and were soon generally regarded as oppressive tyrants.

In 1187 CE Saladin recaptured Jerusalem, and it was never again in Christian hands.

Mongols

In the thirteenth century Islam had to face the onslaught of another wave of invaders, the Mongols of Central Asia. By 1221 CE their savage leader

Ghenghis Khan had reached Persia. Ghenghis died in 1227 CE, but the hordes swept on, led by his grandson Hulagu. In 1258 CE he took Baghdad, the last Abbasid caliph was murdered, and the glittering city virtually wiped off the face of the earth.

Mamlukes

The success of the Mongols was a serious shock to Muslim morale, but it was mercifully short-lived. In 1260 CE the Mongols were halted by the Mamlukes in Palestine. The Mamlukes were descendants of Turkish slave-soldiers who had risen to be military rulers in Egypt. As a result of their success, Cairo became the centre of the Islamic world, and its al-Azhar University became the most important seat of orthodox Islamic learning. The Mamluke dynasty lasted from 1250 to 1517 CE.

Timur the Lame

In 1379 CE Islamic lands suffered another Mongol onslaught under the brutal Timur the Lame (usually known as Tamburlaine). There were wholesale massacres. Heads of his victims were piled up into pyramids, one of which, outside Delhi, had 80 000 skulls! After this monster died, most of his conquests reverted to their former owners.

The gunpowder empires

After the Mongol storm with its violent upheavals, the Islamic world saw the rise of three more great Empires – the Ottoman, the Safavid and the Mughal. These were sometimes known as 'gunpowder empires' because the extent of each kingdom was dependent on how far from the power centre soldiers could transport their 'modern' guns without the capitals being overthrown because they were too far away. In practice, the distance an empire could stretch seems to have been equivalent to about three to four months' travelling time.

Each of these empires had courts of dazzling grandeur, far removed from the simple ways of the Prophet.

The Safavids ruled in Persia from 1500–1722 CE, a Sufi-Shi'ite empire founded by Shah Isma'il. It reached its highest point under Shah Abbas during 1587 to 1629 CE. This empire was finally destroyed by continuous border warfare with the Russians, and the rise of the militant Qajar dynasty.

The Mughals (who were actually descendants of the Mongols) were founded by Babur. His grandson

Akbar (1556–1605 CE) ruled virtually the whole of India. The West regards him as the greatest Mughal emperor, but he was not an orthodox Muslim. He was interested in all other religions, and even put forward one of his own. Devout Muslims objected to the fact that he put the phrase 'Allahu Akbar' on his coins, for it can either mean 'God is the Greatest' or 'Akbar is God'.

They preferred his great-grandson Aurangzeb (1658–1707 CE) who was a militant Muslim. His persecution of Hindus, however, led to hatreds that were later to split India.

Aurangzeb

Mughal power was gradually broken because of internal strife, the resentment of the poor against the rich, the dissatisfaction of displaced royalty, and eventually the growing influence and domination of European powers, especially the British.

From 1295 to 1925 CE Muslim fortunes were centred in the Ottoman Turks, who took Constantinople as their capital and adapted the Cathedral of Saint Sophia (Holy Wisdom) to a mosque.

The Ottomans reached their heights under such rulers as Selim the Grim (1512–20 CE) who defeated the Safavids and Mamlukes, and Suleiman the Magnificent (1520–66 CE) whose conquests included Egypt, Syria, Iraq, the coasts of North Africa and the Red Sea, Rhodes, and the Balkans as far as Hungary.

In the nineteenth century the Turkish Empire gradually began to dissolve. Turkey was known as the 'sick man of Europe'. Many countries broke away from Turkish dominance, and finally there was a revolution within Turkey itself. The caliphate was abolished in 1924 by Mustafa Kemal, known as Ataturk, who set up a socialist republic and deposed the last Ottoman, the thirty-sixth of his line. Since that time there has been no official caliphate.

FOR DISCUSSION

▶ The Christians identified the Muslim army with the forces of Satan, and vice versa. Both sides prayed to win. Does the fact that the Muslims won prove that the Christians were really forces of Satan?

▶ God does not take sides in battles, but judges the motives and lives of individuals.

QUICK QUIZ

▶ How did the Abbasid caliphs go beyond the spirit of jihad?

▶ What were Moors?

▶ What is the modern name of al-Qahira?

▶ Who captured Jerusalem for the Christians?

▶ Who killed the last Abbasid caliph?

▶ Who made a pyramid of skulls at Delhi?

▶ What is the name of the chief Muslim university?

▶ Which Muslims captured Constantinople?

▶ Name the greatest Ottoman conqueror.

▶ Who put an end to the Muslim caliphate?

FOR YOUR FOLDERS

▶ Why did the Pope declare holy war on the Muslims in 1095 CE? Was this war really against Islam? Were the Christian principles at the start any different from those of Islamic jihad?

▶ Explain what is meant by
  a Mongol, and
  b Mamluke.
  Both these conquering forces eventually became Muslim. Should Islam bear the blame for their bloodthirsty reputations?

The reaction against the West

In Muslim countries 'reform' means two things – an improvement in the living conditions of the poor, and a fight against moral and spiritual corruption.

Attempts at the first kind of reform were made by a few Ottoman and Mamluke rulers, but most were regarded by their subjects as corrupt and unfit to hold office. There was a growing admiration for and dependence on the Western powers.

In the eighteenth and nineteenth centuries European traders had established themselves throughout all Muslim territories. They attempted to:
- establish good routes to distant places, both over land and sea
- protect military outposts and missionary settlements
- help with projects to improve irrigation, water supply and the control of disease
- convert all 'native peoples' to the Christian faith
- alter the Islamic patterns of education, which were of no use to their way of life.

Most Europeans had very little awareness of or sympathy with Islam, and generally feared the examples of cruelty and ruthlessness shown by various Eastern rulers (particularly in Turkey), and felt challenged by the Muslim refusal to accept Christianity. Most Europeans believed Christianity to be more civilized, gentle and compassionate, and obvious good sense.

The bad habit grew of comparing the best ideals of one faith to the worst practice of individuals in the other. Few Christians could understand why devout Muslims rejected their beliefs in the Trinity, or the need for a saviour. They did not realize that the 'savage tribesman' who owned nothing, and knelt with his head on the sand, regarded his faith and way of life as being infinitely superior to the corruption, lack of morals, and 'atheism' of the West, whose leading religious thinkers had fallen into the sin of shirk.

Wahhabism

Islamic reform really began in Arabia under Muhammad abd al-Wahhab, who campaigned to see Islam restored to its original purity. He was violently opposed to:
- the complicated schools of Islamic theology that had rendered Islam no longer pure and simple
- the excesses of Shi'ite fervour, and the 'worship' of Muhammad's family and other saints
- low standards of morality

- lack of belief in the unique nature of God, or the worship of other powers alongside Him
- any intrusions from foreign powers.

His mission to see Islam return to the golden age of Madinah was taken up by the Saudi prince Abdul Aziz and their campaign eventually led to the rise of the kingdom of Saudi Arabia.

Al-Wahhab's ideas influenced many other reformers, including al-Afghani, Muhammad Abduh and Rashid Rida in Egypt, who began the twentieth-century campaign for Islamic unity.

Barbarity?

Muslims in the modern world are still accused of cruelty and barbarity, specifically:
- inhumane punishments for various offences
- terrorist activity
- hijackings and taking hostages
- bitter hatred towards enemies, especially Jews.

Islam is accused of hypocrisy, and the behaviour of certain individuals is certainly no advertisement for the faith.

Punishments

Some harsh punishments *are* laid down by Islam, and may be carried out in the stricter countries. These are generally for serious offences against another person's property, life or honour.

The devastating effects of alcohol on Western society have been well observed, and both drunkenness and theft are despised. People could be flogged for drinking alcohol, and hands are cut off for theft.

Muslim scholars sometimes point out that Jesus' teaching on the subject ('*If thy hand offend thee, cut it off! It is better to go through life maimed than with both hands to enter hell*' Mark 9:43) is supported by the Qur'an, and wonder by what standards Christian scholars pick and choose which of the commands they will keep. The deterrent seems to work. You will virtually never see one-handed people in Islamic countries.

Punishment is not done publicly for the sake of barbarity, but so that all may observe that justice has been done. Muslims strongly disapprove of trials and punishments being carried out in secret, with the possibility of inhumane treatment and torture.

What may seem barbaric to the West is taken as a point of honour to Muslims. It is well known that the Prophet swore he would cut the hand off his own daughter himself, if he caught her stealing. It was to be the same justice for all, with no preferential treatment.

One story about Ali tells of his care and attention to a thief whose hand he had amputated, who later loved him so much he became one of his most devoted followers.

We would readily welcome an interpretation of the Qur'anic text which could explain that the expression 'to cut off the hand' was not to be taken literally. What I refuse to do is to abandon Islamic principles . . . . We do not cut off the hand of any who steal to eat. Anyone under such necessity is not to blame, but the fault would lie with society. It is the responsibility of society to make sure everyone has enough for their needs. Only he who steals for stealing's sake, and without compulsion, is open to this penalty.

Take another case: adultery. There has been no question within Islam of stoning the adulterer or adulteress, as has been falsely maintained. The punishment is flogging – 100 lashes – no more and no less – and the fault is so grave it deserves this punishment.'
(From M. Bianco, *Gadafi, Voice from the Desert;* Longman 1975 p.99)

THINGS TO DO

▶ Colonel Qaddafi of Libya, a country in which Qur'anic punishments are literally carried out, is one of those most keen for legal experts to use ijtihad (see p. 98) to see if a modern interpretation of the spirit of the laws of punishment can be found.

Although Qaddafi is often accused by the press in the West as being a trouble maker and terrorist, his supporters regard him as someone who has genuinely attempted to 'purify' the Islam of his country, and free it from the tyranny of non-Muslim corruption.

Laying aside political issues, read the extract given below from one of his speeches, and look at the picture. What does this information tell us about the attitude of one of the world's modern Muslim leaders?

FOR YOUR FOLDERS

▶ Why did many people in Muslim territories welcome the arrival of European traders at first?

▶ Look at the aims of the European traders. Which of these do you think might cause alarm to a devout Muslim, and why?

▶ Give a brief outline of the main aims of Wahhabism.

▶ Explain why Muslims consider that the law and its punishments should be *seen* to be done.

TALKING POINTS

● Citizens in the West demand that Muslims living in their countries should obey the laws of the land, and indeed, they are obliged to do so. Should they therefore accept the same principle when living in Muslim countries, and accept Islamic law?

● Many people living in Muslim countries do not wish to live according to the strict rules of the Muslim faith. (This includes many natural citizens of those lands.) Have they a right not to do so?

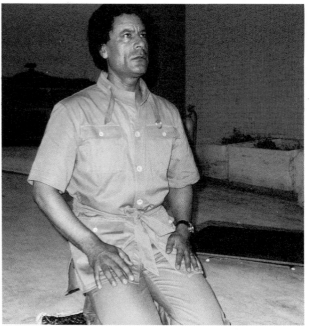

Qaddafi at prayer

Yasser Arafat

One jihad of our present century has proved to be particularly bitter – the jihad against Zionism. Many people think this means that all Muslims hate all Jews, but this is completely untrue.

It is important to realize that anti-Zionism is not criticizing someone's religion. Zionism is not the same thing as Judaism. Zionists are Jews, or their supporters, who have campaigned to be given a homeland of their own in which they can live in peace. Many Jews, suffering and persecuted throughout the world, dreamed of going to Jerusalem and having the land of Israel 'restored' to them, even though they and their families had never been to Palestine, a land occupied by Arab peoples for far longer than any Jewish occupation.

Many Christians, educated with the Bible and with a traditional fear of Islam and a guilt for the way Jews had been treated in Europe, shared this desire for a Jewish homeland.

The history of the Zionist campaign is very complicated. It goes back to the turn of the twentieth century and the settlements made in the Middle East by the superpowers after the First World War.

To the shock of many people (Arab, and many British when they found out the truth), these settlements were not arrived at honestly or justly. The Arabs, who had dealt in good faith with British politicians, discovered that the word of a British gentleman could be broken. Today we have access to the Cabinet papers of the time, and can see for ourselves the shameless pressures, intrigues and deceptions.

Beyond any doubt, the ordinary people urged on by their religious feelings (whether Jewish, Muslim or Christian) had no intention of behaving dishonourably, and all believed that God supported their cause.

Nevertheless, people and governments were manipulated by certain individuals for their own motives, and the sense of shame and dishonour this has aroused has caused a bitterness that will not go away until consciences have been cleansed.

Support for Zionism was greatly increased in the Second World War when the secrets of the Nazi concentration camps were revealed, and horror and repulsion gave fresh impetus to the movement to provide a secure home for surviving Jews.

But was the Zionist ambition reasonable? Did it take into account the settled population already in existence in Palestine, for whom the influx of Jewish people meant a choice between submission to alien rule or exile?

Had the Zionists not realized there would be strong opposition? Or had they just decided to over-rule it, by force if necessary?

Palestine was not an empty land, nor could it hold more than a very small fraction of the Jews scattered throughout the world. The muslim view was that the Jews should be compensated by being given good land in Germany, or perhaps a state in the USA.

Eventually, in 1948, the British granted the Jews the right to live in Palestine, and the resulting upheavals created today's Palestine problem. Many inhabitants became refugees and fled to Jordan, their properties were seized and taken over, or bulldozed flat. Individuals, known as Fedayeen, swore to die rather than allow the Jewish immigrants to take their lands. Many groups were formed, and together are known as the PLO (Palestine Liberation Organization). Under leaders such as Yasser Arafat and Abu Jihad (killed in 1988) they have campaigned for a restoration of their own state. Their 'acts of terrorism' are mild in comparison to the Israeli reprisals aimed at keeping them out, and they cannot see why hijacking a plane gets worse publicity than hijacking someone else's country.

A six-day war in 1967 gave a decisive victory to

the Jews (who are now generally called Israelis), but another war in 1973 made the West realize that the dispute was not going to fade away.

Until recently the Israelis could rely on massive support from the West, particularly the USA, and the Arabs were relatively very weak. Now the renewed confidence of Arab nations, based on the oil the West desperately needs, has altered the picture drastically.

Many Christian pilgrims to Jerusalem are very surprised when they discover Arab resentment against the West. They seem to be completely ignorant of the desperate situation there, an ignorance that is hard to explain away.

In August 1988 King Hussein of Jordan gave up his interest in the territory known as the West Bank – the area captured by the Jews in 1967. Only time will tell what will happen now, as both sides are convinced they have right on their sides.

November 2nd, 1917

Dear Lord Rothschild,
  I have much pleasure in conveying to you, on behalf of His Majesty's Government, the following declaration of sympathy with Jewish Zionist aspirations which has been submitted to, and approved by, the Cabinet.
  'His Majesty's Government view with favour the establishment in Palestine of a national home for the Jewish people, and will use their best endeavour to facilitate the achievement of this object, it being clearly understood that nothing shall be done which may prejudice the civil and religious rights of existing non-Jewish communities in Palestine, or the rights and political status enjoyed by Jews in any other country.'
  I should be grateful if you would bring this declaration to the knowledge of the Zionist Federation.

The Balfour Declaration of 2 November 1917, reproduced in *History of the Holy Land*, Weidenfeld & Nicolson 1969)

'Let the Arabs be encouraged to move out as the Jews move in. Let them be compensated handsomely for their land and let their settlement elsewhere be carefully organised and generously financed.'
(1944 Annual Conference Report of National Executive of British Labour Party)

'What do our brethren do in Palestine? They were slaves, but now that they have found freedom this change has awakened in them an inclination to despotism. They treat the Arans with hostility and cruelty, deprive them of their rights, offend them without cause and even boast of these deeds; and nobody among us opposes this despicable and dangerous inclination.'
(Asher Ginzberg, from Mayhew and Adams, *Publish it Not*, Longman 1975, p.142)

'In Palestine we do not propose to go through the form of consulting the wishes of the present inhabitants of the country . . . . The four Great Powers are committed to Zionism. Zionism is of far greater importance than the desires and prejudices of the 700 000 Arabs who now inhabit that ancient land . . . . The Powers do not propose to consult them. In short, so far as Palestine is concerned, the Powers . . . have made no declaration of policy which . . . they have not always intended to violate.'
(A.J. Balfour, Memorandum to Lord Curzon, 11 August 1919 (Public Record Office Doc FO 371/4183)

'I remember that my Labour friends were, like myself, greatly concerned about this proposal. We have never contemplated the removal of the Arabs, and the British Labour Party, in its pro-Zionist enthusiasm, went beyond our intentions.'
(Chaim Weizmann, *Trial and Error*, Hamish Hamilton 1949)

FOR YOUR FOLDERS

▶ Revolutionary movements are not the same as religion. How far do you consider this to be true of the jihad against Zionism?

▶ How far do you consider the Palestinian campaign against Israel to be justified under the rules of jihad?

▶ Explain why many Muslims came to distrust the West as a result of the Palestine problem.

THINKING POINTS

● Is it right for Jews to fight to acquire, but wrong for Arabs to fight to hold?

● Israel has been idealized because of the horrors of the Second World War. The West supported Zionism to ease its guilty conscience.

● The dispute is so bitter because it has involved dishonour and injustice on all sides.

Women soldiers on guard in Tehran

Poster from the Islamic Revolution in Iran showing Ayatollah Khomeini as Moses and the defeated Shah as Pharoah

Although there are many Muslim countries, there are not yet any perfect Islamic states based on Muhammad's model at Madinah. A Muslim state can be defined as one in which the majority of the population is Muslim and which has many Muslim features.

Organized efforts to establish Islamic states have been going on in several countries. These include the Brotherhood (or Ikhwan) in the Middle East, the Jamaat-i Islami in Pakistan, Bangladesh and Kashmir, the Milli Salamat in Turkey and the Masjumi Party in Indonesia. These are just some of the many movements.

They believe that all citizens of an Islamic state should enjoy freedom of belief, thought, conscience and speech. They should be free to develop their full potential, both in earnings and household. They should enjoy the right to support or oppose any government policy they think right or wrong.

An Islamic state is duty bound to implement the laws of the Qur'an and Sunnah.

Many Muslims, who long for world wide spiritual revival, and to see the whole world dedicated to the service of God and governed by just and humane laws, cannot regard it as a coincidence that the discovery of oil, with all its potential for doing good or evil, should occur just as knowledge of Islam was really beginning to spread. The Devil never sleeps!

Fear of terrorism

Deep convictions lead to roused passions, desperate actions, unjustifiable 'accidents', indiscriminate violence, and wrong decisions – all in the name of principles, whether these be the cause of nationalism or God! And for these principles, many fervent Muslims are quite prepared to kill or to die.

Muslim revivalists cannot accept:
● atheism or materialism
● departing from the revelations of the Qur'an
● corruption
● capitalism
● communism
● tyranny
● hypocrisy.

Their leaders may well be feared by politicians struggling to keep the peace or building up national economies, but they are generally admired as heroes by the deprived and downtrodden masses who have:
● observed the luxurious living, and perhaps corruption, of certain leaders
● not benefited from the booming economies of 'Muslim oil'
● 'benefited' in ways they repudiate as evil, i.e. being provided with alcohol, pornographic films, banks that take interest, etc.

For these reasons, amongst others, many rulers of countries regarded as being Muslim are in fact highly opposed to 'Muslim revivalists' and brand them as terrorists and trouble makers, whereas the revivalists see themselves as reformers and freedom fighters set against tyranny, corruption and the weakening of Islamic standards. Much depends on your point of view.

Less militant Muslims wish to see peace and progress, and a building up of their nation's welfare not ruined by continuous war and insecurity, and are therefore opposed to the more extreme movements. Some are quite happy to adapt to Western ways, and accept as much as seems good to them.

Ayatollah Khomeini

Shi'ite fundamentalism

When civil war broke out in Iran it was between the religious leaders led by the Ayatollah Khomeini (on behalf of the people who were being driven to poverty and despair, tortured and harassed by secret police) against a ruler of immense personal wealth and power who was considered to be under the influence of greedy foreign nations out to take advantage of the country's new oil wealth.

However one interprets the jihad, one notable feature was the fact that large numbers of the armed forces were convinced of the rightness of the Ayatollah, and abandoned their commanders. The Supreme Commander, the Shah, was regarded in the same way as Pharaoh who oppressed the slaves in Egypt until God sent the Prophet Moses to defeat him. Western media did not regard the Shah as an evil man, and are only just beginning to realize how seriously Islamic revivalists rate their war against corruption.

> *'Pharaoh said:*
> *"I will cut off your hands and*
> *your feet, and crucify you all!"*
> *They said: "No matter, we shall*
> *simply return to our Lord. You take*
> *vengeance on us only because we believe*
> *the signs of God. O God! Pour out*
> *on us patience and constancy, and*
> *take our souls unto Thee!"'*
> (surah 7:123–6, see also surah 26:50–52)

The Islamic revolution in Iran, whatever your opinions of it, has rekindled hope in Muslims all over the world – to the distress of nations anxious to preserve peace at all costs, and fearful of disrupting the oil economy of the world.

In 1978 few could understand why millions of Iranian men and women marched to their deaths for the sake of an old man exiled to France who, in imitation of the prophet, had never eaten a heavy meal or slept on a bed in his life.

The mixture of longing for purity, plus spiritual awareness, has led to Islamic reform movements in many countries – Yemen, Algeria, Morocco, the Sudan, Libya, Syria and Indonesia. They are usually represented as rebellions or terrorist unrest.

FOR DISCUSSION

▶ *'The most excellent jihad is to speak the truth in the face of a tyrannical ruler.'*
(Hadith)
▶ Being wrong when you think you are right is the chief danger of fighting for your beliefs.

THINGS TO DO

▶ Make a list of some of the modern Muslim brotherhoods or revivalist movements. Explain why these are often banned by governments who fear their fanaticism.

FOR YOUR FOLDERS

▶ 'Religion and politics are two separate things. Religious leaders should not get involved in politics.' How far do you think a Muslim would agree or disagree with this statement? Give reasons for your answer.
▶ 'When tyrants are overthrown by violence, those who have put them down by force become oppressors themselves.' How far do you think this is true?

Key

Countries with Muslim majority (over 50% of population)

*'He is not of us who fights
the cause of nationalism;
he is not of us who dies in
the cause of nationalism.
Nationalism means helping
your people in unjust causes'*
(Hadith)

The map shows the present spread of countries with a Muslim majority, and the list opposite gives some idea of figures.

Muslims form over half the population of some 46 countries, and make up over 80 per cent of the population in 32 countries.

The number of Muslims is growing rapidly, especially in the Far East, Africa and Russia (where about 25 per cent of the people are now Muslim, not Communist).

The whole political and religious scene in the Middle East is confusing to Europeans, as they observe many instances of Muslim fighting Muslim.

Nevertheless, there are patterns. It is important to realize that:

- not all Arabs are Muslim (some are Christian, some Marxist, etc.)
- not all Muslims are perfect
- many people in strict religious countries desire the freedom to enjoy things Muslims would regard as corrupt.

The key movements in the Muslim world are for:

- socialism – to improve the welfare of the people, and to remove religion from politics
- nationalism – the urge for each country to be independent

- Pan-Arabism – the desire for all Arabic-speaking peoples to unite
- Pan-Islam – the desire for all Islamic peoples to unite.

(The word 'pan' means 'all'.)

Pan-Arabism and Pan-Islam are similar, but with important differences.

Both are against any atheist political system, and nationalism, which they insist divides people instead of bringing them together.

Pan-Arabism aims to see a new empire of unified states, on the same lines as the United States of America (USA) or the Union of Soviet Socialist Republics (USSR). It wants a Union of Arabic Republics.

Although all Muslims try to learn Arabic, millions of them are not Arabic and want a different kind of unity. Pan-Arabism implies a 'land bloc', whereas Pan-Islam implies a 'mind and heart bloc'.

Pan-Islam is the movement for:

- true Islamic government under God
- a new rightly-guided caliph (preferably a descendant of Muhammad)
- unity of all Islamic sects, especially Sunni and Shi'ite

- the reform of society
- the reform of Islamic higher education
- peace and justice for all
- freedom from tyranny (especially Western corruption, Soviet atheism and Zionism).

The campaign against atheism may well sweep Islam through the USSR and China. It may also take firm hold in the more southern countries of Africa and in the 'atheist' West.

Intellectuals have already brought Islam into the universities, and immigrant populations have provided the framework, although many are reluctant to convert non-Muslims to Islam.

No one is converted to Islam 'by the sword'; but millions are becoming aware in their hearts that God exists, and that the day has arrived when individuals from every country in the world can say 'I am Muslim, and I belong to the Ummah'.

Country	Number of Muslims	Percentage of population
Afghanistan	17.7m	99%
Algeria*	15.3m	98%
Bahrain*	0.22m	99%
Bangladesh	63.3m	85%
China	93.5m	11%
Egypt*	33.4m	93%
Ethiopia	17.2m	65%
India	69.0m	12%
Indonesia	125.0m	95%
Iran	31.5m	98%
Iraq*	9.6m	95%
Jordan*	2.5m	95%
Kuwait*	1.0m	98%
Lebanon*	1.7m	57%
Libya*	2.2m	100%
Mauretania*	1.2m	100%
Morocco*	16.8m	99%
Nigeria	59.8m	75%
Oman*	0.75m	100%
Pakistan	63.0m	97%
Palestine*	2.6m	87%
Qatar*	0.17m	100%
Saudi Arabia*	8.0m	100%
Sudan*	14.3m	85%
Syria*	6.0m	87%
Tanzania	9.3m	65%
Tunisia*	5.2m	95%
Turkey	37.6m	99%
UAE*	0.32m	100%
UK	1.5m	2.7%
USSR	60.0m	25%
Yemen (N)*	6.0m	99%

(Based on the 1975 census)
Arab countries marked*
The figures for regions under Soviet rule are:
Azerbaijan – 78%; Kazakhstan – 68%; Kirghizia – 92%;
Tajikistan – 98%; Turkmenia 90%; Uzbekistan – 88%.

FOR DISCUSSION

▶ Look at the figures for the Muslim population of the USSR. Over a quarter of Russian citizens are now Muslims. What should happen democratically when the figure reaches 51 per cent? How far do you think the modern 'glasnost' with the West might be a result of the growing power of Islam in the East?

FOR YOUR FOLDERS

▶ Make a list of the chief aims of Pan-Islam, and explain briefly how it differs from Pan-Arabism.
▶ Why do many socialists and communists regard Islam as a serious threat? Although Islam approves of many aspects of socialism, it can never accept communism. Can you explain why?

THINGS TO DO

Muslims can be found in all the countries of the world, but the table shows some of the highest percentages per population.
▶ Which countries had the highest percentage of Muslims in 1975?
▶ Add up the approximate number of Muslims in the Arab countries (marked*) given here in 1975.
▶ Add up the approximate number of Muslims in the non-Arab countries given here in 1975.
▶ Which countries had the largest number of Muslims in 1975?
▶ How many Muslims were there in the UK?
▶ How many Muslims were there in the USSR?

77 COURSEWORK

	Knowledge	Understanding	Evaluation	Total
Topic 1	8	16	9	33
Topic 2	8	16	9	33
Topic 3	9	13	12	34
Topic 4	25	45	30	100

Check the regulations for your GCSE coursework with your teacher, to make sure you know what assignments are necessary, and how the marks will be allocated according to knowledge, understanding and evaluation.

For long assignments, the length required is usually about 3000 words, or around twelve sides of A4, and short assignments are about 1000 words, or four sides of A4. Your teacher should have worked out a marks grid so that you will not be penalized by being given incorrectly weighted instructions.

For example, if the marks ratio is 25%, 45%, 30%, the grid should look something like the one above.

This job must be done first. Grids can be adjusted, so long as the totals balance.

Examples of coursework assignments

1 MUHAMMAD (8/16/9)

Knowledge: Write a short biography of Muhammad, indicating his major achievements.
Understanding: Explain and comment on the reaction to Muhammad's mission as expressed by (a) Khadijah and Ali (4), (b) the people of Makkah (4) and (c) the people of Madinah (4). (i.e. Why do you think they either believed in him or rejected him?) How did Muhammad's life before his call prepare and fit him for his later mission as a prophet of God (4)?
Evaluation: To what extent do you think Muhammad should be regarded as the 'founder' of Islam? Give reasons for your answer (9).

2 AKHIRAH (9/3/12)

Knowledge: Choose three relevant passages from the Qur'an or Hadith and state clearly what each reveals about individual life after death, judgement, and the future state of existence (9).
Understanding: Explain the idea of Judgement Day (4) and the ways in which this belief can (a) alter the character of an individual (3), (b) have an effect on the way people treat each other (2), and (c) have an effect on the way a person practises faith throughout an average day (4).
Evaluation: Do you think God should always allow free will? Should He interfere with the laws of nature to protect people from such things as floods, earthquakes, fires, wars, etc.? Why do you think God does not protect humans from such things, or their personal tragedies? Would it be a better universe if we did *not* have free will, or the dangerous possibility of making wrong choices? (12)

3 QUR'AN AND HADITH (9/13/12)

Knowledge: Give an account of the origin and compilation of the Qur'an (4). Explain the difference between the Qur'an and Hadith (1). In what ways do Muslims show their respect for the Qur'an (4)?
Understanding: Why is the language of the Qur'an thought to be so important (1)? Choose two passages from the Qur'an, Prophetic Hadith and Hadith Qudsi, and state what each of these teaches about the nature of God (12).
Evaluation: To what extent is it important for Muslims to base their lives on the standard of the Qur'an? How far is it possible to extend the principles of the Qur'an and Hadith to cover problems in modern society? (Examples might include the problems of abortion, taking drugs, censorship, care of old people.) (12)

4 PILLARS OF ISLAM (8/16/9)

Knowledge: Describe the major features of the five pillars of Islam (8).
Understanding: Give an explanation of the purpose and significance of these pillars, and the fundamental beliefs behind them (3 marks each, 4 for prayer).
Evaluation: Which of the pillars do you consider to be the most important, and why (3)?
How far do you think the practices of Islam are effective in creating the feeling of ummah ('one family'), and why is this important (6)?

5 PRAYER (8/16/9)

Knowledge: Give an outline of Muslim preparations for ritual prayer. Where do Muslims pray? What are

the rules of expected conduct during prayer (8)?
Understanding: Explain the meanings given by Muslims to the terms and ideas and movements found in the ritual prayers. What do these prayers reveal about their attitudes and feelings towards God, Muhammad and the prophets, themselves and others (16)?
Evaluation: Give a personal view of the Kalimah Shahadah. Explain why it might be (a) easier or (b) harder to live a life dedicated to God *after* such a declaration has been made (4).
Is Du'a prayer a sign of faith or weakness? Argue the case for both points of view (5).

6 THE MOSQUE (8/16/9)

Knowledge: Present information, with illustrations and diagrams if you wish, to show the major features of a mosque, drawing special attention to the features common to every mosque. A special study could be made of a famous mosque (e.g. Blue Mosque, Istanbul; Regent's Park, London) or a local mosque in your community (8).
Understanding: Explain the purpose, use and significance of these features; of the reasons for the design and decoration of the mosque; of the way visitors and worshippers are expected to behave in the building; the use of the mosque for various functions, e.g. communal prayer, social events, rites of passages (16).
Evaluation: Consider the following issues:
a Should Muslims spend a great deal of money on building a mosque when that money could help the hungry (4)?
b In what ways does the existence of the mosque contribute to the feelings of ummah in Islam (4)?
c Could you be a Muslim without going to the mosque (4)?

7 HAJJ (8/16/9)

Knowledge: What difficulties are sometimes faced by pilgrims making the Hajj (a) in preparation for it, and (b) on the pilgrimage itself? Explain how the state of ihram is an important aid to the correct Hajj mentality (8).
Understanding: Explain how the experience of Adam and Eve (4), Ibrahim and his family (4) and the prophet Muhammad (4) all have a profound effect on the pilgrims on Hajj. In what ways do Muslims have their faith deepened and strengthened by the experiences of Hajj (4)?
Evaluation: Assess the importance of Eid ul Adha as part of the Hajj, and its effectiveness in binding together the whole ummah or family of Islam (9).

8 FESTIVALS AND SPECIAL DAYS (8/16/9)

Knowledge: Construct a calendar of Muslim festivals for the present year (2), and write an account of how Eid ul Fitr is celebrated (6).
Understanding: Explain the meaning of sacrifice and self-sacrifice (4). Explain fasting as a Muslim act of worship, and the right and wrong attitudes of mind and reasons for fasting (4); explain why Muslims do not over-celebrate Maulid an Nabi or Muharram (4); explain the limitations of design on Eid cards (you could illustrate this with your own design if you wish) (4).
Evaluation: Do you think Muslim festivals are seen primarily as religious or family occasions? Give reasons for your answer. What would you say is the value of a regular cycle of festivals (9)?

9 MARRIAGE (8/16/9)

Knowledge: Describe carefully how and why marriages are arranged in many Muslim families. Give an account of the actual ceremony and its implications (8).
Understanding: What are the responsibilities of the mother (5), the father (3), and the children (3) in a Muslim home? How is living in an extended family different from the 'nuclear' family situation (2)? What are the conditions under which a Muslim man might take more than one wife into his household (3)?
Evaluation: Is the extended family an advantage or a disadvantage in helping a family to grow together in loyalty and love (3)? How can the taking of more than one wife be quite consistent with the spirit of Islam (4)? How important to you think it is for a person to marry someone who shares the same beliefs (2)?

10 SHARI'AH (8/16/9)

Knowledge: Give an explanation of what is meant by Shari'ah. How are the rules of Shari'ah arrived at for situations in the ever-changing modern world (8)?
Understanding: Explain the main aims and ideals of Shari'ah, giving full examples from the Qur'an and Hadith. How does living according to Shari'ah build up the feeling of ummah, being one family (16)?
Evaluation: How far is living according to Shari'ah possible for a Muslim in Western society? Should Muslims be prepared to change their way of life in order to be like non-Muslims?

GLOSSARY

Abd   servant
Adhan (Hassan, Azan)   the call to prayer
AH   after the Hijra (Hegira)
Akhirah   belief in life after death
Allah   God
Allahu Akbar   God is great
Amal   putting faith into action
Angel   messenger from God, visible under certain conditions
Ansars   citizens of Madinah who helped Muslims
Arabesque   decorative flourish in writing or art
Arkan   a pillar of the faith
Ayat   a verse of the Qur'an

Baitullah   House of God, the Ka'ba
Barzakh   place of waiting, after death
Bedouin   wandering tribespeople
Bismillah   'In the name of God'

Caliph   'Successor', ruler for God on earth
Calligraphy   decorative writing
Chador   black veil sometimes worn by Muslim women
CE   Christian Era

Dhikr   means of attaining mystic state
Din   the Faith
Du'a   personal prayer or supplication

Eid ul Adha   Feast of sacrifice that ends the Hajj
Eid ul Fitr   Feast to break the Ramadan fast

Fard (or **wajib**) things which must be done
Fatiha   the first surah in the Qur'an
Fiqh   technique of working out Shari'at law

Ghusl   complete bath for ritual cleansing

Hadith   sayings and traditions of Muhammad
Hadith Qudsi   sayings of God not found in the Qur'an
Hafiz   someone who has learnt the Qur'an by heart
Hajj   pilgrimage to Makkah
Halal   allowed
Hanif   a devout person
Haram   forbidden
Harem   'forbidden' rooms, private part of a house
Hejab   the veiling of women in Islam (see also Purdah)
Hijrah   the migration from Makkah to Madinah
Hujurah   Muhammad's burial place in Aisha's room

Ibadah   worship, being a servant of God
Iftar   breakfast
Ihram   state of religious 'separation' or purity
Ihsan   realization of existence of God
Ijma   scholarly agreement to form a decision
Ijtihad   use of reason to decide correct action
Imam   a teacher
Iman   faith or belief
Injil   the revelation given to Jesus
Iqamah   the invitation to worship
Iqra!   Recite! – the command to Muhammad
Islam   submission to God

Jamaah   congregation or communal prayer
Jamra   pillar representing Ibrahim's temptations

Jahannam   hell
Jihad   striving, holy war in defence of God's will
Jinn   a non-human being, perhaps made of fire
Jum'ah   Friday (day of Jamaah prayers)

Ka'ba   the 'Cube', shrine of God in Makkah
Kafir   an unbeliever
Kalimah   'the word', declaration of faith
Khalifa   see Caliph
Khitan   circumcision
Khutbah   sermon
Kiswah   the black cloth covering the Ka'ba
Kitab   book
Kufr   unbelief
Kursi   'seat', the stand for the Qur'an

Lailat ul Miraj   The Night of Ascent to Heaven
Lailat ul Qadr   the Night of Power (when Muhammad received his first revelation)

Madrasah   school
Makruh   action disapproved of but not forbidden
Mandub   recommended actions
Masjid   a place of sujud (bowing down)
Maulid an Nabi   birthday of Prophet Muhammad
Mihrab   niche indicating direction of Makkah
Mimbar   pulpit for giving Friday sermons
Minaret   tower from which call to prayer is given
Mosque   place for communal prayer and activities
Mubah   actions decided by conscience
Muezzin (Mueddin)   the person who calls to prayer
Muharram   New Year
Mullah   a teacher
Mystic   someone who knows God through intuition

Nabi   a prophet
Nafs   instinct to do either good or evil
Niyyah   intention

Pbuh   'Peace be upon him' (said of the prophets)
Purdah   covering all but eyes, hands and feet

Qiblah   the direction of Makkah
Qiyam   standing during prayer
Quraish   the leading tribe in and around Makkah
Qur'an   the Revealed Book

Rabb   Master, i.e. God
Rak'ah   a sequence of movements in ritual prayer
Ramadan   the month of fasting
Rasul   a prophet
Rouh   the human soul
Risalah   prophecy
Ruku   bowing during ritual prayer

Sadaqah   charity, acts of voluntary giving
Sahifa   the revelation given to Ibrahim
Salah   ritual prayer five times daily
Salat ul Janaza   funeral prayers
Saum (Siyam)   fasting from sunrise to sunset
Say (Saai)   Hajj procession from Safa to Marwa
Sema   sacred dance used in Sufi mysticism
Shahadah   declaration of faith
Shahid   someone who dies for the faith, a martyr

Shari'ah   the way of life followed by Muslims
Shi'i   (Shiat Ali) – sect of Muslims who insist on a descendant of Muhammad as caliph
Shirk   sin of associating anything with God
Subha   string of prayer beads
Sufi   a mystic
Suhur   early meal before fasting begins
Sujud (Sajda)   kneeling before God in prayer
Sunnah   the way or example set by Prophet Muhammad
Sunni   Muslim who follows the orthodox way
Surah   a chapter in the Qur'an

Ta'alaq   divorce procedure
Takbir   shutting out all distractions before prayer
Taqwa   consciousness or awareness of God
Tasbih   see Subha
Tauhid   the doctrine of the one-ness of God
Tawaf   circling Ka'ba seven times on Hajj
Tawrat   the revelation given to Moses
Tayammum   symbolic washing done without water
Tughyan   arrogance, taking powers for oneself

Ulama   learned scholars
Ummah   the 'Family' of Islam
Ummul Kitab   the 'mother of books', the Qur'an
Umrah   pilgrimage to Makkah not in Hajj month

Walima   a feast
Wudu (Wuzu)   ritual washing before prayer
Wuquf   time of 'standing' before God during Hajj

Zabur   the revelation given to David
Zakah   giving one-fortieth of savings for God's service
Zulm   tyranny

PLACES

Al-Aqsa   mosque in Jerusalem, traditionally place from where Muhammad ascended to heaven
Al-Badr   site of Muhammad's first battle against Makkans
Al-Quds   the 'Holy', Jerusalem
Arafat   Mount of Mercy, where Adam and Eve met after God forgave their sin
Madinah   (Madinat an-Nabi) the city of the Prophet, formerly Yathrib
Maqam Ibrahim   place where Ibrahim prayed beside Ka'ba
Makkah   city of Ka'ba shrine, Muhammad's birthplace
Mina   place where Ibrahim 'sacrificed' Isma'il, place of stoning the Devil on Hajj
Mount Nur (Mount Hira)   Hill of Light. Place where Muhammad received his first revelation
Mount Thawr   place where Muhammad sheltered in a cave during Hijra
Mount Uhud   site of second battle against Makkans
Muzdalifah   where pilgrims on Hajj camp, and collect pebbles to stone the Devil
Safa and Marwa   places where Hagar searched for water

Taif   mountain oasis where Muhammad was rejected
Yathrib   original name of Madinah
Zamzam   well by Ka'ba, revealed to Ibrahim's wife Hagar

PEOPLE

Abd al-Muttalib   Muhammad's grandfather
Abdullah   Muhammad's father
Abu Bakr   friend of Muhammad; first caliph
Abu Lahab   uncle of Muhammad who opposed him
Abu Sufyan   uncle of Muhammad who opposed him
Abu Talib   uncle of Muhammad who adopted him
Adam   the first created man
Aisha (Ayesha)   youngest wife of Muhammad, daughter of Abu Bakr
Ali   adopted son of Muhammad, son of Abu Talib, who married Muhammad's daughter Fatimah. Fourth caliph (first Shi'ite caliph)
Amina   Muhammad's mother
Amr   a military leader
Azra'il   the angel of death
Bahira   Christian monk who recognized Muhammad as a prophet
Bilal   Ethiopian slave, first caller to prayer
Dawud   the prophet David, king of Israel
Fatimah   daughter of Muhammad who married Ali
Hafsa   Umar's daughter, wife of Muhammad
Hagar (Hajara)   wife of Ibrahim
Halima   Bedouin woman who reared Muhammad
Hamza   Muhammad's uncle, a famous warrior
Harun   the prophet Aaron, brother of Moses
Husain (Hussein)   grandson of Muhammad
Iblis   the devil
Ibrahim   Abraham, the 'father' of Jews and Arabs, and 'friend of God'
Isa   the prophet Jesus, worshipped by Christians
Isma'il   the prophet Ishmael, son of Abraham
Israfil   the angel who takes souls to judgement
Jibra'il (Gabriel)   the angel who transmitted revelations to Muhammad
Khadijah   first wife of Muhammad
Khalid   early warrior of Islam
Maryam   the Virgin Mary, mother of Jesus
Mika'il   angel that protects the faithful
Muawiya   the fifth caliph
Musa   the prophet Moses
Nuh   the prophet Noah
Shaytan   Satan, the devil, the chief Jinn
Suleiman   the prophet Solomon, son of David
Umar (Omar)   friend of Muhammad, the second caliph
Ummayyads   one of leading families of Makkah
Uthman (Othman)   friend of Muhammad, third caliph
Waraqa ibn Nofal   Christian cousin of Khadijah
Yazid   son of caliph Muawiya
Zaid ibn Haritha   adopted son of Muhammad
Zaid ibn Thabit   Muhammad's secretary who compiled the written Qur'an

INDEX